Social Work Editor: Lisa Gebo
Assistant Editor: Susan Wilson
Marketing Manager: Caroline Concilla
Marketing Assistant: Jessica McFadden
Project Editor: Jennie Redwitz
Print Buyer: Mary Noel
Permissions Editor: Susan Walters
Production Service Coordinator: Andrea Bednar,
    Shepherd, Inc.

Text Designer: Andrew Ogus
Copy Editor: Jeanne Patterson
Illustrator: Deb Goedken
Cover Designer: Roger Knox
Cover Image: Roger Knox
Cover Printer: West Printing Group
Compositor: Shepherd, Inc.
Printer/Binder: West Printing Group

For permission to use material from this text, contact
us by
    web: http://www.thomsonrights.com
    fax: 1-800-730-2215
    phone: 1-800-730-2214

Library of Congress Cataloging-in-Publication Data

For more information, contact
Wadsworth/Thomson Learning
10 Davis Drive
Belmont, CA 94002-3098
USA
http://www.wadsworth.com

International Headquarters
Thomson Learning
290 Harbor Drive, 2nd Floor
Stamford, CT 06902-7477
USA

UK/Europe/Middle East/South Africa
Thomson Learning
Berkshire House
168-173 High Holborn
London WC1V 7AA
United Kingdom

Asia
Thomson Learning
60 Albert Street, #15-01
Albert Complex
Singapore 189969

Canada
Nelson Thomson Learning
1120 Birchmount Road
Toronto, Ontario M1K 5G4
Canada

 This book is printed on acid-free recycled paper.

DEDICATION

To those who empowered us:
Marilyn L. Flynn and Wynne S. Korr

CONTENTS

PART III BEYOND THE SURF 227

Chapter 7: Designing Websites for Agencies and Practice 229

Chapter 8: Future Social Work Practice and the Web 271

PREFACE

Social workers must adapt to a new, promising, yet daunting technology: the *Web*. You will become a better social worker through using this book because you will be able to get the most current information from the Web, critically analyze it, and incorporate it into professional social work. We hope you will enjoy using the tremendous resources it offers at your fingertips.

WHY THIS BOOK?

The authors have been using the web for teaching and practice since it first emerged in the early '90s. We were struck then by the awesome potential it held for case management and wraparound services, for political advocacy and activism, and for countless other dimensions of research and practice. We have not been disappointed

We began teaching our students how to use the web as our own familiarity and comfort grew. We also started teaching various skills to colleagues and practitioners at local, regional, and national conferences. As we did this we noted several key problems:

Practitioners and students often seemed fearful of the web. One dimension was technical phobia. People were afraid of using the machines because the early programs and Internet connections were fragile and difficult to use. While this has improved, it still remains a problem for many of us. In addition, many of use were—and are—fearful because it seems quite alien to our work. Indeed, we are a profession of "people persons" and prefer to work directly with colleagues and consumers instead of through machines. So we began to teach people to plunge in!

We also noted that people remained too reliant on obsolete printed lists of websites. In addition, only the large, popular search engines were being consulted, many times in inefficient and inadequate ways. This remains a problem, largely because of the avalanche of information that gets added to the web every day. So we began to learn basic and sophisticated search skills and to teach them.

Critical thinking was another concern. We live in an era where the "as seen on TV" problem of uncritically accepting electronic information is commonplace. While web-based information can be invaluable for social work, many websites are incomplete, deceptive, or intentionally fraudulent. Worse yet, really poor or dangerous websites can be deceptively glamorous. So we began to teach critical thinking skills about the web and to sensitize students and colleagues to some of its dangers and drawbacks.

Many agencies are now coming on-line, and this alerted us to yet another problem: incomplete and inadequate website information for non-profit organizations. We have noted a subjective trend while preparing materials for teaching and writing this book. Many agencies offer websites that are just glorified telephone book-level advertisements. These fall far short of what integrated websites can accomplish for promoting and encouraging service delivery. All too often we see takeoffs of commercial websites that have been designed by technically oriented people, not practitioners. This results in skimpy and incomplete information. So we began to teach the basics about what sound website design could mean for our profession.

Finally, we noted our need to ponder just what the web may do to our profession as we adapt it into practice. It is vital that we control it rather than allow ourselves to be controlled by it. As a result, we decided to write this book and create the two companion websites for faculty and for students that are available from the publisher.

OUR POSITION AND VALUES

Some people gloat about how they have been able to remain completely computer illiterate and still carry on. Akin to this, people may often tell you stories about how they looked at the Web once and found nothing but inane twaddle. Still other people insist that they can completely screw up a computer simply by looking at it cockeyed.

We take the position that these myths are foolish and dangerous. First, they are grounded in ignorance. Can you imagine a telephone-illiterate social worker? We take telephone technology, along with those trusty fax machines, dictation equipment, word processors, and a host of other communications tools for granted. Most of us couldn't practice without them. Computers are no different. They are only communications machines, just like telephones but fancier. And they are just as important.

And dangerous. The nature of practice is drastically changing because of the information age. Finding something out about people from a diverse culture you have not encountered, learning the latest trends in legislation and programs, or getting mentoring from supervisors or colleagues once took tedious trips to the library, many phone calls, and maybe a couple of in-service training sessions. All of this can now be done immediately from a connected computer.

Social work consumers too are using the Web. Self-help groups abound. People learn about the latest treatments, trends, and resources within a short time; or they can be completely "information impoverished" because they do not have access. Abundant information—and some pretty scary misinformation—can be easily accessed by anyone who is literate and capable of using a computer. We need to learn how to use the Web because of these consumer realities.

Learning to use the Web—and to use it well—is an acquired skill. It is vexing, challenging, and at times so frustrating that we would all like to throw the dratted machines into the nearest dumpster. When mastered though, computers can genuinely enhance our practice. Just as social workers had to adapt to telephone in practice a century ago, we must now adapt to computers. Realtime practice on literally a global scale with all sizes of client systems is now possible. A family counselor in Des Moines can work with a couple in Manila. A social worker in Vancouver can arrange an adoption in Bucharest. A refugee worker in Addis Ababa can comb foundations in New York. An advocate in Oregon can monitor legislation and directly lobby Washington, D.C.

All of this is now possible—instantaneously possible—because of the communications technologies that have recently evolved and will continue to grow in scope and sophistication in the future. We have the obligation to learn how to use these and to use them equitably, safely, and ethically. To do less is foolish and dangerous.

ACKNOWLEDGMENTS

Many people have contributed time, ideas, and support to us. We deeply appreciate the support our spouses Katherine Vernon and Jack Lynch provided. Our colleagues Lynn Adkins, Sandy Baughn, Andrea Bednar, Shirley Bigna, Marge Epstein, Colleen Galambos, Lisa Gebo, Judith Halseth, Beth Kiggins, Leslie Krongold, Kim Mann, Steve Marson, Dawn O'Shea, Gerri Outlaw, Jeanne Patterson, Jennie Redwitz, Kris Ruddle, Jill Scheer-Doerfert, Cheryl Shearer, Marshall Smith, and Susan Wilson provided wonderful ideas, helpful insights, and frank criticism. This was invaluable. We would also like to acknowledge our reviewers, whose helpful comments have strengthen our thinking and this book.

Molly Davis, George Mason University

Grafton H. Hull, Indiana University Northwest

Donna McIntosh, Siena College

Ginny L. Raymond, University of Alabama, Tuscaloosa

Robert F. Rivas, Siena College

Katherine Shank, student

Jose B. Torres, University of Wisconsin, Milwaukee

We have departed from how other colleagues have written about the Web in one significant way: we have provided only minimal listings of Web resources. This is for practical and philosophical reasons. Printed lists of websites become quickly obsolete because the Web is so volatile. The intent of this book is to teach you how to find, evaluate, and use information *on your own*. If you need lists of resources, we suggest you use the *meta-lists* at the back of Chapter 4 as a starting place.

Finally, a word about our style. We are pretty irreverent about computing. We think that keeping a humorous frame of mind is vital. Computers are just objects filled with hopelessly complex innards and gizmos. Nothing more. They are not sacred. They are not sentient. They are simply tools. Keep this in mind! We use the minimal technical jargon we can. After all, we are social workers, not computer programmers.

IMPORTANT! READ THIS PART TWICE!

There are details you need to know before you begin using this book!

First, this book is already obsolete! Well, it is not entirely out of date, but parts of it probably are. The Web is changing so fast that it is impossible for any printed book to completely keep up. New versions of the browsers will have come out. Some of the instructions will have changed. The pictures of actual webpages will be different because their webweavers will have updated them. Some websites will have moved. Others may have entirely vanished. The Web is a very volatile place.

So why bother with a book? The day may come when books are completely electronic, but not just yet. You use barter, currency, checks, and credit cards to buy things, don't you? Each of these technologies was once new but never replaced the older ones. Computers are the same. Books will remain vital for some time to come. And we hope this book strengthens your practice!

In addition, heaven only knows what kind of computer and connection you are using! No two college labs are ever configured exactly the same way. The same goes for computers in homes and agencies. It does not matter if you are using a Macintosh or an IBM-type of computer. It does not matter if you are using the latest computer or a venerable 386 you got at the Goodwill. The important point to remember is *the technical nature of how your computer actually works may be different from what is described in this book.*

We have written for a typical-use situation but you still may have to adapt, ask questions, and get help. Follow the examples in this book as suggestions. View the illustrations as general aids. We have written this book primarily for the IBM-type of personal computer because they comprise about 90 percent of those available. We have specifically chosen to use the Windows '95 operating system because it, too, is very common. If you are using something else, such as Windows '98 or Windows NT, you may encounter minor differences between what we have said and what your machine does. We have also provided extra directions for Mac users whenever possible.

This book is written for the two most common *browsers,* the Netscape Communicator/Navigator Version 4.0 and the Microsoft "Internet Explorer" Version 4.0. Both browsers work very well and in much the same way, as do others that can be found in the marketplace. In order to keep this book as short as possible, we have intentionally omitted many of the accessories common to most browsers. There are many other fine books that will help you learn more about the technical dimensions of browsers.

Ask for specific help when you need to. You are going to have to do this in practice anyway. You might have a Mac at home but use an IBM-type computer at work. You might use one browser at the agency and another at the library. As a result, you will need to be flexible when using this book, just as you have to be flexible when using computers in practice.

We have written this book based on the assumption that the reader has at least a basic familiarity with personal computers. This includes how to navigate windows (mouse and scrolling skills), multitasking (switching between the Web and word processing), and basic E-mail (sending, receiving, and reading E-mail messages). If you are not able to do these, you will need to find help beyond what this book can offer.

We have focused the exercises onto the major issues within each chapter with one exception. Chapter 3, Security and Confidentiality, contains quite a few technical instructions. Since the types of computers and connections the readers will be using are vast, we present this as information for practice but are not able to provide a hands-on experience.

Mastering the Web takes time. It is a developed skill that gradually emerges after hours of solitude, frustration, and delight. We hope this book empowers your practice!

DISCLAIMER

This worktext and related web material is presented solely for educational purposes. During the course of using this worktext and related web material, readers may encounter sample information that may be potentially offensive to individuals, professions, and organizations. It should be noted that such materials and references do not represent the views or endorsements of the authors, social work colleagues, the social profession, or the Publisher, Brooks/Cole-Wadsworth Publishing Company, or any of the publisher's affiliates. Neither the Authors nor the Publisher, nor any of the Publisher's affiliates, assume any responsibility or liability arising out of this material.

PART I

BASIC CONCEPTS

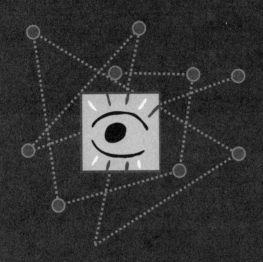

CHAPTER 1

The Web and Social Work

 Some ideas to consider . . .

. . . Future social workers may practice *on-line* as well as *ftf* (face-to-face).

. . . The *World Wide Web* holds vast resources for all dimensions of practice.

. . . It is possible to exchange electronic information on a planetary basis.

CHAPTER OVERVIEW

Learning to use the World Wide Web (the Web) is like learning to play the recorder or draw pictures. Almost anyone can learn these, but it takes genuine skill to do them well. Many six-year-olds can turn on a computer, point and click the mouse, and get something from the Web onto the screen. Yet professional use of the Web is far more involved. This chapter begins the journey:

- How the Web Connects to Social Work
- Basic Definitions and Concepts
- A Metaphor for Understanding the Web
- How Does the Web Work?
- Watch the Horizon

If possible, go through this chapter while at your computer! It really helps!

HOW THE WEB CONNECTS TO SOCIAL WORK

Just What IS This "Web" and What Does It Have to Do with Social Work?

The World Wide Web (simply called *the Web* by most folks, but also called *the Infobahn* or *the Information Superhighway*) is the fastest growing part of the Internet.

In fact, if you have a speedy computer, a good Web browser, and a reliable Internet connection, *the Web may be all you really need for many new dimensions of social work practice!* No kidding! It is becoming the universal way to travel the Internet; and many of the older applications such as *E*-mail, FTP (file transfer protocol), list-servs, gophers, and newsgroups are gravitating to the Web. This is called *convergence.* These separate communications features are merging into the more seamless Web. This is why it is so easy to use in comparison with what was hot just a few years ago. You do not have to become an expert to use the computer.

Simply put, the Web creates the ability for many computers to talk with each other and exchange information. Period. Just as telephones easily link people across the world, computers are gaining the same ability. There is nothing mysterious about the telephone; you just use it. The Web is becoming the same. It is evolving into potentially *the* source for information on an unimagined scale. Consider the following possibilities:

■ What if you need to quickly develop a handout for caretakers of Parkinson's disease victims for members of a support group you run? Where could you find the latest information on research, treatment choices, pharmaceutical developments, and architectural adaptations? You can find this information, cut and paste it, and develop a custom handout for the group members. All from the Web.

■ What if your supervisor asks you to research policy choices on female circumcision so the agency's board of directors can form policy? Consider how much you need to know about people from other cultures and our own before you suggest anything. Daunting, isn't it? How could you quickly find out more about beliefs, values, spiritual views, social rules, laws, and many other dimensions of different cultures? Tremendous resources are available at your fingertips. All from the Web.

■ Suppose the police drop off a homeless man at your agency. He is extremely disoriented and tells you he has been blacking out, stumbling, and biting his tongue. He shows you a bottle of medicine he is taking. He tells you he has been taking this medicine for only a few days. Can this medicine possibly be related to the problems he is having? You can find out. All from the Web.

■ Imagine that the alcohol on a colleague's breath every morning makes you wonder if they are "impaired." You could research impairment in the National Association of Social Worker (NASW) Code of Ethics. You could review your own professional obligation to this colleague and our profession. You could probably join a discussion group on the subject and get some mentoring. Then you could take action. All from the Web.

■ How do you prevent disclosure and confidentiality problems in practice when you can easily circulate information throughout the planet? Divulging toxic information such as very personal case details can wreck lives. Different approaches to information security and electronic communications can be directly researched to prevent this. All from the Web.

■ The grant is due in the mail tomorrow, and you really need statistics describing how many poor people live in your county. You especially need fine-grained information to show that your agency has a good command of the issues. You can find this information and put it into the grant in about a half hour. All from the Web.

Many people are under the impression that the Web consists of flashy companies trying to sell you something along with pornography and other exploitive
horrors. While these can certainly be found, nothing could be further from the
truth. The resources available for social work are immense and growing every day.
You must learn how to find, evaluate, and use what is out there for practice. The
chances are very good that you will come to rely more and more on the Web for
information and resources as your practice matures.

CSWE Curriculum

Let's examine some of the basic issues by looking at each of the nine Council on
Social Work Education (CSWE) curriculum content areas (CSWE, 1994, pp. 100, 138)
and how the Web affects them. We examine many issues in this book through
these categories, and the learning exercises at the back of each chapter are based
on them. It is mandatory that *all* social workers, BSW *and* MSW, study all nine
areas to become professional social workers.[1]

PRACTICE   Social workers practice with systems that range from individuals to communities. Knowledge, values, and skills enhance the well-being of people and help
ameliorate environmental conditions. Practice includes understanding client
strengths and problems in the interactions among individuals and between people
and their environments.

We practice with many different sizes and types of systems, ranging from individuals to communities and larger units. Did you know that it is now possible to
counsel people on-line through E-mail and websites? If you need to find a support
group for your clients, chances are you can find several on the Web for any specific
issue or problem. You probably can find a lot of information about municipal
programs and services just from a few local websites in your area. Web-supported
practice resources are rapidly emerging, and you will need to know how to find
them more and more as the Web evolves and matures (Weinberg, 1996; Giffords,
1998; Schopler, Abell, & Galinsky, 1998; Rondero, 1998).

POLICY AND SERVICES   Policy includes the history, mission, and philosophy of the
social work profession. Political and organizational ways to influence policy, the
formulation process, and frameworks for analysis are included. Services consist of
publicly and privately funded efforts to help people attain or maintain optimal
health and well-being.

Want to keep abreast of the latest proposals floating through your state legislature? Want to find out what changes to services and funding patterns are being
proposed? Chances are good that you can find immediate up-to-date information
on countless policy issues. Policy-making and policy-influencing organizations
that range from federal organizations through local municipalities are now offering information about themselves and their activities directly on the Web. If your
local county or state is not up to speed, it is probably just a matter of time before

---

[1]   A synopsis of these areas is provided for your convenience and reference in the exercises. The entire texts for both BSW and MSW requirements are available on the CSWE
website: http://www.cswe.org/accreditation.htm

it starts providing webpages with information about proposed legislation, policies, and services. Your ability to professionally advocate and influence legislation will increase too! You can now easily E-mail all federal senators and congresspersons and give them your opinion on impending legislation. You can find out countless details about specific services by using webpages that give this information free of charge. Need to update your resources list for your agency? The Web is one place to start (Schwartz, 1996).

FIELD/AGENCIES   Social workers practice in a wide variety of settings including countless social, human, educational, and health agencies and organizations. The agencies may be staffed either largely by social workers or instead by a comparative few. Services may range from few to many, and the people served may be similar or quite diverse.

Can you imagine an agency that has no telephones? "Webless" agencies are going to become rare in your future, too. Field agencies have an uneven distribution of computers right now. Some agencies have only a few older ones that are not connected to anything, while others use systems that can easily access global communications. Use differs too. Some agencies only use computers for word processing, scheduling, budgeting, accounting, and similar managerial tasks. Others use them extensively to make their services known and available to client systems, find out information, and generally support many different practicing professionals such as social workers, teachers, attorneys, doctors, and nurses. The authors expect that the shift to using computers as a way to access information and support professional field activities, as opposed to simply managing them, is going to continue. Students and practitioners will be expected to be able to master Web communications as more agencies come on-line. If your agency does not have a website now, chances are good it will in the future, and you may play a part in its design (Marson, 1998; Butterfield, in press).

SOCIAL AND ECONOMIC JUSTICE   Social workers seek to end all forms of human oppression and discrimination. This includes using strategies geared toward achieving individual and collective social and economic justice and combating the causes and effects of institutionalized forms of oppression.

As long as we are talking about policy, did you know that you can find many websites that help you choose strategies for promoting economic and social justice? Many advocacy groups and organizations are now on-line, and *NetActivism* is emerging as a credible way to take action (Schwartz, 1996). Current news items about poverty and empowerment are available with a few keystrokes. You need to know how to find this on the Web to advocate for issues (Galambos & Neal, in press).

POPULATIONS AT RISK   The dynamics and consequences of discrimination, economic deprivation, and oppression put people at risk. Some of the categories for populations at risk include people of color, women, gay and lesbian persons, the elderly, poor people, religious minorities, ethnic and cultural minorities, and people who are physically or mentally challenged.

Information about many different groups of people, neighborhoods, and communities that are at risk is also available on the Web. Need to know the latest on immigration policy? Want to find out more about support groups for Alzheimer's victims and their families? Need to find major funders for children's programs? Is there a local support organization for lesbian and gay persons? Our profession is centered on populations at risk. We need to learn how to find, evaluate, and use this information as more and more comes on-line (Galinsky, Schopler, & Abell, 1997; Finn, 1995).

DIVERSITY   Social workers must learn differential assessment and intervention practices, because we work with diverse populations. These include but are not limited to groups distinguished by race, ethnicity, culture, class, gender, sexual orientation, religion, physical and mental ability, age, and national origin.

Even in its current disorganized and, frankly, chaotic state, the Web reflects human diversity on an awesome scale. Do you need to learn more about a specific group of people you have never met before or studied? Chances are very good that you can find excellent information about many diverse religious, cultural, social, ethnic, racial, and national groups of people. As our society becomes more and more diverse, we all need to learn from each other as we become interdependent. Discerning use of the Web is an excellent beginning (Miller-Cribbs & Chadiha, in press).

HUMAN BEHAVIOR IN THE SOCIAL ENVIRONMENT (HBSE)   Social workers need to master knowledge about the social systems in which individuals live, such as families, groups, organizations, institutions, and communities. This includes understanding biological, social, psychological, and cultural systems as they affect and are affected by human behavior. Social and economic forces on individuals and systems must be learned.

Human development as it relates to biology, psychodynamics, society, economics, culture, and organizations has wide-ranging dynamics. The impact of social and economic forces on the individual or on the agency can be astounding. Every single human developmental stage has a host of websites. All of these issues, ranging from blunt information to subtle discussions, are available on the Web.

VALUES AND ETHICS   Social work is a profession with specific values and ethics. These are reflected in our conduct toward client systems, the profession, other colleagues, and society at large. Values include individual worth and dignity, mutuality, acceptance, confidentiality, honesty, and the responsible handling of conflict. People have the right to make independent decisions and to participate in the helping process. Social workers respect diversity and strive to make social institutions more humane and responsive. These and other values are further specified in several codes for ethical conduct.

We are the "good guys and gals." Our values and ethics are publicly posted for the world to see and to hold us accountable. It is important to keep in mind that the full spectrum of human values and ethical stances are on the Web. This includes some horridly racist, sexist, ageist, and homophobic sites. Unethical, criminal, and cruel dangers are out there, too. You need to master skills for discerning the values and ethical bases for websites, even when these are intentionally hidden by the organizations that sponsor them (Finn, 1990; Marson, 1999). Not everyone is a "good guy or gal."

RESEARCH   Social work is research grounded. This includes mastering scientific approaches to developing practice knowledge and service evaluation. It includes qualitative and quantitative approaches and attention to ethical standards for scientific inquiry.

There is probably at least one website somewhere in the world for almost any topic or issue you can imagine. The information can range from really first-rate scholarly data to questionable and even fraudulent information. Hard statistical data can often be dredged up, but is it accurate and timely? Qualitative information is abundant, but can you trust the sources? You need to know how to find and evaluate Web-based data toward evaluating your practice, discovering new information, conducting research, and advancing our profession (Holden, Rosenberg, & Weissman, 1996).

SUMMARY   In summary, the Web touches every facet of social work education and practice. This will increase. The potentials for good and evil are certainly present. The Web can help in our practice, but it can hurt people too. We have the obligation to know how to use the Web in effective, equitable, and ethical ways that are compatible with sound practice.

BASIC DEFINITIONS AND CONCEPTS

You do not need to know how your telephone works to use it, do you? You really do not need to know very much about how the Web works in order to access and use it either. You just need to understand a few key terms to get started.

First, the Web is part of something much larger called the **Internet.** This is a *part-whole* relationship. The Internet consists of countless computers and networks that exchange information in many different forms. It can provide you with data and software goodies you can download; "gopher pages" that contain text files; Web pages that have graphics, sounds and animations; and much more. In short, the Internet is simply a term for the extensive network that enables computers to link together on a planetary basis. The Internet is the *whole.* The Web is one of these networks, or *parts,* and a part that is getting bigger and bigger. Eventually, most of the tasks we do on the Internet may be done on the Web.

You need to know a little more. First, the **Web** actually consists of millions of computers that can be linked together in almost any fashion. *Websites* (discussed in the next section) are simply computer files that are kept on special computers called **servers.** While usually more complex and expensive than your personal computer, servers really are not very different. They simply provide files to anyone authorized to access them. Through using many different technical goodies that we really do not need to get into, the system works in a way that allows most server computers to link together. With this networking, almost anyone can access available information. The Internet and the Web look a little like Figure 1–1.

Note that you can go almost anywhere in the world from any single computer. The important point to remember is that the Web is a part of the Internet, and, together, the ability to share information is truly vast.

Just What, Exactly, Are Websites, Webpages, and All Those Other Confusing Terms?

Think of the Web as a vast library with millions of books on every subject you can imagine. Each book is actually a **website.** Each website has text, illustrations, and some degree of organization. The contents of the book are the **webpages** that, all

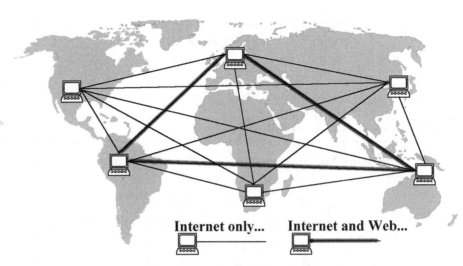

FIGURE 1-1 What the Internet and Web might look like.

together, make up each website. Like books, websites generally have more than one page. Most websites have a few webpages, and some can number in the thousands.

Just like books, the Web is *somewhat* controllable by the reader. You choose to pick up a book, browse through its contents, and decide whether you want to put it down for another, skim it, or read it from cover to cover. Using the Web is no different in this regard.

We said *somewhat*, didn't we? There are some real differences. Paper books are static and have to be reprinted every so many years. Webpages can be updated or completely changed, or they can vanish in an instant. This makes the Web very up-to-date and volatile: "subject to change without notice." The technology is in its infancy and far less reliable than good old ink and paper. Just as it took hundreds of years for the book to evolve, the Web is changing and renewing itself. What you learn about it now will be ridiculously obsolete within a few years. Yet, the Web remains an unparalleled resource for social work practice.

A METAPHOR FOR UNDERSTANDING THE WEB

The Web is generally known by its name because people think it resembles a spider's web. There is even folklore of arachnid images: Web crawlers creep along like spiders. *Lycos,* a search engine, is the species name for a tough little spider you really do not want as a houseguest. Yet, this is not a very helpful image anymore, and maybe it never was. The Web is not as orderly, symmetrical, or organized as one any self-respecting spider would ever build. The following is a metaphor that is more realistic.

The Web is like the Wild West, but not the syrupy Hollywood version. It is not very well mapped. It is full of muddy tracks and dirt roads that sometimes lead everywhere and sometimes lead nowhere. Traveling can be very slow and tedious with a lot of waiting. It is very easy to get lost. The Web has interesting wildlife too, including pack rats and more than a few rattlesnakes. And it is fraught with social conflicts and cultural factions. Do not be deceived by the Information

Superhighway metaphor. Maybe the Web will become paved in the decades to come, but for now it is a very messy, muddy, and sometimes hostile territory that no one owns and everyone shares.

HOW DOES THE WEB WORK?

A little technical jargon goes a long way, but you need to know a few basic terms. Technically, the Web consists of

> HTML files called *webpages*
>
> that are combined together to make *websites*
>
> that are put on *server* computers
>
> that *dynamically link* with each other.

You are probably familiar with word-processing programs for computers such as Microsoft Word and WordPerfect. Just like them, webpages are written with programs that take text and put it into a different computer language called **html** or *hypertext markup language.* Creating webpages is not all that different from typing that case report, grant proposal, or research project in a word processor; and some word-processing programs allow you to convert your text to Web documents with ease. The big *difference* is that by using html and perhaps other goodies like JAVA to animate pictures or JAVA SCRIPT to animate words, you can make the text extremely interactive. Printed text is not really going anywhere, is it? It just sits on your page. The html text—the stuff webpages are made of—lets you jump around at will anywhere within a document and even jump to other websites with no difficulty. This is an understatement: when we say *jump to other websites,* we mean websites all over the planet! Websites are like books full of webpages, ready for your access, but far less static than paper books.

To be able to read webpages, you need a specific type of computer program called a **browser.** Browsers display Web documents and allow you to scroll through them and navigate from one to another. Other programs such as JAVA permit special effects, and VRML or virtual reality markup language allows fancier capabilities, but in the main most of the Web consists of html documents organized as websites that have to be viewed with a browser. The websites are kept on the servers we described. When you connect your personal computer or one in a lab with a browser and server, your computer can be dynamically linked to millions of others.

Dynamically linked is the understatement of understatements. In general, any server can access another as long as there is a way for a compatible connection to be made. This can be through telephone lines, microwaves, fiber optics, and many other conduits. Just as you can now dial almost all telephones in the world, most web servers on the planet can connect with each other at will.

The key issue is that, as of this writing, there are probably over fifty million webpages in the world and perhaps as many as eighty million (Bray, n.d.). Estimating how many websites and webpages are really available is very difficult and perhaps not very useful anymore. Think of the Web as a map of the world from maybe three hundred years ago. Whole continents were unmapped back then, and many features were completely unknown. (Smith, 1997). But regardless of its actual nature and size, the Web holds vast amounts of information on a scale never before created by any human civilization. Within this vastness are countless websites that are useful for social work.

Accessing the Web is becoming commonplace. At least 45 percent of homes in the United States have a personal computer (*Wall Street Journal,* 10 March 1998/Edupage[2]). Roughly 750,000 people are on the Web at any given time. America On Line (AOL), one of many **Internet Service Providers (ISPs)** has over thirteen million subscribers (*Investor's Business Daily,* 28 August 1998/Edupage). This means that many client systems now enjoy access. Yet, this is producing problems as well. Electronic traffic now doubles at least twice a year, making for a very crowded Internet. This creates a *bandwidth* problem, meaning that the demand for the Internet and the Web is beginning to exceed what the technology can deliver (*Information Week,* 16 March 1998/Edupage). Premium connections to the Internet are beginning to emerge so companies can avoid *gridlock* (*CIO,* 15 November 1998/Edupage). The *Internet 2* initiative to develop a separate network for scientific research and communications is underway, largely to alleviate the crowded Internet. **Intranets,** electronic networks *within* companies but not connected to the outside, are also rapidly increasing (*Investor's Business Daily,* 16 October 1997/Edupage). This means that accessing the Internet may become problematic in the future.

Another problem is based on race, economics, and class: poor people have less access. Social workers need to master the Web because we may often be the main conduits for client access. We will also need to advocate for more equitable distribution of Internet resources as services to the poor become more and more on-line. A few cities (i.e., Oakland, California) are already beginning to legally require Internet access in public housing (*Government Technology,* September 1997/Edupage). Nevertheless, *information poverty* is a new form of disenfranchisement—and oppression—that is likely to increase (Novac & Hoffman, 1998).

Access also produces social and personal consequences. There is some evidence that excessive use of the Web can become addicting to the point where families break up (*Associated Press,* 15 August 1997/Edupage). Web use can be a lonely experience and can contribute to depression (*New York Times,* 30 August 1998/Edupage).

Access also is geopolitical: the third world has far less access. Developing nations are concerned that North American and European countries will create international policies that lead to a permanent dominance of the Internet and Web by the Western world (*TechWeb,* 9 March 1998/Edupage).

What does all of this mean? The Web certainly provides many helpful resources for social work, and this will increase in the future. Yet, we will also experience problems as well, and we will need to be attentive to equity and empowerment issues as the world becomes ever more knitted together by the Web.

---

[2]   Edupage citations follow the references at the end of the chapter. Edupage is a news service that provides three weekly summaries about information technology as a public service. It is produced by EDUCAUSE, an international nonprofit association dedicated to transforming higher education through information technologies. The website is www.educause.edu

WATCH THE HORIZON

We have just covered the basics. This book only takes you through the silent side of the Web because the majority of resources available are, at present, without sound or important animations. (OK, that snazzy sound and video greeting from the agency's executive director are cute, but are they really all *that* important?) This will be changing in the near future, so we want you to be aware of some trends.

Multimedia-configured computers (computers with sound cards, speakers, and even tiny TV cameras) are becoming commonplace. While agencies may tend to buy the cheaper nonmultimedia machines to save on expenses (technology is a faucet that never stops dripping), this may not last long. Websites with sound are going to become more and more common, especially as people strive to make the Web more disability friendly. While multimedia are rather limited to the commercial and entertainment sectors at this time, it is quite possible that in the future we will see more and more useful websites that offer sound and movie capabilities. Imagine being able not only to read about different cultures but also to experience native speakers who interpret their world for you. Imagine being able not only to exchange information about a case but also to directly exchange pertinent verbal and visual information online. Imagine not only learning about current legislation but also directly hearing people—including yourself—speak about the issues. These scenarios are quite possible.

In addition, cheap and easy videoconferencing with colleagues, students, and clients at remote locations is also becoming possible. Tiny video cameras are now available that, coupled with audio peripherals, make it possible to "CU-SeeMe" in a fairly inexpensive way over the Web. While still in its infancy (most *see-you-see-me* programs compress the video pictures, making them jerky and strobe-light-like), this technology may rapidly expand and improve in the near future. *Video-streaming* technologies that allow you to view direct realtime pictures without having to download them to the computer's memory are evolving. *Webphones* that allow you to talk directly with someone else are available now, although the quality of speech is sometimes clunky and garbled. These may eventually give way to communications on a par with the best telephone quality.

Electronic books are emerging. They may come in several forms such as simple downloading to your computer or to another type of appliance (*Associated Press*, 23 October 1998/Edupage). You may soon even be able to make your own postage stamps off the Web that will be honored by the United States Post Office (*Investor's Business Daily*, 20 November 1998/Edupage). Disk storage may soon take a quantum leap: IBM is currently developing a ten-billion-bit disk drive. That amounts to 725,000 double-spaced pages, far more than any human is likely to write during a lifetime (*Atlanta-Journal Constitution*, 30 December 1997/Edupage). Voice-activated computers for cars may soon be available from Intel, perhaps drastically altering where social workers have to work (*San Jose Mercury News*, 29 December 1997/Edupage).

The implications for practice are extensive. In the near future, you will be able to directly hold case management conferences on-line, interview clients, and conduct many other face-to-face dimensions of practice from a computer terminal, perhaps in your own home, where you work, or in your car. We want you to remember: this book is about the beginning of what the Web can do. As technologies such as television, cable, radio, computing, and others converge together into more seamless and blended audiovisual environments, the dimensions for practicing ethical social work will change and may change dramatically.

If we ignore technology as a profession, non-social workers are going to do it for us, at us, under us, on us, and over us, but not with us.

Exercise 1
Expectations

■ This is a paper exercise. You do not need to use a computer.

■ The purpose of this exercise is to sharpen your awareness and understanding of the nine different content areas and how they may relate to the Web.

■ In addition, your thinking about the "horizon" issues discussed in this chapter should be sharpened.

DIRECTIONS

If we were surfing the Web right now, we might find websites that hold different types of information for each of the areas that follow. Professional social work websites such as organizations and agencies, consumer-based websites such as self-help and mutual support groups, education- and research-related websites, commercially related websites, and those of other professions could be found.

Speculate about each of the following nine areas by writing one or two sentences per question. Refer to the section on CSWE curriculum for definitions of the areas.

Example: Field/Agencies

What information would tell you that you are in an agency's website?

I'd look for their name, probably a board of directors, and a description of the services offered.

Practice

What type of content do you think a "practice-related" website should contain?

Field/Agencies

What information would tell you that you are in an agency's website?

Policy and Services

How would you know you are in a website that relates to social welfare policy?

Social and Economic Justice

What information in a website do you think would tell you it is related to social and economic justice?

Populations At Risk

What you think would constitute a website for a specific population at risk?

Diversity

Describe a diversity-related website you would expect to find.

Human Behavior in the Social Environment (HBSE)

How would a website reflect human behavior in the social environment, such as different developmental stages?

Values and Ethics

How can you spot the values and ethics bases for a website?

Research

What information would you expect to find in a research-related website?

Summary

This chapter discussed why you need to learn to use the Web in social work and provided examples from practice and education. A very simple explanation of the Web, how it works, and a glimpse toward the "horizon" was described. The next chapter takes up the basic skills you need.

Questions for Discussion

What kinds of computers have you seen at various social welfare agencies? How were people using them?

How *technologically literate* should social workers be? What is important to master?

Should technology be a tenth area for social work students to study along with the other nine?

What factors prevent clients from getting access to the Web?

What are the issues clients may face when they do not have direct access to the Web, especially as the "horizon" comes closer and closer?

References

Bray, T. (No date). Measuring the Web. [On-line]. Available: www5conf.inria.fr/fich_html/papers/P9/Cover.html

Butterfield, W. (in press). Human services and the information economy. *Journal of Computers in Human Services, 15*(2/3).

Council on Social Work Education: Commission on Accreditation. (1994). *Handbook of accreditation standards and procedures* (4th ed.). Alexandria, VA: Author. [On-line (in part)]. Available: http://www.cswe.org/accreditation.htm

Finn, J. (1990). Security, privacy, and confidentiality in agency microcomputer use. *Families in Society: The Journal of Contemporary Human Services,* 283–290.

Finn, J. (1995). Computer-based self-help groups: A new resource to supplement support groups. *Social Work with Groups, 18*(1), 109–117.

Galambos, C., & Neal, C. (in press). Macro practice and policy in cyberspace. *Journal of Computers in Human Services, 15*(2/3).

Galinsky, M., Schopler, J., & Abell, M. (1997). Connecting group members through telephone and computer groups. *Health and Social Work, 22*(3), 181–188.

Giffords, E. (1998). Social work on the Internet: An introduction. *Social Work, 43*(3), 243–251.

Holden, G., Rosenberg, G., and Weissman, A. (1996). World Wide Web accessible resources related to research on social work practice. *Research on Social Work Practice, 6*(2), 236–262.

Marson, S. (1998). Major uses of the Internet for social workers: A brief report for new users. *Areté, 22*(2), 21–28.

Marson, S. (1999). *On-line ethics.* [Monograph submitted for publication].

Miller-Cribbs, J., & Chadiha, L. (in press). Integrating the Internet in a human diversity course. *Journal of Computers in Human Services, 15*(2/3).

Novak, T., & Hoffman, D. (1998). Bridging the racial divide on the Internet. (This working paper is a longer version of the article published in *Science*, April 17, 1998.) Project 2000, Vanderbilt University. [On-line]. Available: www.cybergrrl.com/fs.jhtml?/views/hottopic/art251/

Rondero, V. (1998). Computer technology in social work settings: Issues, considerations, and implications for the profession. *Information Technology for Social Work Practitioner's and Educator's Conference Proceedings* (pp. 40–50). Columbia, SC: School of Social Work, University of South Carolina.

Schopler, J., Abell, M., & Galinsky, M. (1998). Technology-based groups: A review and conceptual framework for practice. *Social Work, 43*(3), 254–267.

Schwartz, E. (1996). *Net activism: How citizens use the Internet.* Sebastopol, CA: Songline Studios.

Smith, Z. (1997). The truth about the Web: Crawling towards eternity. *Web Techniques Magazine, 2*(5). [On-line]. Available: www.alexa.com/company/internet_stats.html

Weinberg, N. (1996). Compassion by computer: Contrasting the supportiveness of computer-mediated and face-to-face interactions. *Computers in Human Services, 13*, 51–63.

Edupage Citations[3]

Associated Press. (15 August 1997). Time to log off. [Reported in Edupage, August 18, 1997]

Associated Press. (23 October 1998). E-books to come singing down the wire. [Reported in Edupage, October 25, 1998].

Atlanta-Journal Constitution. IBM developing 10 billion bit drive. [Reported in Edupage, December 30, 1997].

CIO. (15 November 1998). Premium ISPs on the rise. [Reported in Edupage, November 22, 1998].

Government Technology. (September 1997). Oakland ends welfare as we know it . . . By adding the Net. [Reported in Edupage, October 12, 1997].

Information Week. (16 March 1998). ISPs say Internet demand exceeds technology. [Reported in Edupage, March 18, 1998].

Investor's Business Daily. (16 October 1997). Intranet use exploding. [Reported in Edupage, October 16, 1997].

Investor's Business Daily. (28 August 1998). AOL just grows and grows. [Reported in Edupage, August 30, 1998].

Investor's Business Daily. (20 November 1998). E-stamps on the way. [Reported in Edupage, November 22, 1998].

---

[3] Edupage is an on-line news service. To subscribe to Edupage, send a blank message to edupage-subscribe@educause.unc.edu. For more information visit: http://www.edu-cause.edu/pub/pubs.html

San Jose Mercury News. (29 December 1997). Computin' down the highway. [Reported in Edupage, December 29, 1997].

TechWeb. (9 March 1998). Third world protests tax-free Internet. [Reported in Edupage, March 10, 1998].

Wall Street Journal. (10 March 1998). Nearly half of U.S. homes own a PC. [Reported in Edupage, March 10, 1998].

Additional Readings

Gralla, P. (1998). *How the Internet works* (4th ed.). Indianapolis, IN: Que Publishers Inc.

Grant, G., & Grobman, L. (1998). *The social worker's Internet handbook.* Harrisburg, PA: White Hat Communications.

Grobman, G., & Grant, G. (1998). *The non-profit Internet handbook.* Harrisburg, PA: White Hat Communications.

Hahn, H. (1999). *Harly Hahn teaches the Internet.* Indianapolis, IN: Que Publishers Inc.

Jaffe, J. (1998). *Quick guide to the Internet for social work.* Needham Heights, MA: Allyn & Bacon.

Karger, H., & Levine, J. (1999). *The Internet and technology for the human services.* Reading, MS: Addison Wesley Longman, Inc.

Kasser, B. (1998). *Using the Internet* (4th ed.). Indianapolis, IN: Que Publishing.

Walker, M. (1997). *How to use the Internet* (4th ed.). Emeryville, CA: Ziff Davis Press.

Wendland, M. (1998). *The complete "no geek-speak" guide to the Internet.* Grand Rapids, MI: Zondervan Publishing House.

Additional Websites

Hobbes Internet Timeline (History Timeline) http://www.isoc.org/zakon/Internet/History/HIT.html

General Telephone Onternetworking (1998) *BBN Timeline* (History Timeline) http://www.bbn.com/timeline/

Marketing Automation Products (August 06, 1998) *Internet Marketing* (Projected statistics for Internet use) http://www.mapsys.com/ma3inews.htm

Leiner, B., et. al. (20 February 1998) *A Brief History of the Internet,* version 3.1 (Internet History) http://www.isoc.org/internet-history/brief.html

Barry M. Leiner, Vinton G. Cerf, David D. Clark, Robert E. Kahn, Leonard Kleinrock, Daniel C. Lynch, Jon Postel, Larry G. Roberts, Stephen Wolff

Browser Basics

Some of the many things you can do on the Web . . .

. . . Lobby about the latest legislation on practice.

. . . Find out more about cultures you do not know very well.

. . . Create lists of resources for clients.

. . . Paste excerpts and quotes into an academic paper.

. . . Follow the news on emerging events in the profession.

. . . Download relevant files and software.

. . . Help a client shop.

. . . Find out if a specific conduct is addressed in the NASW *Code of Ethics*.

. . . Discover many more things than can be imagined.

CHAPTER OVERVIEW

There are plenty of fat books on how to use the Web, and, if you really need to master it comprehensively, you may need to get one. Actually, there are also many excellent resources on the Web itself, so consider mastering this chapter and Chapters 4 and 5 on how to search the Internet before you buy supplemental books! Its cheaper! This chapter will take you through the basics:

- How to Start
- Browser Basics
- URLs: Life of the Web
- How to "See" a Webpage
- Saving and Using What You Have Found
- Copyright Issues
- Error Messages

If possible, go through this chapter while at your computer! It really helps!

FIGURE 2-1 Netscape Communicator and Microsoft Internet Explorer icons.

HOW TO START

You need a software program called a **browser** installed in your computer to navigate the Web. *Browser* is just a name for programs that allow you to view webpages and navigate between them, just as we call writing programs *word processors.* Many types of browsers are available, but most do the same things. Our emphasis is on *Netscape Communicator 4.0* (the Navigator part of it) and *Microsoft Internet Explorer 4.0,* because these are the predominant browsers currently available. We call them *Navigator* and *Explorer* for convenience. Both browsers perform the same functions. There are others, too, and most of these instructions will fit them as well. Some university labs may offer several browsers, and brand-new computers often come with one or more of them already installed and ready to connect.

IMPORTANT: While browser programs have not been around very long, it is vital for you to *use an up-to-date version.* The older ones are far from satisfactory. (Yes, a two-year-old browser *is* old!) If you do not have at least the *Netscape Navigator 3.0* or its Microsoft equivalent, *you need to advocate* having it installed in your labs or *download* an up-to-date version to your private computer. Earlier versions of browsers will not support you well and are far less versatile. Using an obsolete browser is like eating a sandwich when you could have a five-course, served banquet. If this is an accurate description of your situation, solve this problem *now!* Both Navigator and Explorer are available *free* to educational institutions, non-profit organizations, and personal users, so there is no excuse!

If your computer has the browser installed and the Internet connection is ready, all you have to do is turn on your computer, wait for it to fully turn on in the Windows or Mac version, and find the *icon* (little picture and caption) for the Netscape Communicator or the Microsoft Internet Explorer (Figure 2-1).

Roll the mouse until the *cursor arrow* is over the icon. The arrow may change to a hand. Double-click the left button on the mouse (IBM type of computer) or the single button (Mac type). This should start the browser and get you on your way to the Web.[1] Depending on the browser, you should get something similar to one of the screens shown in Figure 2-2.

---

[1] Most campus computer labs have this or a similar configuration. If you are at home or at your agency, your connection may be different.

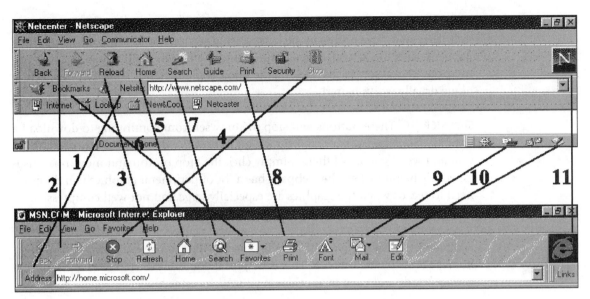

FIGURE 2-2 Netscape Communicator and Microsoft Internet Explorer control buttons.

BROWSER BASICS

Before we go on, let us become a little bit more familiar with the browser. Ignore whatever is in the browser's window, and look at the rows of buttons and graphics at the top and bottom of the screen. (Depending on settings, you may only have text-labeled buttons, pictures, or both as in Figure 2-2.) The Netscape and Explorer browsers have similar buttons that do essentially the same thing. We are going to show you the *basic* buttons and features (indicated by number in the figure) you need to get going.

What the Buttons Do for You

NETSITE OR LOCATION/ADDRESS (1)   The Netsite or Location/Address white boxes tell you the *Uniform Resource Locator* or *URL* (the webpage's address) for the page you are currently viewing. (A discussion of the URL is found later in this Chapter.) If you highlight this URL by holding the mouse button down and scrolling so that it covers the whole URL, you can type in a new URL. Then press the return key on your keyboard, and the browser will take you to the new webpage. However, while you *can* do this, there are serious security reasons *not* to do so. To go to another webpage, it is better to click on the upper-left File menu choice and scroll to the Go To (Explorer) or Open Page (Navigator) box instead where you can type in a new URL. Make this a habit. These dangers are discussed in the next chapter, but for now remember that the Netsite or Location/Address box shows you the Web address for the page that is currently in the browser's main window.

BACK FORWARD/BACK FORWARD (2)   If you have visited several webpages, the Back feature will take you to the previous webpage you saw, and you can keep on going if you like. The Forward button will take you forward in the same way. These buttons only work when you have visited several webpages. Using them is much easier than reentering the URL and sometimes faster than the navigation provided on the webpage.

RELOAD/REFRESH (3)   Webpages sometimes get bogged down or just do not work well. They may have problems such as missing sections or freezing up. When this happens, click the Reload/Refresh button and the browser will reload the current webpage. This is sort of like kicking the photocopier when it jams, but this technique usually works better!

STOP/STOP (4)   These buttons will stop the browser from continuing to download a webpage. Some webpages take f-o-r-e-v-e-r to download, and you may not want to wait and see any more of them. Simply click the Stop button and move on. This is especially helpful when the webpage has a lot of peripheral graphics you do not need to see, or when the graphics are especially large and not well compressed, which makes them download at a tedious pace.

HOME/HOME (5)   Clicking on the Home button will take you back to the default homepage set by the browser. This is helpful if you want to start over again during surfing but do not want to shut down your Web connection.

BOOKMARKS/FAVORITES (6)   If you learn to use the Bookmarks/Favorites utilities, you can go directly to and never have to type the URL again! Both Netscape and Explorer have similar ways to enter, organize, and edit bookmarks. Click on this button and follow the prompts to build your list. When you want to go to a specific place, click the Favorites or Bookmark button again to summon your list. Select and click on the website you want, and you are on your way!

If you are at a public workstation, office connection, or campus lab, this feature may only work if you save your Bookmarks/Favorites onto a separate floppy disk. This is because the Bookmark or Favorites feature may be partially disabled. Imagine the mess that would result if fifty users a day bookmarked their favorite places on the same computer! Bookmarking onto a floppy disk is also a good idea for keeping confidential records of your work. (Directions are provided in Chapter 3.)

SEARCH/SEARCH (7)   The Search buttons will take you to Internet search engines. We discuss how to use these in Chapter 5. Do not develop the bad habit of simply clicking this button and using the first engine that comes up! If you must, click this button and explore several of the search engines just for fun. You can always click on Home if you get lost! We teach you better ways to search the Web in Chapters 4 and 5.

PRINT/PRINT (8)   Clicking on the Print button will usually print the current webpage you are viewing. This depends on how the browser is connected via the computer to the printer. You may get everything you see, only what you see on the screen but not the full webpage, only text with no pictures, or completely wasted paper.

MAIL ICON/MAIL (9)   If the browser is set up to support E-mail, clicking on the Mail button or icon will bring it up. This feature can be very handy, because you can conveniently send a message and then easily get back to *your still-connected and working* browser. The only easier way to use the Web and E-mail together is to use Web-based E-mail where everything is done in the browser.

EDIT ICON/EDIT (10)   Depending on how the browser has been configured and if the software is available, clicking on the Edit button or icon will bring up the

WYSIWYG (pronounced *wizzywig,* What You See Is What You Get) editor for creating your own webpages or editing the page you are viewing. Forget it for now.

BROWSER LOGOS (11)   Both the Navigator and Explorer logos have animations. The Explorer's *e* spins, becomes the earth, and goes back to being *e*. Navigator's animation shows comets streaking over the earth. When the logo is actively showing you these animations, it means the browser is busy downloading the website file to your computer. Downloading websites sometimes takes a long time, and, especially if you are on a slow computer or have a wretched connection, nothing appears to be happening on the screen except for the logo animation. Just be patient. The webpage is ready to view when the animation stops.

From time to time, a webpage may not load into the computer. As a general rule, if the logo is not moving and the results on your screen are useless, wait twenty seconds. If the computer does not continue displaying the webpage, consider clicking the Stop button and then clicking the Reload button.

There are many other features and buttons on these browsers, and your screen may not look exactly like the ones in the figure. Mastering any browser takes time. However, familiarity with these few buttons is all you need to start surfing the Web!

TIP: Both the Navigator and Explorer browsers have excellent Help features on the top lines of the window. Clicking on Help and following the prompts will lead you to tutorials for all of the browser's features. The Help source often comes directly from the Web, so you may need to have your browser connected to the Web when you use it.

URLS: LIFE OF THE WEB

We do not have the foggiest idea of what the homepage in front of you really looks like, so let's go to a common one every self-respecting social worker should know by heart: the homepage for the National Association of Social Workers (NASW). In order to do this, you need to learn how to get out of your computer's default homepage, which brings us to something called **Uniform Resource Locators,** or **URLs,** pronounced by some folks as *Earls,* as in Duke of . . . , and others as *Urals,* those large mountains in the middle of Russia. Still other people spell it out as U-R-L. There is no agreement at this time, so take your pick.

URLs are the key addresses you must have to go to specific websites. URLs are similar to phone numbers with access codes, area codes, and numbers: you must enter correctly or you will get a wrong number. Entering a URL is like telephoning an agency on a referral for a client: you can call the main number or instead go to the right extension if you know it. If you do not enter the URL correctly, you will know it because you will immediately get a "wrong-number" type of error message. Usually this is the No DNS (No Domain Server) message, and it usually means that the browser could not get to the website you requested. (Error messages are taken up at the end of this chapter.)

URL Anatomy

Figure 2-3 offers a helpful way to understand what URLs actually mean. Imagine that you are addressing a "snail-mail" envelope.

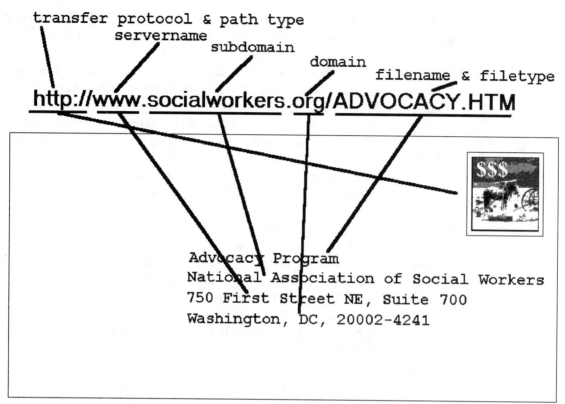

FIGURE 2-3 Anatomy of a URL.

URLs have a common structure that is fairly predictable. This makes it somewhat easy to know ahead of time where you are headed. The URL for NASW is

http://www.socialworkers.org

The first part of the URL—http://—is the server command. This command tells the browser *what kind of server* you want to connect to. The *http* means *hypertext transfer protocol,* and is the most common command on the Web, but you may occasionally use other URLs that begin with *gopher://* or *FTP://* or *telnet://* or *news:*. Not to worry. This is what makes the Web so wonderfully versatile.[2]

Generally, the *http://* part of the URL does not have to be typed in unless you are working with an older browser such as Netscape 3.0. More up-to-date browsers will type this in automatically. The Navigator browser will automatically queue in the *www* and *.com* part of commercial URLs too, a nice feature.

The next part of the URL is the *Internet address* for the Website. The part of the URL that distinguishes it as the NASW's is

www.socialworkers.org

---

[2] *Gopher* files are text only and run on computers called *gopher servers* that predate graphic-capable Web machines. You may still encounter them. After all, why buy a new server if you are only going to put text files on it? *FTP* stands for *file transfer protocol* and is another older way to transfer files and programs from another computer to your own. *Telnet* allows your computer to guest on another distant one, a nifty feature if you are at another location and want to check your E-mail. *News* is the way to dial into newsgroups. Most browsers now integrate and automate these other features on the website, making life much easier.

You can often learn a little more by dissecting the Internet address further. The first part, often *www* for *World Wide Web* tells you the name of the *host* machine at a specific location. Not all URLs have it anymore. The next part, *socialworkers,* is a *subdomain,* usually nested within a larger domain. Finally, the *last three letters* in the Internet address tell you the *largest domain* of the URL. This is the *.org* part of NASW's URL. All URLs must have a domain.

Knowing the domain part of the URL is extremely helpful because you can usually tell where you are going. There are six common **domains** in the domain-name system:

.org	stands for *organizations,* usually nonprofits.
.net	stands for *network* sites, the folks who try to keep the Web alive and well.
.com	stands for *commercial* websites that usually have a for-profit dimension.
.edu	stands for *educational* and research institutions.
.gov	stands for *government* websites, ranging from small to vast.
.mil	stands for the *military,* who crafted the Internet in the first place so everyone could have a nice chat during World War III. Cheery thought.

TIP: Memorize these six domain names, and you will find surfing much more informative!

URLs can get a lot more complex, but we get to that in a bit. The other helpful fact to keep in mind is that you can *sometimes tell where you are going on the planet* by reading the URL. For example, some URLs include international designations:

fr	stands for *France.*
ja	stands for *Japan.*
au	stands for *Australia.*
ca	stands for *Canada.*
ch	stands for *Switzerland.*
us	stands for *United States.*

These are just a few. The comprehensive International Organization for Standardization[3] listing, called the *ISO 3166 Country Designation Codes* list, identifies 239 different countries from Afghanistan (af) to Zimbabwe (zw).[4] These codes can really clue you in on where you are headed if they appear in the URL. Conventionally, domestic URLs within the United States do not have international designations at this point. Some people, especially from the third world, view this as a bit arrogant.

The dimensions of the domain-name system are evolving. First, attempts are underway to create more fine-grained domain names such as *.art* for the arts, *.nom* for personal webpages, *.store* for retail websites, and so on. Barriers are present. New domain names in English may not translate well into other languages. (The

---

[3] http://www.iso.ch
[4] For a comprehensive listing, visit: http://eexpert.com/_gp_dng.htm, http://iso3166.styx.net/, or http://wmbr.mit.edu/stations/ISOcodes.html

current ones do not either.) Second, there is serious resentment by third-world countries over the "westernization" of the Web and its dominance by the developed countries (*Wall Street Journal,* 24 March 1998/Edupage). Ditto the non-English-speaking developed countries (*TechWeb,* 31 January 1998/Edupage). There is considerable debate over this, because an expanded and more useful domain-name system would have to globally meet the needs of many people and organizations. More fine-grained domain names may eventually emerge, but the evolution will be rocky. Even with the present system, it is better than having just an area code and phone number, is it not?

A second type of URL you may encounter is the simple Internet Protocol or IP address. These URLs—the ones the computers *actually* look for—are simply the identification numbers for the actual destination computers, and each number is unique to one machine/Internet location. These addresses have four separate components, which are, from left to right, the geographic region, the organization or service provider, the group of computers, and the specific machine. Sometimes these addresses are benign, but they can also mask more "toxic" places such as pornography or hate-group websites. They usually look like this:

http://123.456.78.901

We talk more about these types of websites in Chapter 3. The important point to remember is that not all URLs are intuitive, and some may be intentionally deceptive.

Finally, URLs often have a lot of extra stuff after the main address. For example, the URL

http://www.socialworkers.org/Code/CDTOC.HTM

will take you to the NASW *Code of Ethics* (NASW, n.d.) Table of Contents. What this URL really does is tell the server to (1) go to the NASW website, (2) open the *Code of Ethics* folder, and then (3) download the file containing the Table of Contents. The actual name of the file is the *CDTOC.HTM* part. We are getting a little ahead of ourselves here, but keep in mind: some URLs can be extremely long and opaque, while others are very transparent.

Opening a Webpage

The best way to open a new webpage for a new website is to type the URL into the Netscape Open Page or Explorer Open box and click on the Open or OK buttons (Figure 2-4). *Let's go to the NASW homepage.*

Pull down the File menu by clicking on it with the mouse button and select the Go To (Explorer) or Open Page (Navigator) box. Type in "www.socialworkers.org" (without the quotation marks) in the white selection box, and press the Open button to summon the website. Depending on how fast your computer and its connections are, you should see the NASW homepage (Figure 2-5) in several seconds or a minute or so.

Examining the Webpage

Most webpages[5] have text plus graphic files, and the NASW homepage is no exception. The logo picture in the top middle of the page is a *graphic* and may take

---

[5] Do not forget, websites may have changed since this book was published, so the webpages may look different from what is shown in the figures.

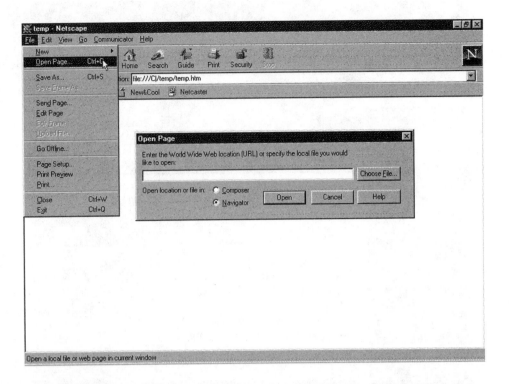

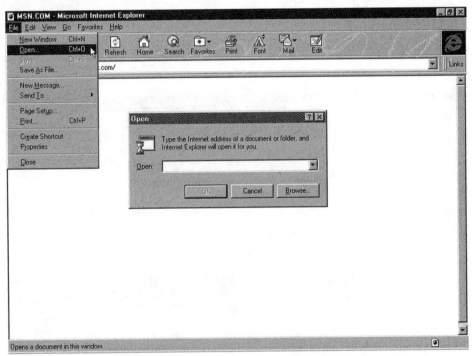

FIGURE 2-4 Type the URL in Navigator *Open Page* or Explorer *Open* box.

longer to load than the text. Do not click your mouse yet! Roll and scroll the cursor all around the screen, and notice where the cursor changes from the arrow to the small hand, showing you where there are hypertexts or hyperlinks to somewhere else within this website or beyond it.

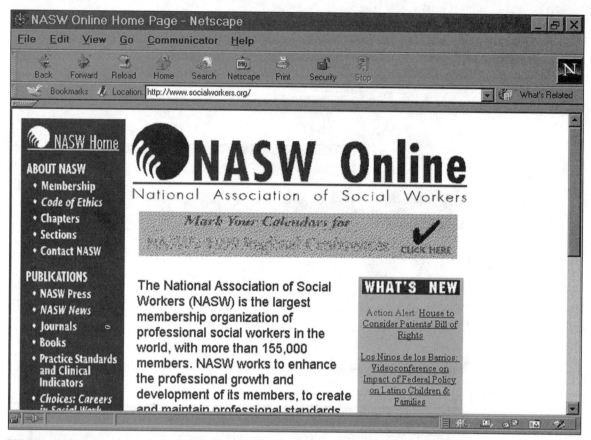

FIGURE 2-5 National Association of Social Workers homepage. (Used by permission of NASW.)

FIGURE 2-6 National Association of Social Workers chapter webpage. (Used by permission of NASW.)

Navigating beyond the Homepage

Let's try navigating within the NASW website. Click on the Chapters button in the top left (you do not have to be a member of NASW to use these resources, by the way, but you should be!) The new webpage should appear (Figure 2-6).

Compare the new page with the previous one. Note two important changes. First, while the new page looks similar, it is different in its layout. Also note that the URL in the Location/Address box has changed automatically to

http://www.socialworkers.org/CHAPTERS.HTM

The Location/Address box always shows the *current* webpage you are viewing.

HOW TO "SEE" A WEBPAGE

This sounds pretty dumb, does it not? After all, any sighted person can obviously see the page on the screen in front of them, can they not? While this is true, it is very important to *always look at the full document!* A typical homepage, especially for professional organizations and agencies, has three design elements: the header, the body, and the footer. We explore these features in a little bit, but you need to first develop a very good habit by mastering a vital RULE: ALWAYS look over the whole webpage, top to bottom and side to side, when exploring a new homepage. Scroll bars will appear when there is more to the page than shown on the screen. Use them!

Examine Figure 2-7. This is the complete homepage for NASW, although you may only see about a third of it at a time on your computer screen. Note the *header* or top part. This generally *tells you where you are.* Usually you will find the name of the organization sponsoring the page, logos or graphics that echo this, and other verbal and visual cues to orient you. Some navigation may be present, such as links to other places on the website. Navigation is often in a left-hand column too, as in this example.

The *body* contains *the main information* about the website, such as its purpose and contents. Links within the site to different sections or topics within the website are common, and links beyond to other websites are common, too. In general, the links will be a different color or otherwise highlighted in a different way from the normal text.

The *footer* usually has navigation aids within the website, and these are sometimes redundant with other parts of the page. Linkages to other resources at other sites sometimes appear here, too. Source, signature, creator, sponsor, dates, and contact information are often present, especially on well-designed webpages such as this one.

Naturally, there are many variations, but this design format is fairly predictable. Just do not forget; the RULE: ALWAYS look at everything first! You may find some nice surprises and some pretty awful ones at times, too!

SAVING AND USING WHAT YOU HAVE FOUND

One of the advantages to using the Web is that you can easily circulate, modify, and use electronic copies of almost anything you find. For example, you could research foster care and save pertinent website contents into a word-processor file.

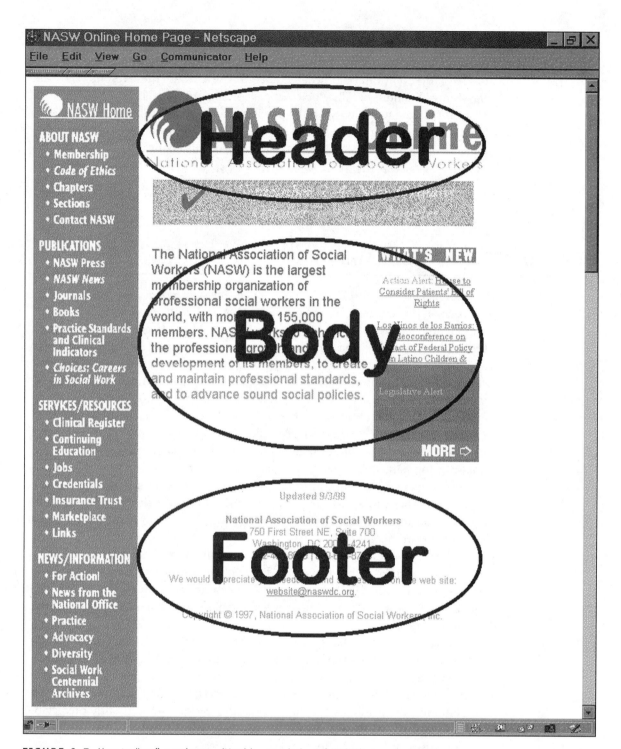

FIGURE 2-7 How to "see" a webpage. (Used by permission of NASW.)

You could then edit the materials and, *voilá!*, have a handout for a workshop. You could E-mail the information to colleagues or post it to a discussion group. You could save the information as an html file and display the website as needed to clients and colleagues without depending on an Internet connection. Saving and using Web-based text can be done fairly quickly and easily once you learn how to capture the information. First, save a copy of the URL itself in a Bookmark or Friends file for later use. This helps keep track of websites you have visited. (More on these in Chapter 3.)

Printing a Hard Copy

Sometimes you need hard (paper) copies for reference or practice. These are very convenient, especially for sharing with clients or colleagues. A paper copy is the most portable, because no computer is necessary. For example, a client with Parkinson's disease might want to know the latest information on experimental treatments. You go to a website, find the information, print it, and give it to the client. *The advantage of having a hard copy is that the client does not need a computer and can refer to the materials at a convenient time.*

The easiest way to make a hard copy of a webpage is by clicking the Print button at the top of the browser. Both Netscape and Explorer have this icon/ button. Pressing this button should give you a hard copy of the webpage if your system is connected to a printer. If the button is not visible, then simply pull down the File menu from the top left corner of the screen and select Print from the keyboard. (This applies to both Navigator and Explorer.) If all is connected well, the printer should generate a copy in short order. If not, you are going to have to troubleshoot.

Several factors can affect printing quality. First, obviously, you must have a printer that is turned on, filled with paper, and linked to your computer. Since there is tremendous variation in how computers are configured, we cannot go into detail in this book, but do become familiar with your printer's characteristics prior to getting on the Web. If you are in a computer lab at school, chances are you are linked to a printer somewhere. Ask for directions if needed. If you are at home, you are probably familiar with your own system.

Clicking on the Print button may produce several results:

The entire page may print just as it appears on your screen.

Only the text, and perhaps a few of the graphics, will print.

You get an error message and maybe something to line the cat's box.

This variation is due to different computer-printer linkages and software configurations. Laser printers, for example, generally can handle pictures just fine if properly set up, while older dot-matrix printers produce rather hopeless graphics. The only suggestion we have is that it is helpful to know the idiosyncrasies of your system and where to get help.

Making Electronic Copies

A far more versatile approach is to make an electronic copy of all or part of the webpage.[6] There are two ways to make an electronic copy: save it as it is written in the html language, or save it as a text file for a word processor. Most modern word-processing programs will allow you to do either or both.

---

[6] If you want the entire document, you can go to the edit menu and choose Select All or simply press and hold down the Control key and then press the A key. The whole file will be highlighted, and you can then copy it.

Saving the Webpage as an html File

You can save the webpage as an html file *and bring it up on the browser even if you have not connected to the network.* This can be really handy if you want to show a webpage to someone, because you might not always be able to get back to the one you want if the server is busy, if a system (yours or the remote server) goes down, or if webpages get moved around or changed at the website.[7]

■ Go to the File menu on the browser (both Netscape and Explorer have this same choice), pull the File menu down, and click on the Save As line. You will get a prompt that asks where you want to save the file.

■ Generally, you can save the file anywhere you like on the hard drive, such as in a designated folder. To stick with the NASW example, you might create a folder on the hard drive called *NASW* and use it to store part of the NASW website for further reference.

■ If you are at a public workstation such as a school lab or are at an agency (and especially if the material has confidentiality implications), you will need to save the file to the floppy drive on a separate disk you have brought with you instead of on the computer's internal hard drive.

■ As a general rule, give the file a simple name so you can remember what it is for.

■ Click the prompts as they appear until you have saved the file in a location you can easily find again on your computer or on a separate disk. Be certain that the file has the *.htm* suffix attached to its name.

IMPORTANT: This procedure saves the current webpage as an html file. If you want more pages from the site, you have to save each one separately, although there are commercial software programs that will copy far more pages or the entire website if you want to. In addition, remember that graphics files are often very large and can take up an inordinate amount of space. Just a few graphics files can easily fill up a 3.5-inch floppy disk. Pay attention to how much room the graphics files may need before proceeding. If the website is largely made up of text, it should usually save to a floppy disk without problems. If there are abundant graphics, you may need a larger storage device such as a *Zip* or *Jazz* drive or writable CD.

What Can You Do with the Copy?

Now that you have a copy of the complete webpage on your computer, you could show it as a resource webpage to a client or colleague or include it in a demonstration for a class or consumer group. The easiest way to display a "captured" webpage is to open the browser and select the Open Page (Navigator) or the Go To (Explorer) option from the File menu. Click on the Choose File button, and follow the prompts until you have selected the file. Click the OK button in the Open choice box and then the Open choice when the name and location for the file appear in the white box.

As an alternative, open the Open Page or Go To box and type in the name and location for the file in the Location/Address box. Just be sure to substitute the location of the file on the hard disk, such as *c://* instead of entering the *http://.* If

---

[7] Your computer may be making electronic copies anyway, but you need to be able to control and manage them. We get into this more in Chapter 3.

you have named the copied webpage *NASW.htm* and put the file in a folder called *Resource,* the URL you would enter into the Open Page choice box would be

C:/Resource/NASW.htm

This presumes you intend to save the file to your *C:* drive (IBM type). Otherwise, simply substitute the drive location you have used. The nice thing about all of this is that you can show a webpage, and often a whole website, without being connected to the Web.

Depending on the software available, you could also include all or part of the webpage in a presentation program such as PowerPoint or Astound. This skill is beyond this book, but do be aware that you may have this ability. It can create excellent presentations. You can probably open the html webfile as a textfile in your word processor, too.

You can open the file in most word processors as such *if* the word processor can translate the file from html to a general textfile, or if it will allow you to write html files. If you do not have either of these word-processing features, you are sunk, but most modern word-processing programs will allow you to do these without difficulty. You might lose some or all of the formatting. You may not get the graphics, because some word processors cannot read .gif or .jpg files, which are the types of graphic files used to display pictures on the Web. At minimum, you certainly can save and open the text, thus avoiding tedious retyping! The only downside is that you will copy the whole webpage when you follow this process, and you may want just a small part of the webpage.

Saving All or Part of a Webpage to a Word Processor

Another approach to copying materials is to use the Copy and Paste feature found in most browsers. This allows you to copy part or all of a website's text and transfer it to somewhere else on your computer, such as the word processor. This approach has *a major advantage* over directly printing a hard copy or making a full electronic copy of the webpage's html file. *Textfiles are far more manipulable,* and you can do a lot more things with them, such as inserting text from the Web into term papers—with citations of course!—or making handouts on resources available for clients. The possibilities are endless.

Copy and Paste is far more efficient if you want to copy just a part or section of a webpage instead of the whole thing. For example, perhaps you need to teach non-social-work colleagues about the mission of our profession at an in-service training session. From surfing the NASW homepage, you may have found that clicking to the *About NASW* page takes you to the NASW Mission Statement. You go there and

■ Open your word processor and create a blank page (or E-mail box program; this method will copy stuff to E-mail messages, too!).

■ Switch back to the browser and its website.

■ Highlight the desired text in the website by clicking on the left mouse button at the beginning of the section you want to copy. Keeping the mouse button down, scroll down until you have highlighted what you need. Then let the mouse button up. The part you want to copy should be back-highlighted in another color, usually darker than the text (Figure 2-8).

■ Go to the Edit choice at the top of the browser. Click down and select the Copy feature. You can also hold down the Control and *C* (IBM only) buttons

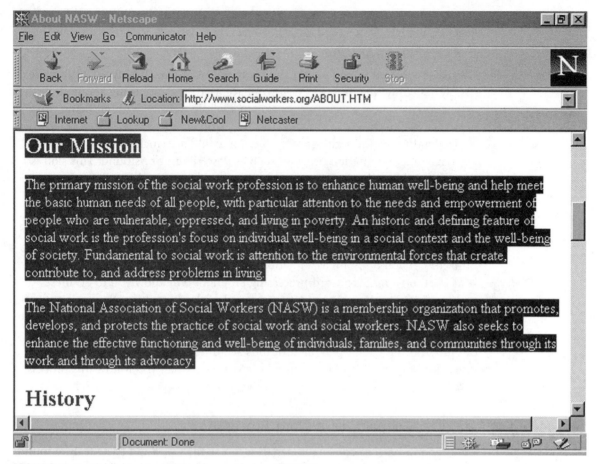

FIGURE 2-8 Highlighted text. (Used by permission of NASW.)

together and get the same results or click the word processor's Copy button, too, if it has one. The program will automatically copy the text to the computer's Clipboard.

■ Now return to the word processor (or open an E-mail message box if you are sending the text as a message to someone else).

■ Locate the cursor where you want to insert the desired text, and click the Paste feature or button. Instead, you can press the Control and *V* keys together on the keyboard (IBM only); go to Edit and pull down the menu, then select Paste; or simply hold the Shift and Insert keys together (IBM only) on your keyboard. Any of these methods will usually work.

Voilá! The text from the webpage should be entered directly into the word processor. The only problem with this approach is, as in the alternative described earlier, you may not have much luck copying pictures or graphics.

The easiest way to copy a graphic file from a webpage, at least with Navigator and IBM-type machines, is to highlight the graphic with the left mouse button, release it, and then click the right mouse button and choose the Save Image As choice. Just follow the prompts, and you can save the image to the computer's hard disk or other storage device if available.

While this is not entirely within the scope of this book, some information about graphics may be helpful. Websites generally display two types of graphics files: .jpg and .gif. Many word processors do not accept these types of graphics

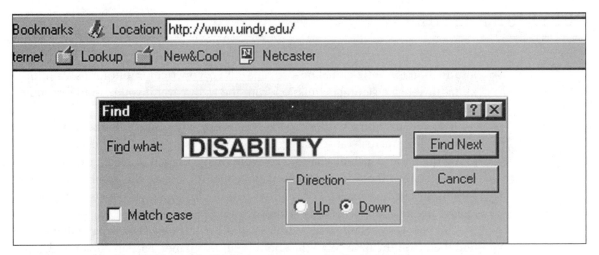

FIGURE 2-9 Using the *Find* feature is like having a search engine for each webpage.

files. As a result, you may have to convert Web graphics from the .jpg and .gif formats to perhaps a .bmp (bitmap) format that the word processor can recognize. You will need an intermediary graphics-editing program to do this. There are enough technical hassles—such as how many colors you need, file compression choices, and the like—to make this an acquired skill in its own right. If you do want to use graphics from the Web in written media, then you may need to use one of these graphics-editor programs.

These approaches extend the use of the text information you find on the Web. They circumvent tedious retyping!. You can cut and paste part or all of the saved document into other textfiles such as agency reports or term papers without having to do much more than giving them a cursory edit and citation. *What you have created is a very easily manipulable file that can be printed, sent to another person as an E-mail enclosure or attachment, or otherwise treated as any other textfile.*

The Find Feature

The Find feature, available on both browsers, lets you search for specific words or word fragments within a webpage. This feature is extremely useful when searching through a long document, especially one with poor navigation aids. For example, perhaps you want to read about disabilities in a bill being considered by your state legislature. Since many state legislatures are now on-line, accessing a specific bill is quite possible. If you are able to get to the proposed legislation on the Web, entering *disability* into the Find feature will take you to every single use of the word in the text.

The Find feature (Figure 2-9) can really help you locate specific information in large, cluttered, or text-dominant webpages. To access it, pull down the Edit menu and simply select the Find feature, then follow the prompts. Using Find is like having your own personally controllable search engine built into every single webpage.

TIP: The Find feature is useful but not very smart. If you actually enter *disability* instead of *disabilities,* you only find *disability* inclusions in the text. A better strategy is to cut off the end of the search word so it looks for the root term, such as entering *disabil* when you use Find. This use of the root instead of the complete word, called **stemming,** will result in bringing up both forms of the term you are after.

COPYRIGHT ISSUES

While you can copy almost anything on the Web for your personal use, use of the information for professional purposes has direct copyright implications. At minimum, investigate getting permission from the webweaver if you plan to distribute any information in any way beyond personal use.

If you are a student writing a paper, then copying webtext into the paper is generally legitimate because you are engaged in personal learning. Just be certain to use quotes and include citations to avoid being accused of plagiarism. We strongly suggest that you also make paper copies of at least the homepage and the specifically cited webpage(s) of websites you cite for academic papers and projects. Make sure the complete *URL* is included.

The Web is so volatile that websites can disappear between the time that you find them and the time you write about them in a paper. Backup copies of the homepage and cited page(s) are very cheap insurance and proof of legitimate scholarship.

Copying the same information into an agency's brochure, report, or other non-personal usage is an *entirely different matter*. Always assume that every webpage you visit has a legitimate legal copyright owner (Templeton, 1998). *Get permission(s) in writing before you proceed* (Daunt, 1998).

Ignorance of copyright laws and obligations is no excuse for violation or professional misconduct. When in doubt, find out! Several Web resources are listed at the back of this chapter. In addition, the following resources may be helpful if you have to negotiate policy regarding copyright use for your placement or agency:

■ Check the NASW *Code of Ethics* (NASW, n.d.,). See especially Section 4, Responsibilities as Professionals, and subsection 4.08 on acknowledging credit.

■ Refer to your school's plagiarism/fair use policy. Almost all colleges and universities have adopted guidelines and policies on plagiarism and fair use.

■ Consult the *Publication Manual of the American Psychological Association, 4th ed.* (APA, 1994). The Ethics section is very helpful.

■ Consult a librarian. Many professional librarians address copyright issues all of the time and can often help or refer you to pertinent resources.

ERROR MESSAGES

To err is human, but to really foul up, you need a computer! Clichés aside, the Web is new, emerging, and often very fragile. Things go wrong far more often than we would like. This section addresses what to do when things do not work!

When You Have Entered a URL and Nothing Seems to Happen or Change

First, is the browser working? Both the Netscape and Explorer icons in the upper right corner of the window have animations that tell you when the browser is active. The comets streak past the dark planet on Netscape, and the Explorer has an *e* that turns to become the earth and then the *e* again. This is helpful, because, if nothing other than the animation is happening on your screen, then you know the browser is working and looking for something or downloading a webpage. Just wait and be patient.

Sometimes you may be trying to access a URL on a server that is on the other side of the planet. Long-distance downloads—especially at times when their server may be at its peak load or when there are many intermediary connections between your system and the remote location—can really take a long time. Again, all you can do is wait.

Did you press the Return or Enter key? Sometimes we forget!

Finally, if the webpage you are after has a lot of graphics on it and if these files are fairly huge and not well compressed, then downloading may be tedious.

When the Known URL Does Not Work

Pay attention. This happens a lot! Several things can go wrong with reliable URLs that you think are accurate, and most browsers will usually give you a clue about why it did not work by giving you error messages. There is a basic hierarchy to the errors:

- Nothing happens because your computer is not really connected and you are not really getting out onto the Web.

- Your connection is fine, but you are not getting to another link because you have an incorrect URL, you goofed when typing it in, or the server that hosts the website is not turned on and working.

- You cannot get to the website because too many other people are already using it, just like the busy signal on the telephone.

- You are getting to the webpage you want, but you get an error message or nothing is there. Instead, you may get a "This website has moved" type of message, or "Error 404."

- Deep mystical experiences are happening on the Web with no ontological meaning beyond their existential essence. (We have been meaning to warn you about this.)

We discuss these problems in the following sections.

IF NOTHING HAPPENS   Nothing happens. The Netscape planet/comet animation or the Explorer *e* simply twiddles interminably. If nothing has happened for about two minutes, click on the Stop button. Then check your connection by trying another known and reliable URL. If you can get the new URL, then your connection is fine, but something is wrong with the server you are trying to access, or it may simply be overloaded with too many other souls using it.

When nothing happens and the planet or *e* animation has stopped, first try clicking on the Refresh (Explorer) or Reset (Navigator) buttons. This will make the browser try to reload the webpage again and often works. If this does not work, and if you have already visited a previous webpage somewhere and know that your connection and browser are working properly, then try clicking on the Back button or arrow and then going forward. Depending on how your browser is configured and how it is storing webpages, you may get everything back. Finally, if the system just is not going anywhere, you may have to shut down your Internet connection and then reestablish it. Do not do this if you can avoid it because you will probably lose your previous work.

A second type of error message, the ! Network Error, happens when your network connection is on the fritz. Given how fast high-speed modems operate, they can make mistakes in transmitting data. Try the following strategies:

- Click the Reload or Refresh button at the top of the browser.
- Click the link again (if you are having problems connecting from a link on a webpage).
- Try disconnecting and reconnecting your link.

YOU KNOW YOUR CONNECTION IS FINE BUT YOU ARE NOT GETTING TO ANOTHER LINK   This is an extremely common problem. The usual message (Figure 2-10) is "There was no response . . ." (Netscape), "Internet Explorer cannot open . . ." (Microsoft), or "No DNS" (Netscape, not illustrated). These messages are roughly equivalent to the busy signal on your phone but can mean other things are wrong too. One of several problems has usually happened when you get these messages.

The most common problem is that you did not enter the URL completely and accurately into the browser. Typing a comma (,) instead of a period (.); forgetting to add the domain (.edu, .org); or putting in the wrong domain (.com when it should have been .net) will stop you dead in the water or take you to an entirely different ocean. Browsers are rather obsessive-compulsive and cannot tolerate even teensy mistakes, much less the weensy ones! *Check your spelling and punctuation for complete accuracy.*

A related problem is *case sensitivity.* "No DNS" or "Internet Explorer cannot . . ." can happen when you have not entered the URL in the correct case. Some servers handle *capital* letters and the *lowercase* small letters quite well, but others are very sensitive to the differences. For example, entering the URL

http://www.capital.edu/file.htm

may get drastically different results from entering

http://www.capital.edu/FILE.HTM

Server computers (and all the other gizmos between where you are and where you want to go) do not always work well, especially with long, arcane, and somewhat nasty URLs such as

http://its.somewhere.com/lost/on_theInter.net/80:-and/Icantf.ind/it.html

Correctly entering a long URL can still produce a "No DNS" or "cannot open" error message because the length may induce problems. When this happens, a good strategy is to *cut off the right-hand parts of the URL between the slashes, one at a*

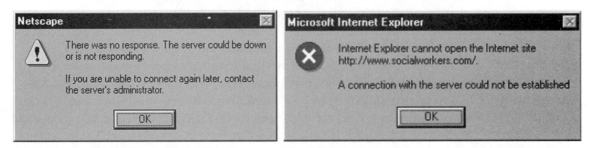

FIGURE 2-10 Typical "busy signal" messages for Navigator and Explorer browsers.

time, until you get to a webpage that can take you to the file you wanted in the first place. This strategy works well but only when there are good links in the website that will let you move forward within it to find your target. To do this, you would enter

> **http://its.somewhere.com/lost/on_theInter.net/80:-and/Icantf.ind**

If this does not work, try

> **http://its.somewhere.com/lost/on_theInter.net/80:-and**

If this does not work, try

> **http://its.somewhere.com/lost/on_theInter.net**

If this does not work, try

> **http://its.somewhere.com/lost**

If this does not work, try

> **http://its.somewhere.com**

And if this does not work, something may be very wrong with the server, the connection, or the URL in the first place! This approach sounds tedious, but it really is not very hard and will often provide good results.

"BUSY SIGNAL"   Another common problem that brings up the "No DNS" or "cannot open" error message is that the website you want to visit is too busy because of other people accessing it. Try reconnecting later, especially if the URL has worked in the past or if you are certain that it is accurate and available.

The message can also mean that the website's server is turned off. You cannot do anything about this except to try later.

ERROR MESSAGES   Another error message typically shows itself when your computer actually is not connected when you think it is (Figure 2-11). When this happens, check to see if you can put your computer back on-line by pulling down the File menu from the top left of the window and selecting the Go On-line choice (Navigator) or making sure the Go Off-line choice is not checked in the File menu (Explorer).

Other error messages can be informative too. For example, you may occasionally get a "cannot open site graphics" message. This error message happens when the webpage you want is not available. It does not mean it is completely gone, and you may find it later because someone turned the server on again. It can also mean the file no longer exists or the links to it have been removed. People often take files off their webpages but do not clean up the links.

FIGURE 2-11 Navigator and Explorer off-line messages mean the computer is not connected.

Try any of these three approaches:

- Click the Refresh or Reload buttons.
- Retry the URL.
- Try the URL-shortening technique already described. You may be able to go forward and find the webpage you are looking for if the file you want has been retitled or relinked.

There are still other error messages, like the "404" and the "403". When you get into a website just fine but try to go to a link that is no longer there, you often get a "404 Error" message telling you the webpage is not available. If you are trying to get into a restricted/passworded part of a website, you will generally get a similar "403 Error" message. Forget it. You are not going to get there!

You frequently will get a *"This site has moved!"* notice on the webpage. One of the more vexing problems on the Web is that people keep changing URLs. There are several reasons for this, such as the organization got a new server or they switched their ISP (Internet Service Provider). If you are lucky, the old provider will direct you to the new one and may even have a hypertext link that will take you to the new location. When this is not the case, the only thing you can do in this case is make the best-guess attempt at what you think the URL probably looks like and hope for the best. This actually is not hard once you have a little practice on the Web, especially with commercial sites that want everyone to visit them. (We take this up in Chapter 4. The other strategy is to use a search engine or hierarchic directory as described in Chapter 5.)

DEEP MYSTICAL EXPERIENCES   Finally, there are the deep mystical experiences that happen on the Internet with no ontological meaning beyond their existential essence. Well, what we really mean is that two things can happen that are completely baffling.

"Black Holes"   "Black holes" are specific webpages that will lock up your system. Some are practical jokes. Others are simply ill-programmed by mistake. You know you have probably stumbled into one when the navigation buttons stop working. The only thing you can do is to click on the Back button and try to graciously leave. This happens when the black hole is rather benign. If this does not work, you may have to exit the browser completely and then turn it on again. In extreme cases, you may have to exit and completely shut down the computer and then turn it on again and reestablish the connection. While rare and usually confined to personal webpages, various pranks abound, so beware. In addition, commercial websites sometimes "seize" your browser, too, and will not let you return to where you were. They disable the Back and Forward buttons. The only way out of this arrogance is to summon up and click on the browser's History or completely exit the browser and, with a new connection, bring the browser up again.

No One Knows   You can encounter problems that completely defy explanation, even from the "experts." Technical assistants often feel that they must appear knowledgeable and may mumble in jargon as they wander away, having failed to fix your problem. Be nice, because it is good manners and you may desperately need them later; but remember, the Web is fragile, evolving, imperfect, and not always well understood even by people who hold advanced degrees in computer programming.

Once again, do remember that clicking on the Help section in most browsers can be most worthwhile. Also remember that real mastery of any complex software takes time, and browsers are no exception.

Exercise 2A
Narrowing Areas, Topics, and Issues

- This is a paper exercise. You do not need to use a computer.
- The purpose of this exercise is to focus your thinking onto one of the nine specific areas, a topic within in it, and different issues within the topic.
- This work will carry over into the next exercise.

DIRECTIONS

A. *Circle the one area* of the nine listed that *most* applies to your issue or as directed by the instructor:

- Practice
- Field/agencies
- Policy and services
- Social and economic justice
- Populations at risk
- Diversity
- Human behavior in the social environment
- Values and ethics
- Research

B. *List three topics* within this single area that interest you: (refer to Chapter 1 for more information on the areas)

    1. _____

    2. _____

    3. _____

C. *Circle the one topic* that interests you the most from the three.

    Write one sentence that explains why you have this interest.

D. *List three issues* within the one topic that you would like to understand better:

    1. _____

    2. _____

    3. _____

E. *Circle the one issue* that interests you the most from the three.

    Write one sentence that explains why you have this interest.

F. *Describe this issue* in one paragraph of three to five sentences:

_____

_____

_____

G. *Read the paragraph* you have just written, and *choose one or two words that best crystallize* the issues within the area and topic. Strive for direct, specific words.

The word(s) is (are):

_____

Exercise 2B
The Paper Web

- This is a paper exercise. You do not need to use a computer.
- The purpose of this exercise is to focus your thinking onto how all of the nine social work areas relate to each other in terms of the issue you want to work on.
- This is a holistic activity that will help you produce key words in the next exercise.

DIRECTIONS

A. *Write the one area, topic, and issue* you chose in Exercise 2A: Narrowing Areas, Topics, and Issues *in the center* of the following diagram.

Example

If your area of interest is "populations at risk," the topic is "AIDS," and the issue is "children with AIDS," then write those words in the *italicized center part* of the diagram.

Area: _____

Topic: _____

Issue: _____

Area: _____   Area: _____

Topic: _____   Topic: _____

Issue: _____   Issue: _____

Area: _____   *Area:* _____   Area: _____

Topic: _____   *Topic* _____   Topic: _____

Issue: _____   *Issue:* _____   Issue: _____

Area: _____   Area: _____

Topic: _____   Topic: _____

Issue: _____   Issue: _____

Area: _____

Topic: _____

Issue: _____

B. Write the eight *other areas* in the diagram *around* the central area in the places provided.

C. Think of a topic and issue in each of the surrounding eight areas that directly relate to your central issue and write them down.

Example

If your central area is "populations at risk," the topic is "AIDS," and the issue is "children with AIDS," the "diversity" *area* might contain the *topic* "other cultures" and the *issue* "medical care attitudes."

SUMMING IT UP

Look over your work and answer the following question in one paragraph:

What would anyone looking at this diagram conclude about the central and related issues?

Exercise 2C
Key Words

NOTE: This is a critical exercise for many of the other exercises in this book. MAKE A COPY!

■ This is a paper exercise. You do not need to use a computer.

■ The purpose of this exercise is to generate useful key words that will help you find what you are looking for on the Web.

DIRECTIONS

A. *Circle the one area* of the nine listed that was central to all the others in Exercise 2B: The Paper Web (to help your instructor know what you are doing).

Write the one or two crystallized words from Exercise 2A, G, in the center column for the area.

Review each of the remaining eight areas from Exercises 2A and 2B.

Generate one or two key words that crystallize the issues for each of the eight areas, and write them in the center column for each area.

Practice

_____   _____   _____

Issue word(s):

Field/Agencies

_____   _____   _____

Issue word(s):

Policy and Services

_____   _____   _____

Issue word(s):

Social and Economic Justice

_____   _____   _____

Issue word(s):

Populations at Risk

_____   _____   _____

Issue word(s):

Diversity

_____   _____   _____

Issue word(s):

Human Behavior in the Social Environment

_____   _____   _____

Issue word(s):

Values and Ethics

_____   _____   _____

Issue word(s):

Research

_____   _____   _____

Issue word(s):

B. For each of the issue word(s) in the center column, write a corresponding word (words) in the _left column_ that is (are) _similar but more general in nature._

Example

If your center area and issues are "populations at risk" and "children with AIDS," you might write "autoimmune diseases."

C. For each of the issue word(s) in the center column, write a corresponding word (words) in the _right column_ that is (are) _similar but more specific in nature._

Example

If your center area and issues are "populations at risk" and "children with AIDS," you might write "infants," or "Hispanic," or any other more narrowing term that you are interested in.

Exercise 2D
Cut and Paste

- This is a computer exercise. You will need a Web-connected computer and a working word processor.
- The purpose of this exercise is to begin seeing how the key words and issues generated in the last exercise may relate to our profession.
- Another purpose is to help you learn more about organizations that relate to social work. (There are many more!)

DIRECTIONS

A. Read through the key words list you generated in Exercise 2C.

Choose any one of the nine areas listed and circle it.

- Practice
- Diversity
- Field/agencies
- Human behavior in the social environment
- Policy and services
- Values and ethics
- Social and economic justice
- Research
- Populations at risk

Write one sentence that succinctly describes the area, topic, and issue you have chosen.

B. Choose and visit *three* different websites from the list at the end of this exercise that you think should have something related to your area, topic, and interest.

Thoroughly "surf" each website by looking through its webpages for items that are relevant to your interest.

Example

The *Clinical Social Work Federation* has its own code of ethical standards, and some of these might be relevant to your issue. Perhaps the "Responsibility to clients/Informed consent" section relates to your issue.

C. If/when you find something on the website that is related to your interest as defined by the key words, highlight it and then cut and paste it into a separate word-processor document. Copy just a paragraph or so of text, and do not worry about the graphics. Take enough information to illustrate the connection between your key words/issue *and* the organization. If you cannot find anything on the website, then copy a paragraph of text as an example of what you did find. (This proves you did the assignment!)

D. In the word-processing document:

Type the name of the website/organization you visited above the pasted text from the website.

Type the key words that you used to stimulate your thinking below this.

Insert the text from the website.

Write a short paragraph below the pasted text that either explains how it connects with your issue or describes your activities and lack of results.

Tips

Remember: the Edit and Find features can really help on larger or visually confusing webpages!

Do not get carried away! This assignment should take about twenty minutes per website.

Organizations to Visit

American Network of Home Health Care Social Workers
http://www.homehealthsocialwork.org

American Association of State Social Work Boards http://www.aasswb.org

American Association of Marriage and Family Therapy http://www.aamft.org

American Board of Examiners in Clinical Social Work (ABE) http://www.abecsw.org/

Association for the Advancement of Social Work with Groups (AASWG)
http://dominic.barry.edu/~kelly/aaswg/aaswg.html

Association for Community Organization and Social Administration (ACOSA)
http://www.bc.edu/bc_org/avp/gssw/acosa.htm

Association of Baccalaureate Social Work Program Directors (BPD)
http://www.rit.edu/~694www/bpd.htm

Association for Oncology Social Work
http://www.biostat.wisc.edu/aosw/aoswhello.html

Australian Association of Social Workers (AASW) http://www.aasw.asn.au

British Association of Social Workers http://www.aosw.org

Canadian Association of Social Workers http://www.intranet.ca/casw-acts/

Clinical Social Work Federation http://www.cswf.org

Computer User in the Social Services Network (CUSSN)
http://www.uta.edu/cussn/cussn.html

Council of Nephrology Social Workers http://www.kidney.org/Cnsw/

Council on Social Work Education (CSWE) http://www.cswe.org

Group for the Advancement of Doctoral Education
http://www.sc.edu/swan/gade/index.html

Gay, Lesbian, Bisexual, and Transgender Caucus
http://www.geocities.com/WestHollywood/Heights/4168/

Institute for the Advancement of Social Work Research
http://www.sc.edu/swan/iaswr/index.html

International Federation of Social Workers http://www.ifsw.org

Inter-University Consortium for International Social Development
http://www.sc.edu/swan/iucisd/index.htm

Israel Association of Social Workers http://www.isassw.org.il/index.htm

National Association of Black Social Workers http://www.nynet-ac.com/~nabsw

North American Association of Christians in Social Work http://www.nacsw.org

National Association of Social Workers http://www.socialworkers.org

National Institute for Social Work (UK) http://www.nisw.org.uk

National Organization of Forensic Social Work http://www.nofsw.org

National Network for Social Work Managers http://www.socialworkmanager.org

National Organization of Deans and Directors (NADD)
http://www.sc.edu/swan/nadd/

Society for Social Work Leadership in Health Care http://www.sswlhc.org

Summary

Modern browsers are fairly automated, and using them is reasonably easy once you understand what the buttons and commands will do. Entering the correct URL (Uniform Resource Locator) is vital to successful navigation. Once the desired webpage has been found, it can be electronically sent to other people or the contents can be edited and used in other ways. Errors can arise from several problems such as faulty connections and mistyping. While basic browsing is rather easy, it takes time to develop skill and confidence.

Questions for Discussion

Is it important to learn to use more than one browser and type of Internet connection? Why?

What about learning more than one platform, such as being able to use both the Mac and IBM types of computers? Is this important? Why?

What would be the most transparent type of Internet address (URL) for you and the consumers?

What, in your opinion, is the most ideal type or form of browser you would like to see? What designs would you like?

References

American Psychological Association. (1994). *Publication manual of the American Psychological Association* (4th ed.). Washington, DC: Author.

Daunt, R. (Document posted on Web, August 11, 1998). The risks of ignoring Internet website copyright issues. *CyberCouncil Internet Law Newsletter.* [On-line]. Available: http://www.iplawyer.com

National Association of Social Workers. (No date). *Code of Ethics.* Washington, DC: Author.

Templeton, B. (Document posted on Web, August 11, 1998). *10 big myths about copyright explained.* [On-line]. Available: http://www.templetons.com/brad//copymyths.html

Edupage Citations

TechWeb. (31 January 1998). Europeans voice disappointment over U.S. domain plan. [Reported in Edupage, March 10,1998].

Wall Street Journal. (24 March 1998). Domain group blasts U.S. plan for domain name distribution. [Reported in Edupage, March 10, 1998].

Additional Readings

O'Hara, S. (1998). *Netscape beginners guide to the Internet for Windows and Mac.* Scottsdale, AZ: Coriolis Group Inc.

Pfaffenberg, B. (1997). *Official Microsoft Internet Explorer 4 book.* Redmond, WA: Microsoft Press.

Additional Websites

Cyberspace Law Center *Search engine for legal issues on the Internet* http://www.cybersquirrel.com/clc/index.html

Copyright Office, Library of Congress (Cornell University) *37 Code of Federal Regulations* (Chapter II) http://fatty.law.cornell.edu/copyright/regulations/regs.overview.html#202.2

Brinson, J., & Radcliff, M. (1996) *An intellectual property law primer for multimedia and Web* http://www.eff.org/pub/CAF/law/ip-primer

NASW *Links* http://www.socialworkers.org/LINKS.HTM.

Security
and Confidentiality

 Some of the things you need to worry about . . .

. . . Many people can often tell where you and the client have been on the Web

. . . You might as well publish all your activities on the front page of your local newspaper if you do not take some basic precautions

CHAPTER OVERVIEW

Remember the Wild West metaphor from Chapter 1? There are two critters you need to keep in mind: pack rats and rattlesnakes. Your computer, believe it or not, is probably a pack rat, happily stashing away every smidgen of stuff you have ever visited on the Web! And there are more than a few rattlesnakes to worry about out there. Seriously, there are some real dangers associated with using computers in social work practice, and you need to know what they are and how to counter them. In this chapter, you will learn about

- Security and Confidentiality
- Ethical Issues for the Web and Social Work
- Dangers within Your Workplace
- Dangers within Your System
- Dangers from Professional and Personal Value Conflicts
- Dangers by Intent

If possible, go through this chapter while at your computer! It really helps!

SECURITY AND CONFIDENTIALITY

CASE STUDY

Clark

Clark killed himself after being confronted by his minister and three deacons in church over being gay. He was indeed gay, but far from ready to come out of his closet. Severely depressed, his exposure to the congregation and its "trial by gossip" was the final event in his tragic life. He was twenty-two.

The gossip had begun innocently enough. One of his other church members, a secretary at a local counseling center, had used the social worker's computer on her lunch break—with the social worker's permission—to explore the Web. This was just after the worker's session with Clark where they had spent an hour looking for gay lifestyle issues and resources on the Web. Clark had been really impressed with the resources that were available: they had found over ninety promising websites. The secretary had been impressed too, because she reviewed Clark's complete session and immediately knew what Clark's issues were. She was a temporary worker and had not been briefed in the agency's confidentiality policies or signed any agreements concerning information security. She just could not resist looking over what they had covered, and it had been so easy to follow the URLs and history that the computer had recorded.

When asked to recount the counseling session, the social worker stated: "We briefly discussed what resources might be found on the Web and then sat down at the computer for about an hour to look at websites. When we were done, I turned off the browser and we agreed on exploring various sites at the next opportunity. I then wrote my case summary on my computer and forwarded it to the central records file. Clark left the building and I took my lunch break."

ETHICAL ISSUES FOR THE WEB AND SOCIAL WORK

Confidentiality Issues

One of the critical mistakes professional social workers can make is to forget about confidentiality issues on the Web. Imagine for a moment that you were the worker seeing Clark. You helped him view websites and find supports and resources, but it was not enough. Breaching confidentiality can, at times, cost more than the trusting relationship. Anyone with some basic expertise can sit down at the computer and directly view the webpages you and the client just shared, review that competitive grant proposal, or learn that research agenda unless specific precautions are taken.

Clark's case illustrates the more sinister dimension of the Web: *passive* breaches of confidentiality. We would not think of leaving sensitive case materials lying around the office where anyone could see them. Much less would we divulge information about a pending grant application over the telephone to an unknown caller. Web activities require the same concern and habitual vigilance.

Just What Do You Need to Worry about?

The best single guide for professional social work conduct is the NASW *Code of Ethics* (NASW, n. d.).[1] The *Code* can help determine if activities are permissible or not, and what should be done to comply with the *Code*. Let's begin with Clark. Are there any breaches of the *Code* in the case? Yes. Several specific issues are at least out of compliance.

1. SOCIAL WORKER'S ETHICAL RESPONSIBILITIES TO CLIENTS

1.03 Informed Consent

(e) Social workers who provide services via electronic media (such as computer, telephone, radio, and television) should inform recipients of the limitations and risks associated with such services.

Based on the provided case information, the worker did not inform Clark about limitations and risks. Perhaps the tragedy could have been avoided by the worker simply reading a prepared statement—approved by the agency's board—informing Clark about the risks of surfing. This might have changed the nature of the entire session.

1.07 Privacy and Confidentiality

(1) Social workers should protect the confidentiality of clients' *written and electronic records* [emphasis added] and other sensitive information. Social workers should take reasonable steps to ensure that clients' records are stored in a secure location and that clients' records are not available to others who are not authorized to have access.

The Clark case is a direct violation of this part of the *Code*. The worker is culpable. This is because the *Code* specifies that *it is the worker's responsibility* to take "reasonable steps," not that of the secretary, the supervisor, or any other party.

We do not know much more from the case but are left wondering about what happened to the written case notes mentioned by the social worker. Another specific part of the *Code* addresses this:

1.07 Privacy and Confidentiality

(m) Social workers should take precautions to ensure and maintain the confidentiality of information transmitted to other parties through the use of computers, electronic mail, facsimile machines, telephones and telephone answering machines, and other electronic or computer technology. Disclosure of identifying information should be avoided whenever possible.

We have seven victims in this case. Clark is of course the direct victim. There also are his family and friends. The secretary may feel great remorse and guilt for a

---

[1]   State certification and licensure statutes are another source. In addition, some professional organizations such as the Clinical Social Work Federation (http://www.cswf.org/ethframe.htm) have professional codes for conduct as well.

very long time. The social worker is perhaps a victim if the agency did not specify policies and procedures for using computers in compliance with the *Code*. The agency certainly will suffer. Our profession, too, becomes diminished. And humanity loses Clark's possible contributions forever. Just what, specifically, should be done to prevent cases like Clark's from happening?

While the *Code of Ethics* specifies basic conduct for using electronic communications, the technology is so new that more specific policies, procedures, and interpretations have yet to evolve. The NASW Delegate Assembly—the people and process that generate policies and codes for the profession—may produce an interpretive policy statement in the future.[2] Until this transpires, we are left with the *Code* as the major guide. The writers are specifically concerned with the following areas:

- Dangers within your workplace

The most direct practice-directed danger from Web-based communications lies within the workplace. While marketing firms, computer maintenance personnel, and others may, under some circumstances, get access to what you have used your computer for and some hacker may invade your system for heaven knows what reasons, these dangers are probably less serious than what can go wrong directly in the workplace. The risk lies with unauthorized nonprofessionals *in your own network* having access to your Web activities and being able to connect them with what you have been doing.

- Dangers within your system

External access is a serious problem, too. The people who manage and maintain computer systems—within your workplace and at other locations such as your Internet Service Provider (ISP)—often routinely make copies of all Web transactions, E-mail, and other communications as a part of their regular work. This presents the persistent problem that copies of your activities—legitimate copies—often circulate well beyond your knowledge and control. *Just when you thought it was safe. . .*

- Dangers from professional and personal value conflicts

The behavior of other colleagues—both social workers and other professionals—needs to be considered when one can publish any available computer-based communication to the planet with very little effort. Even if your agency has developed excellent security and confidentiality policies and procedures, no assurances can be made that other people or agencies will have them too, understand them, or even honor them.

- Dangers by intent

Some people and organizations on the Web actively try to harm other people and institutions. Two levels exist: passive and active. Hate groups, for example, *passively post* offensive contents to the Web and certainly within the United States have the Constitutional freedom to do so. Other individuals and organizations *actively work* well beyond any law to disrupt and destroy legitimate computing systems. This ranges from the individual pedophile that befriends an adolescent toward molestation[3] to terrorist groups who would like to destroy Western civilization but will settle for the Internet.

---

[2]   The policies and pronouncements from the NASW Delegate Assembly are published in *NASW Speaks* (NASW, 1997). At present, there are sixty-six different policy statements that provide guidance and direction for the profession on a wide range of issues.

[3]   Molestation can be virtual and still traumatic.

Each of these separate problem areas must be addressed with a different strategy. At the outset, keep in mind that professional social work practice is often opposite to what browser designers think is a good idea. We usually want to keep information as narrowly accessible and constricted as possible to ensure security. Browser designers want multiple ways to access information to make browsing easier. This is an inherent conflict.

Most browsers have technical ways to make your communications more secure. However, these are often hard to use and confusing. In addition, different computing systems have different security needs. For example, a large system in an agency with a hundred employees will have different security requirements than, say, a shared personal computer (PC) in a three-person office. The nature of the work, too, will impose security requirements. Highly confidential work—as in the case with Clark—requires different security procedures than recreational surfing.

Because of this range of needs and the variation in computing systems, this chapter can only help you become familiar with very basic issues and procedures. We do not go into the technical issues of how to use certificates, encrypt files, use a proxy server, or design other more complex precautions. Thus, you get the "technical minimum" of things to worry about. But please, please, please remember that you may have to take additional steps beyond the scope of this book to ensure that your communications are as safe as needed for practice. Shared computers have different configurations, so ask about the specifics, especially in the agency or school setting.

Moreover, technological "fixes" rarely solve social problems. Even if you are using a computer with a proxy-firewalled system with exotic encryption that would amaze James Bond, you are never completely safe from the criminal who physically breaks into your office, accurately guesses your passwords, and proceeds to make mischief. (Paper-based information poses the same risk in this case.) We urge you to pay as much attention to simple procedures—such as turning the machine off, locking it up, and locking the door—as you leave as you do to trusting technical whizbangs.

TIP: We strongly suggest that you *never disable security warnings!* You can do this by clicking the "Don't show me the message again" choices in most browsers. Do not do it! The gentle nagging may be worth everything if it prompts you to action.

Just to get you a little terrified, we want you to know something that happens every time you browse a website. When you contact the other server with the website, you do not just look at the files on it. The host server has to know how and where to send the files to your computer so you can look at them. At minimum, the other server will usually find out the name of your service provider, the type of operating system you use, the browser you are using, technical information about its innards and gizmos, and—are you ready for this?—your complete Internet protocol address! It records this information and also may have access to other parts of your computer such as those case records you left on the hard drive last week and forgot to delete.[4] The server can—and will—create and maintain its own files in your computer. Often, you are not even aware of this.

---

4   For more information, visit Cookie Central at http://www.cookiecentral.com/index2.html

DANGERS WITHIN YOUR WORKPLACE

Different types of practice settings have different security and confidentiality needs, depending on the client system and the nature of the work. Workers with clients who have high risk from stigma, such as Clark, will have *different* security requirements than others who surf and make educational websites available to children or gather information for policy deliberations. All client systems need shielding, but people like Clark need it from the real community; children need shielding from inappropriate websites in the virtual community; and the grant writer needs protection from prying competition. At minimum, the following cardinal rule should apply to all professional social work transactions on the Web, especially when clients are involved.

CARDINAL RULE: COVER YOUR TRACKS! Under no circumstances should client names or other personal identifying information ever be circulated on the Web. (Directly identifying clients is a direct violation of the NASW *Code of Ethics.*) This even includes situations where you have obtained the client's permission, because you can never forecast how the information may actually be used. When you work with high-risk client systems, the more benign uses of the Web could be subverted toward the detriment of the clients, agency, or profession. The Web is still far too unsecured and global to risk the exchange of confidential business or personal information except in very restricted instances where you know that confidentiality can be ensured or does not pose any threats. When you do use the Web with various sizes of client systems (and there are countless reasons to do so), you should erase all traces of your work from the computer so the connection with the specific client system cannot be reestablished by an unauthorized party.

What Can You Do?

The first step is to learn what your computer records as it browses. As you surf, your computer is continually copying down Web materials and references to where you are. At minimum, browsers usually record all of the URLs you visit while you are still on-line. This usually results in a copy of all the associated graphics and the actual html file for every page you examine. Pack rat, remember?

The Navigator and Explorer browsers make these records in different ways. It is important to be familiar with the copying features for both browsers—and any others in use for practice—because of your likelihood of encountering and using multiple types in practice. In addition, no two computing systems are configured in exactly the same way, so the same browser will often behave differently on two different machines. For example, your PC on your desk may have all of the copying features described here, while the Mac used in a lab as a workstation will have most of them disabled.

What you can do to promote safe and secure Web use is to make security procedures a reflex. This means developing competencies for both the system you normally use and others you encounter in practice.

Immediate Security

At minimum, always turn your computer completely off when you are done. Never turn over a shared computer that is still running if you have visited places that require confidentiality. This includes disconnecting the Internet connection; the best strategy is to completely shut the computer off and let the next user reboot it. This erases most temporary files in the browser and makes it fairly difficult for the next person to accidentally view what you have been looking at, although more measures are still required. (This was the major mistake made in the Clark case.)

Long-Term Security

This section is a little complex, but bear with us. You need to learn how to completely erase browsing records from your computer. The Navigator and Explorer browsers have different characteristics, and you need to learn the erasure procedures for each because you probably will encounter both. At the outset, it is important to remember that if the computer uses more than one browser (e.g., both Navigator *and* Explorer are in the computer), you have to repeat this process *for each browser you use!*

Let's start with Netscape. To get an idea of just how comprehensive Netscape's records may be, type "about:global" (without the quotation marks) into the Location box of the Netscape browser (Figure 3-1) and press the Return key or click the mouse (works with both IBM and Mac).

If the global history file from the Netscape browser has never been deleted before or set so it does not accumulate information about where you have been,

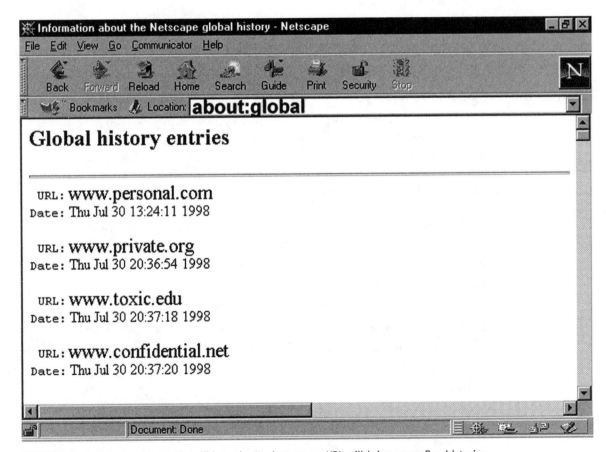

FIGURE 3-1 Entering "about:global" into the Navigator as a URL will bring up surfing histories.

you may see the entire history of your computer's browsing since the moment the computer was first turned on. Surprise! Anyone can retrieve everything you have ever seen on the Web![5] Yikes!

Netscape creates *four different types of session records* that range from transitory to very long-lived. You need to be able to control and eliminate all of them. Netscape records a **temporary history** that is erased when you turn off the computer. In addition, there is a **session history** that may be saved for a specific number of days, depending on the preference entered and set in the browser. The session history file is what the "about:global" command dredges up.

Netscape *caches* all of the files you view in its hard-disk memory somewhere unless you empty it or set the browser to do so. Finally, Netscape records a more permanent **history file** that does not go away when you turn the machine off.

Netscape keeps track of many URLs you use and makes them readily accessible from the Location box for later reference. It does this in a file written by the computer as you browse. The default name of the file is *prefs.js.*[6] Each of these separate files must be deleted or modified if you are going to erase your session completely. Each requires a different procedure.

The following instructions are primarily for IBM-type machines. Directions for Macintosh users are included as noted. Do not forget: Your computer may have different versions of these browsers, so the instructions and figures may not be identical to what you find on your machine.

Eliminating the Temporary History

The temporary history can be viewed in the session by clicking on the Go pull-down menu. Simply exit the browser to delete it. This works for both the Mac and IBM versions.

Eliminating the Session History

Netscape: The session history feature helps you go back to pages you have visited while you have been on line. Depending on how frequently you want it erased, the history may be fairly short from only the current session to much longer for many sessions. To look at the History part of the browser, simply pull down the Communicator menu from the top of the window and select the History option (Figure 3-2). You can select any of the URLs listed on it by directly double-clicking.

To eliminate this feature, which will result in no histories being available the next time you connect to the Web (Figure 3-3),

- ■   Go to the Edit pull-down menu from the top left of the window.
- ■   Select the Preferences choice.
- ■   Select the Navigator in the Preferences window.
- ■   Set the "Pages in history expire after" choice to "0" (the number zero).
- ■   Click the OK button, and resume your session.

You really do not need these histories anyway if you have bookmarked important websites.

---

[5]   This may not happen in a lab or shared network if the history feature has been disabled.

[6]   The file is called *netscape.ini* in the 3.0 version of Netscape.

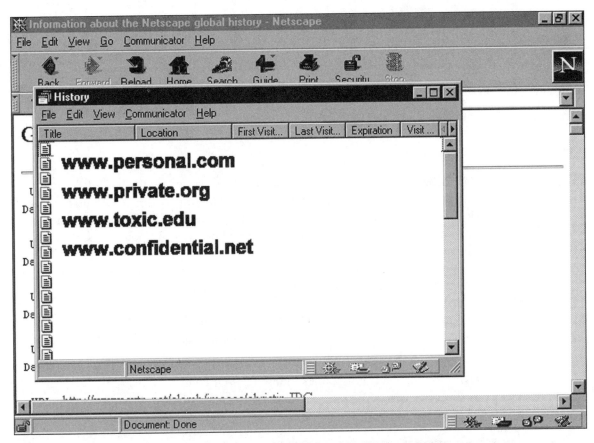

FIGURE 3-2 The Communicator History box shows all of your recent browsing activities.

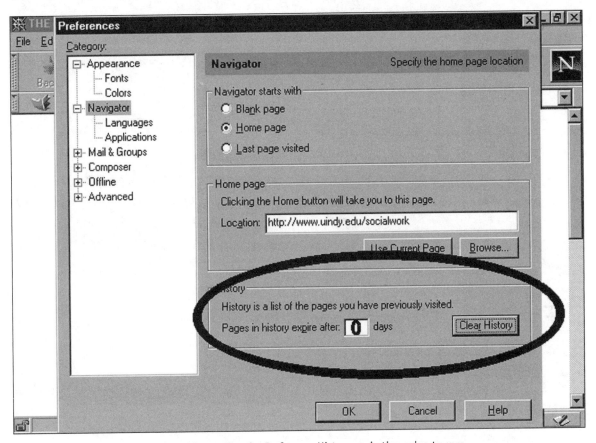

FIGURE 3-3 Eliminate the History by setting the Preference History expiration value to zero.

Setting the "Pages in history" choice to zero will eliminate easy access to your browsing history after you have turned the machine off. It also eliminates the history raised by the "about:global" command, making security much better. It *still* does not completely erase everything!

Macintosh: Macintosh users can follow similar procedures to adjust the history setting.

Eliminating the Files in the Cache

The **cache** feature stores all of the files you have viewed on the hard-disk memory unless you have emptied it, automated its elimination, or are at a group workstation where the cache feature has been disabled. It stores the files in a folder usually named "Cache"; and there may be several on your computer for surfing and others for various E-mail programs.

There are several ways to find cached files on your computer. Any of them will work. The object is to be able to precisely locate individual files in order to modify or delete them. Three ways follow.

The first way, from the Start button in Windows98, works if you know the name of the file, its folder name, or a close term (Figure 3-4):

■ Click on the Start button in the lower left corner of your screen.

■ Select the Find choice; then choose Files Or Folders . . .

■ Presuming that the files you want to find are on the main C:\ drive of the

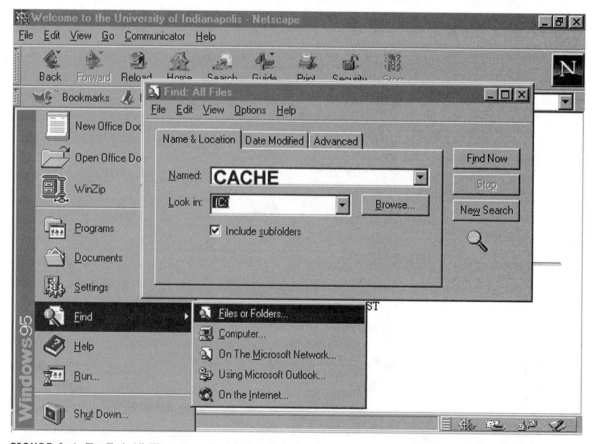

FIGURE 3-4 The Find: All Files approach to find cached files.

computer, enter the name of the file you want to find in the Named: choice box. It does not have to be the complete name of the file. Thus, "Cache" will work and you do not have to look for a "cache.abc" type of specific file.

- Be certain the C: is entered in the Look In choice, unless Netscape is installed on another drive. In that case, you would enter the name of that drive instead.

- Be sure there is a check mark in the Include Subfolders choice so the search feature will look through the entire C: drive.

- Click the Find Now button.

The files you want should be brought up.

A second way, using the My Computer icon in Windows98, works if you know the exact name of the file you want and if the configuration shown may be different on your computer (Figure 3-5):

- Click on the My Computer icon on the main (desktop) screen.

- Click on the C: choice. (You may also have to click on the Program Files folder.)

- Click on the Netscape folder.

- Click on the Users folder.

- Click on the Default folder.

- Click on the Cache folder.

The files you want should be brought up.

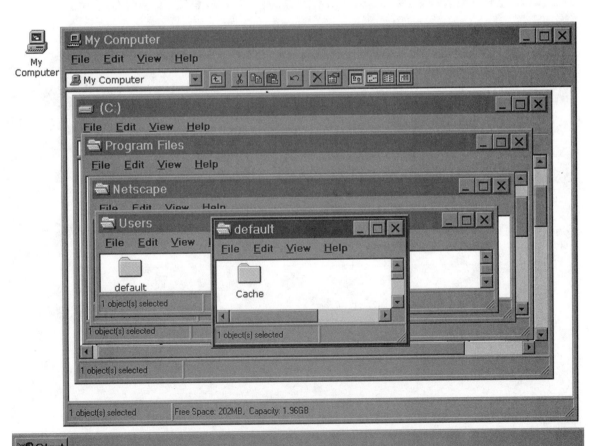

FIGURE 3-5 The My Computer approach to finding cached files.

A third way, from the File Manager in Windows 3.x, '95, or '98 works if you know the exact name of the file you want (Figure 3-6):

- Select the File Manager choice with the small file cabinet icon. In Windows 3.x, the File Manager is usually in the Main menu/window.

- Select the C: drive or other likely location.

Either

- Go to the top of the column on the left and select the C: choice and click on it. This reveals the directory "tree" for the drive. Follow this procedure until you find the file you are after.

Or

- Pull-down the File menu and select the Find choice.

- Enter the specific name of the file you are looking for in the Search For or Named box.

- Be certain that the C:\ is entered in the Start From choice box.

- Be certain that the Search All Subdirectories check box has a check in it.

- Click the OK button.

This procedure should show you the specific file you want.

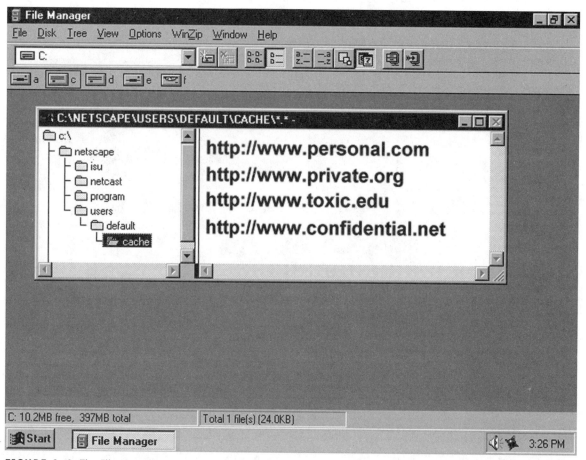

FIGURE 3-6 The File Manager approach to finding cached files.

Any of these methods should eventually allow you to find and modify or delete the specific files you need to ensure security. To manually delete the cache,[7] you first have to find the right cache. There often is more than one because E-mail, network news services, and other programs often have their own caches as well as the one for the Netscape browser (Figure 3-7):

■ Find the Cache folder for the Netscape browser through one of the methods already described.

■ Open up the cache by clicking on it. You should see a list—often quite long—of different Web-related files, such as *.gif* and *.jpg* graphics files and *.htm* files for webpage texts, and other files for access and control.

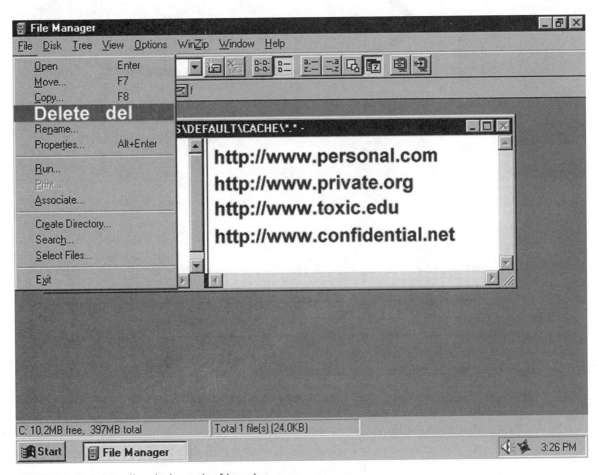

FIGURE 3-7 Delete all cached records of browsing.

---

[7] Here is another worry we will not go into details about, but one you need to beware of. If your computer has a graphics program on it such as PaintShopPro or Adobe Photo Shop, then you can probably view the cache in it. This procedure will bring up every graphical image in the cache, and, as we all know, pictures are worth thousands of words. Thus, you can sometimes guess where a person has been without even using a browser! The simple cure: empty the cache.

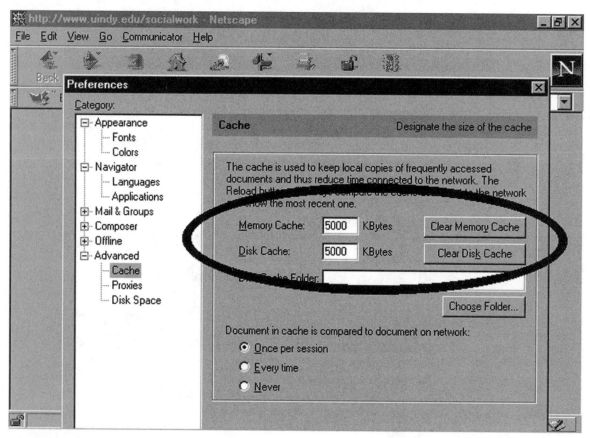

FIGURE 3-8 Clearing both the Memory and Disk caches by the Preferences Cache box.

■ Highlight all of the files *in the Netscape cache folder.*

■ Now delete the cached files. Usually, all you have to do is press the Delete key and follow the prompts. Generally, choosing the Yes To All button will erase all of the cached files.[8]

Here is an alternative method for emptying the Netscape browser cache (Figure 3-8):

■ Start the Netscape browser.

■ Click on the Edit pull-down menu at the top left corner of the window.

■ Select the Preferences choice.

■ Select and double-click on the Advanced choice in Preferences.

■ Click on the Cache folder. You will see two buttons:

Clear Memory Cache Now. Clicking this button and following the prompts will eliminate any cached files from the computer's *temporary* memory. Turning off your computer will have the same effect.

Clear Disk Cache Now. Clicking this button will erase any cached files from your computer's hard disk. Turning your computer off instead will have no effect.

■ Follow the OK prompts, and your disk cache should be eliminated.

---

[8] If you are doing this while still connected to a network, you may not be able to delete the *fat* file (File Allocation Table). Simply delete everything else.

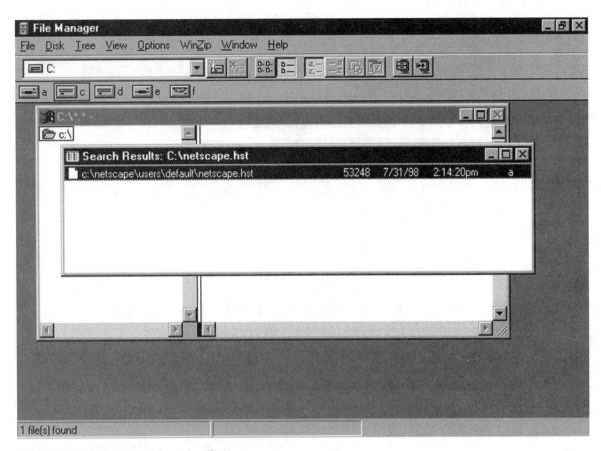

FIGURE 3-9 Deleting files from the File Manager.

Either of these procedures will eliminate all of your cached files, but remember: Your computer will probably fill up the cache again and again every time you surf.

Macintosh: To eliminate the cached files on the Macintosh, you can follow the same procedures but instead look for Cache Folders. If this does not work, then use the Find feature and enter the word *Cache* into it with the Name default activated. Now click the Find button. You should find all of the *.gif* and *.jpg* graphics files from your sessions. Trash them. Then conduct another Find inquiry, but type "html" into the query box, still using the Name default, and click the Find button. You should find all of the webpage files currently cached on your computer. Trash them, too!

Eliminating the Netscape History File

The more permanent history file requires a different treatment. You want to locate your "netscape.hst" file that the browser records somewhere on your C:\ drive. This file may be in the Netscape folder but not always. To be on the safe side, you need to delete this file, too (Figure 3-9):

- Find the "netscape.hst" file on your C:\ drive by using one of the methods already described.

- Select this file *and delete it.*

This will delete the Netscape history file, making it still more difficult to trace your browsing record from your computer. Do not worry about deleting this file, because it will reestablish itself when you use the browser again.

FIGURE 3-10 Navigator's Location pull-down box.

Macintosh: To delete the history file on the Macintosh:

- Find the System Folder and go to Preferences.
- Look for the "Netscape f" folder. If you cannot find it, it may be in the regular Netscape folder. You should find a file titled Global History.
- Delete it by dragging it to the trash can and emptying it.
- Reboot the machine and check to be certain that you have eliminated the history file. You should see a much shorter history file when you use the "about:global" inquiry command.

Emptying the Location box: You may have noticed that some of the URLs you have recently used can be accessed from the browser's Location box by clicking the *down arrow* on the right-hand side of the box (Figure 3-10). The latest editions of Navigator allow you to clear the Location box with a few simple button clicks:

- Click on the Edit choice at the top left of the screen.
- Select the Preferences choice.
- Select the Navigator choice in the Categories box on the left-hand side if it is not already there. You should see a Clear Location Bar button in the lower right part of the screen.
- Click this button and then the OK choice that follows it.
- Exit by clicking the OK choice for the Preferences window.

Earlier editions of Navigator require more complex procedures. To delete the URLs from the Location box, you are going to have to modify your "prefs.js" file (Figure 3-11):

- Find the "prefs.js" file by any of the methods already described.
- Select the "prefs.js" file *but do not delete it!* Instead, double-click on it. The file should come up in the computer's default Notepad word processor.
- Scroll and search through this file until you come to the list of URLs that appear in the Location box. It will look something like the following:

  user_pref("browser.url_history.URL_1", http://www.uindy.edu/");

  user_pref("browser.url_history.URL_2", "http://www.aurora.edu/");

  user_pref("browser.url_history.URL_3",. . . (and so on)

- Select and delete *ONLY* the lines that have "browser.url_history" in them.
- Go to the File pull-down menu in the Notepad located in the top left corner of the window and choose the Save feature.
- Close the window down. The Location box should now be empty.

```
prefs - Notepad
File   Edit   Search   Help

// Netscape User Preferences
// This is a generated file!  Do not edit.

user_pref("browser.bookmark_columns_win", "v1 1 1:10000 2:2996 4:1999 3:1999"
user_pref("browser.bookmark_window_rect", "44,44,480,321");
user_pref("browser.cache.directory", "D:\\CACHE");
user_pref("browser.download_directory", "E:\\");
user_pref("browser.link_expiration", 1);
user_pref("browser.startup.homepage", "http://www.uindy.edu/socialwork");
user_pref("browser.startup.homepage_override", false);
user_pref("browser.url_history.URL_1", "http://www.personal.com"
user_pref("browser.url_history.URL_2", "http://www.private.org"
user_pref("browser.url_history.URL_3", "http://www.toxic.edu"
user_pref("browser.url_history.URL_4", "http://confidential.net"
user_pref("browser.wfe.show_value", 3);
user_pref("browser.window_rect", "0,0,632,436");
user_pref("custtoolbar.Browser.Personal_Toolbar.showing", false);
user_pref("custtoolbar.personal_toolbar_folder", "Personal Toolbar Folder");
user_pref("editor.author", "Robert Vernon");
user_pref("editor.html_directory", "C:\\Netscape\\Users\\default\\Seminar\\")
user_pref("editor.image_directory", "A:\\");
user_pref("editor.last_doc_page", 1);
user_pref("editor.publish_last_loc", "http://socwork@www.uindy.edu/~socwork/"
user_pref("editor.publish_last_pass", "JaaMPfTMMXBG");
user_pref("ghist.location.width", 2399);
user_pref("ghist.show_value", 1);
```

FIGURE 3-11 Editing out the URL history record from the Notepad.

WARNING! Do not delete anything else in this file or your browser may not work when you start it up again! If problems happen, you will have to reinstall the complete browser.

TIP: Is there any way to keep URLs from going into the Location box in the first place? Yes! A simple way to avoid having to erase Location box entries in the 4.0 or better version of Navigator is to *develop the habit of not typing URLs into the Location box* when you surf. (We told you about this in Chapter 2, remember?) If you type the URL into the Location box, the program will remember it by default. Instead, go to the File pull-down menu in the upper left-hand corner and select the Open Page choice. *Enter the URL you want in this box instead of the Location box, and you will not have this problem.*

Take Out the Trash . . .

Do not forget to empty the Recycle Bin if you are using Windows95 or '98 or a subsequent version or empty the Trash on the Macintosh computer!

■ Click on the Recycle Bin icon from your main (desktop) screen. When the screen for the Recycle Bin comes up, you may see files that have not been completely deleted from the computer.

■ Click on the File menu at the top left corner of the screen, and select the Empty Recycle Bin choice. This will highlight all of the files awaiting deletion.

■ Click the Empty Recycle Bin choice to completely get rid of them.

Macintosh: The Macintosh Trash feature procedures are almost identical.

FIGURE 3-12 The Explorer history record.

You Are No Safer with Microsoft's Internet Explorer

Click on the History button in Explorer. You may find a complete history of your Web-browsing activities for the past few weeks (Figure 3-12). In addition, just as in the case of the Netscape Location box, you will probably find a nifty list of every place you have visited by pulling down the Address box. If you have surfed a bit, clicking on the upper left File pull-down menu will reveal all of the websites you have visited, too. Remember: Browser designers' values are different from ours when it comes to retrieving information! They really like redundancy!

Eliminating histories is a little easier in Explorer (Figure 3-13), and you can set defaults so they do not accumulate.

- In Microsoft Internet Explorer, select the View choice from the top of the window and choose the Internet Options choice.
- Now select the Advanced folder in the box and scroll to the Security section.
- Check to be certain that the "Delete saved pages when browser closed" choice is checked. If it is not, then check it.
- Now open the General folder and set the number of days that a history will accumulate to "0" (zero).
- Click on the Clear History button and then choose the Yes option.
- Exit the program by clicking Apply/OK.

This step ensures that the histories and copies of your explored files, other than the URLs you have bookmarked, will disappear when you turn the computer off.

Macintosh: Follow the same procedure using the Find feature. The target file this time is usually titled "history.html."

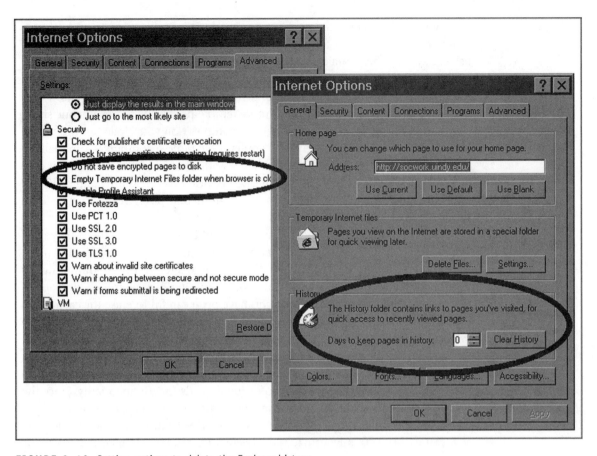

FIGURE 3-13 Setting options to delete the Explorer history.

Remember our worries about nonprofessionals being able to guess where we have been and why? *History and cache files must die!* Again, the greatest danger to safe work on the Web may be more directly connected to your workplace than to some hacker in Peoria. Get in the habit of deleting and modifying traceable files after every session. Constant precautions must be taken whenever confidential information poses risks to clients, practice, the agency, or our profession.[9]

DANGERS WITHIN YOUR SYSTEM

Just when you thought it was safe . . . If you think you have eliminated the pack rat in the computer, there are more in the nest! The computer you are using at home, in an agency setting, or in school is probably tied into another larger computer owned by the ISP that makes copies of all electronic transactions. Sounds like Big Brother? Not intentionally. Files are often copied into large network computers

---

[9] As an alternative to manually managing files, some firms provide utilities that will do some or all erasing tasks for you. For example, *Norton Utilities* has a feature called "Clean Sweep" that eliminates many cached files. Other firms have similar products. These can be most worthwhile because they are great time-savers but remember: 1) These programs must be correctly installed and configured to thoroughly do the job and 2) They only work on the specific machines and systems in which they are installed.

and then regularly emptied, maybe once a week. This is cheap insurance against those occasional nasty system failures. If you back up everything, you can reestablish the system after a major crash. While all of your work may be buried along with everyone else's and chances are good that no one will ever access your records, it remains possible for someone beyond your immediate colleagues or fellow students to retrieve your work. This is a more remote possibility than someone sitting down and intentionally going through the computer on your desk, but it *is* possible. As a result, assume that anything you ever type into a computer—especially if you are in a lab or an agency—probably goes off to other computers where it can be (and often is) recorded. This has drastic implications for security and confidentiality, because the files are well beyond your immediate control and may be legally subpoenaed or simply read by totally unauthorized people.

RULE: When using a networked system—and if you are using the Web, you *are* networked!—always assume that phantom copies are being made of your work somewhere else. Non-social-workers may have access to electronic communications, and anything you summon onto your computer may be more vulnerable than you might assume, even when you have been careful to erase the cache! You probably cannot do anything about *removing* remotely created copies.[10] What you *can* do follows.

First, find out just where copies are being kept, for how long, and just who exactly has access to them. Ask! Then consult and negotiate with the appropriate managerial personnel about your professional needs for confidentiality. Since the specific nature of computing systems varies considerably and agency or institutional policies on backup may vary, too (or worse yet, simply not be in place at all), you will have to advocate for an agreement on the need for confidentiality in Web communications. It is a great opportunity to create policies!

Once you have negotiated a policy or learned what already exists, then inform the colleagues that may be affected and adapt your security routines to it. Of course, in compliance with the NASW *Code of Ethics, you must inform the clients, too.* Develop procedures and protocols for informing all relevant parties, and then implement them. Doing this as a matter of routine will not eliminate the problem, but it will establish an organizational awareness around the issue that at least acknowledges the presence of copies and the potential dangers they may hold.

Another approach is to use *encryption* programs to scramble your work (Electronic Frontier Foundation, 1998). Both Netscape and Explorer browsers have this built in, and there are many others available on the market. These have the advantage of making files unintelligible to unauthorized readers, but the disadvantage is that the authorized receivers must be running the same encryption program with the same settings and must also know what to do. This can get tedious. Encryption is well beyond the scope of this book and applies more to E-mail than to Web surfing. In the agency setting, use a consultant to choose and set up security encryption, because many choices and levels are possible. In addition, you are going to have to teach the correct procedures to everyone who will be using them. This is not a minor undertaking, and you can easily plan on a halfday's training per employee. If backup copies do pose definite risks to a specific client system, we suggest that an agency-wide encryption system be investigated and developed. It is worth the money!

---

[10] Well, you actually can do something about them, but if you know how, you probably do not need to read this chapter!

FIGURE 3-14 The padlock is a security icon.

More Security Issues

If you are not scared yet, there are still more worries . . . While we are on security, there are a few rattlesnakes to watch out for.

In Netscape, Note *the small padlock icon* (Figure 3-14) at the bottom left-hand corner of your Netscape browser screen. As long as the padlock is unlocked, you are not on a secure line and you do not have a secured Web connection that is just between you and the host computer you are connected to. *Any* third party can also directly figure out what is going on during your session.

Click on the padlock icon. You will see many different types of choices and levels of security. We are not going to go into them in detail, because different agencies have different choices, capabilities, and requirements. We do, however, recommend that you consult with your system's manager, often known as the sysop and find out how this feature can be used to your professional advantage. As in the case of encryption, securing lines is beyond the scope of this book, but available consultants can usually set up your system so that it is difficult for another third party to eavesdrop. Using consultants is especially important when designing networked stations in an agency where security needs to be centrally—and habitually—maintained.

At minimum, prompt yourself regularly about security. To ensure that security warnings keep appearing (Figure 3-15),

- Click on the padlock/security icon.
- Click on the Navigator choice. A window with "Show a warning before" check boxes should appear.
- Click on the four choice boxes so that each has a check mark. (They will work when the box has an "X" in it.)
- Click the OK button and exit.

Similar procedures can be followed for the Messenger E-mail feature.

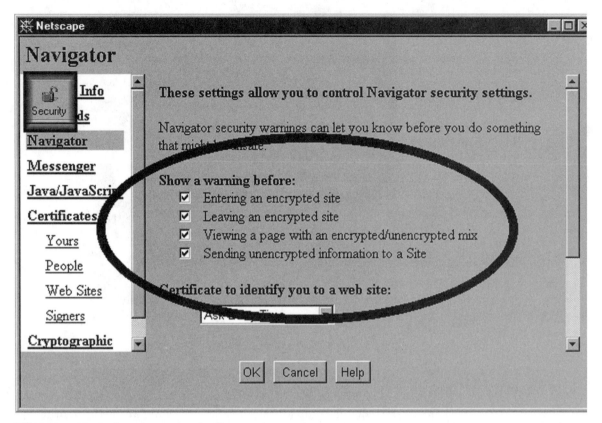

FIGURE 3-15 Navigator's security warnings.

In the Internet Explorer (Figure 3-16),

■ Open the View pull-down menu at the top left line on your screen.

■ Select the Internet Options choice.

■ Go to the Advanced file.

■ Scroll until you find the Security section.

■ Check all of the boxes in the security section so the black dots are on them.

■ Exit by clicking the Apply and OK buttons.

These procedures will make sure that you are continually nagged about security issues. It is so easy to take the Web for granted and view it as a rather benign resource. Remember that the NASW *Code of Ethics* enjoins us to always be mindful!

DANGERS FROM PROFESSIONAL AND PERSONAL VALUE CONFLICTS

Major value conflicts between ourselves and other people, professions, and organizations are common. Why? Ethical standards for professional conduct vary considerably. For example teachers interpret confidentiality boundaries in different—and still quite functional—ways than we do. Thus, other professionals who construct

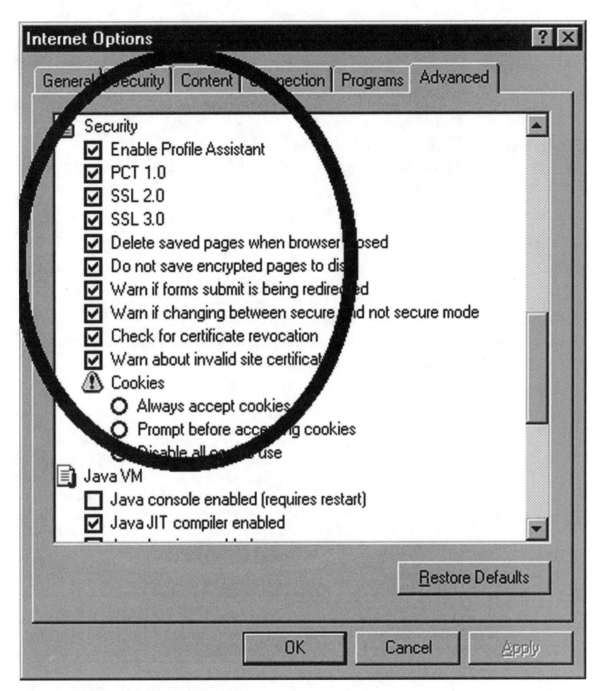

FIGURE 3-16 Setting security options in Explorer.

webpages—such as teachers, health care workers, and law enforcement agencies— have a different sense of confidentiality, security, and professional obligations toward consumers. Potential conflicts are always possible.

Also remember: People will often reveal amazing information to total strangers. The Web is a fertile place for these revelations because of its illusion of anonymity. It is actually as anonymous as an airport. Again, any time you look at a webpage, you are logging into a foreign host server, and that server immediately gets your IP address. Anonymity *is* an illusion.

FIGURE 3-17 A common magic cookie message.

Cookies, Anyone?

One of the more common messages you may receive when on the Web is the "cookie" message (Figure 3–17). What does it mean? Basically, the people who create webpages often want to know more about who is actually using and viewing them. This is especially true in the commercial realm where marketing information is an integral part of business. Enter the magic *cookie*.

A **cookie** is a message sent to your computer from a remote website to find out detailed information about your session. It records what computer and system were logged on, how long you were connected, and your viewing history, including the choices for every single link you followed within the website. It even records how long you looked at each webpage and in what order. In short, it makes a very comprehensive analysis of your visit.

This can be very convenient, especially when you repeatedly shop on the Web, because the foreign computer will automatically default to your previous preferences that an earlier cookie recorded. (They want you to have a nice time and spend money, so they try to please you as much as possible.) Cookies allow companies to freely collect personal information about whoever uses your computer. Usually this information is written to a file on your computer called the "cookie" file. Whenever you interact with a webpage such as by buying something, filling in a form, or responding to a questionnaire, the cookie file can be updated. This information can now become available to *new* websites you look at, along with the firms that have already been added to it, if they have the cookie technology. This can make shopping much easier, especially when you return to a website—all at the price of privacy and confidentiality. The issues are not always very clearly cut or stated (Blankenhorn, 1998).

There are several "types" of cookies. The following is a glib way for you to remember them.

FRESH COOKIES   Some cookies self-return to the sender and make no entries on your computer. This is characterized by a ". . . will be sent only back to itself" message. Generally, this type of cookie is harmless, but you have no way of knowing just how safe it really is, so keep on reading.

STALE COOKIES   Some cookies will persist *in your computer* for a fixed amount of time, probably until they are scrapped. Deleting cookie files is possible; you can follow the same procedures to find and eliminate them as you did with the cache files previously discussed. This gets tedious. Accepting these cookies means they will remain available to unknown firms and organizations for a very long time. Think twice. Do you really want old cookies getting stale and growing fuzzy little green jackets somewhere on your hard drive? Seriously, you do not need 'em! Lose-'em.

There is a second dimension to this. Cookie users can have access to the information you have provided for a fixed period of time, often far beyond any imaginable time for serious use! Why do they do this? Let's explore an example. If you enjoy mountain biking as a hobby and surf a lot of websites on it (hopefully not at work, or only on your lunch hour with your supervisor's permission!), the marketing firm behind the cookie will know that someone who uses your machine is interested in mountain bikes when cookies for websites on mountain bikes are regularly accepted. The marketing firm's clients—maybe a search engine firm working for a commercial corporation making athletic products—now know your interest too. Surf on mountain biking a few times, and guess what Web advertisements you will see when your computer logs into their search engine. Surprise! Mountain bikes and related paraphernalia! Targeted marketing is here, up close and very personal. *You* are the target. So are the clients! Ah, the joys of unbridled capitalism![11] Beware.

ANCHOVY CHIP COOKIES   This brings us to one of the more problematic dimensions of cookies: nasty surprises. Let's imagine that you have a colleague who shares your computer at work. All of a sudden, whenever you use a specific search engine, you get nothing but pornography advertisements dancing about the screen. If you have not been looking at porn sites, then we will give you one guess on who has.[12]

This was no coincidence. Similar nasty surprises crop up in families all the time! Cookies provide a browsing trail that, if unchecked, can easily reveal far more about the user than she or he ever dreamed because of targeted marketing. Considerable amounts of personal information can be gathered with little difficulty. At present, there are no laws or regulations for this practice.

POISON COOKIES   When you click OK and allow a cookie to be set in your computer, you are allowing a foreign computer to read information from and *write to your hard drive*. This means that it is remotely possible for a distant computer to gather

---

[11]   For an example of how cookies are commercially used for marketing research and customer profiling, visit "Double Click" at
www.doubleclick.net
Compare this with Cookie Central's analysis:
http://www.cookiecentral.com/dsm.htm

[12]   One reported study by Digital Detective Services found that one in four corporate computers contained pornography files (Investor's Business Daily, 3 October 1997/Edupage).

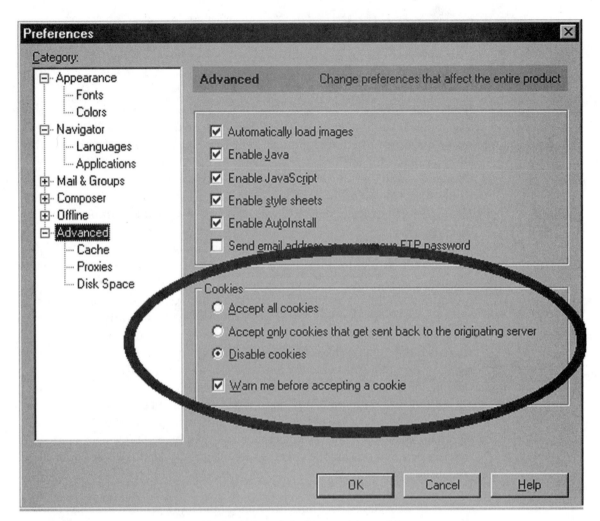

FIGURE 3-18 Controlling magic cookies in Navigator's Preferences Advanced box.

confidential information that is stored somewhere on *your* computer. There also is another very remote possibility of taking on a computer virus. In the agency setting, cookie ingestion—to the point of compromising the agency's security—may lead to demeaning acts of contrition for you. The point is simple: Cookies may look innocent, but you never know what they have been laced with or who is behind them. Most cookies are harmless, and the information they actually gather can also be found in the visited server's log files, but why take any risks?

TIP: We strongly suggest that you do not accept any cookies, except the real ones sold by the Girl Scouts of America. Almost all websites will let you proceed to download if you refuse cookies or have a program that automatically disables them. The capitalist system is not going to collapse if you refuse cookies, and the Web will be a better place.

Thanks, but No Thanks!

If you have never seen a cookie message, your computer is probably ingesting them without your being aware of it. To set your default to refuse cookies, check how the browser defaults for them are set. To do this in Netscape (Figure 3-18)

- Select the Edit pull-down menu.
- Go to the Preferences choice.

FIGURE 3-19 The "Disable all cookie use" choice in Explorer.

■ Choose the Advanced section.

■ Click the Disable Cookies choice so it has a black dot in it.

■ Click the "Warn me before accepting a cookie" choice so it has an "X" in it.

■ Exit the program with OK.

In the Internet Explorer (Figure 3-19),

■ Open the View pull-down menu at the top left line on your screen.

■ Select the Internet Options choice.

■ Go to the Advanced file.

■ Scroll until you find the Security section.

■ Check the "Disable all cookie use" button so a black dot is in it.

■ Exit by clicking the Apply and OK buttons.

Also consider installing an *anti-cookie* program on your machine to help control what information you allow to be circulated. Shareware and commercial programs are available and programs can be installed. These offer reasonable control.

In conclusion, it is vital to remember that not everyone has the same standards for security and confidentiality as our profession. Other professions have different values and processes. People can be beguiled into revealing extensive personal information when they think they are anonymous. Commercial firms (and heaven knows who else) actively attempt to find out more about you, your clients, your agency, and anyone else who consistently uses the Web. Beware. The *X Files* are more than a television program.

Profiling

A final concern for professionally related conflict is **profiling.** This is like the magic cookie approach but much more up front. Some websites, especially commercial ones, often require you to "register" before you are allowed to proceed further in the website. The registration process usually consists of providing personal information in check boxes and lines. This information is then used to add your name and *profile* to the sponsoring firm's database. You have absolutely no control over what happens to it after this. The best way to determine if you want to provide any information is to look for *disclaimers* on the website. These often inform you about why the data is being collected and provide circulation and limitations details. *If* you find a disclaimer, and *if* you are comfortable with the policy, and *if* you trust the firm, then continuing on may be reasonable. That was three *ifs,* was it not? Should you find nothing, provide nothing. E-mailing the webweaver a brief note to tell the firm why you will not use their website (and products) may have an effect. Inform the clients, too!

DANGERS BY INTENT

Any time you are on an active Web connection, your communications can be intercepted by another computer program. There are some real hackers and crackers out there, capable of money theft, extortion, blackmail, or general mischief by screwing up your computer and maybe much more. While this is rare, it does happen. As we mentioned at the start of this chapter, there are passive and active dimensions to this.

Passive Issues

Keep a basic value conflict in mind whenever surfing the Web: *There is always something available to offend someone.* Groups that are antithetical to social work values, such as hate groups, have the right to be on the Web just as much as anyone else. Yet good practice necessitates some degree of judgment. Accidentally sharing a "Holocaust revisionist" website that insists the Holocaust did not happen—particularly with survivors in an adult daycare setting—could certainly be traumatic and cruel. Pornography sites perpetuate the oppression of women and children. They are abundant. Racial hatred sites are appallingly available. The list is endless. You must keep this in mind and act accordingly when working with client systems with stigmas or histories of persecution. Passively offensive websites may be as traumatic as active attacks. While the decision to prevent people from viewing offensive websites *is* a form of censorship, we are obliged to protect populations at risk (such as children). As a result, we suggest that this is a matter for agency policy deliberations. The individual social worker needs to bring these issues to the agency's attention but should not act unilaterally on it.

What does this really mean? If the agency deems it necessary to limit what people will see—for example, children in a day-care setting—then the agency should invest in and install a commercial *filtering software* program to thwart access to the more toxic places on the Web. These programs are not foolproof, but they certainly help. In addition, when possible, have someone such as an assistant or aide *physically present during the session!* If toxic sites are a problem, then teach the workers and aides how to recognize them and take action. At minimum, this may prevent your having to fill out those twenty carbon copies of your agency's "Please Don't Fire Me!" form because clients discovered their children viewing pedophilic websites.[13]

Active Issues

Many actions, some criminal and some not, can make the Web a dangerous place. Intentional predation is possible through Web-mediated E-mail and listservs. News stories of attempted, virtual, and real molestation, for example, are becoming commonplace. Perpetrators, such as a husband searching for an abused wife who has disappeared, can stalk victims. There is criminal mischief—both economic and political—to contend with. Fraudulent investments, for example, are quite possible (Barrett & Lamb, 1998). In addition, "hactivists" engage in virtual civil disobedience. This can result in the intentional vandalization of websites for

---

[13] Additional discussions of work and family-related filtering programs can be found at ZDNet,
http://www8.zdnet.com/products/content/zdim/0212/zdim0010.html
or a search can be conducted for these products.

political reasons ranging from the extreme right to extreme left (*New York Times*, 31 October 1998/Edupage).

Proxy Servers and Fire Walls

The authors, visiting an international conference on the Internet in Chicago in 1997, counted twenty-seven firms selling security systems that ranged in price from a few thousand dollars to enough money to budget a small agency for a very long time. While the baroque and rococo systems that recognize your voice or scan your eyeball (We are not kidding: Some really do this!) are not terribly necessary in most agency settings, a good basic security fire wall may be necessary for any agency dealing with confidential information. What, you may be asking, is a "fire wall"?

Commercial fire-wall programs buffer the interface between your system and the rest of the Internet to prevent close encounters of a malicious kind. These technologies are beyond the scope of this book, but do investigate their use (Stein, 1998). Just remember: These programs are generally designed to protect your computer and its system, not the information in it! The most common danger is from viruses (Butterfield, in press) and "hostile JAVA applets." Both types of programs are intentionally designed to harm your system.

Computer viruses range from minor annoying ones, sort of like head lice in the day-care center, to the genuinely lethal ones that can crash your whole system and give you a very bad day. The tormented souls who create some of them may need a session with their local district attorney. At minimum, be certain your computer system has a virus-checking program installed and operating at all times when you are on the Internet. Be certain that the program is frequently updated, because new strains are constantly being created and circulated. You generally cannot get a virus from E-mail, because it is written in text-based language, but since you are connected with the Internet, anything is possible, even if somewhat remote. Most ISPs offer some degree of protection, and the firm you use may have specific concrete suggestions for additional security. Ask them. This may get more troublesome in the future as more people adopt E-mail programs with *client programs* in them. These types of extra programs can create and open up binary files (not ASCII textfiles) instantly. This ability, as opposed to opening simple textfiles, can be quite lethal because virus infection now becomes far easier.

TIP: Never E-mail any messages to websites you consider suspicious for any reason. Never open an appended file in your E-mail from an untrusted source. Never reveal any personal information.

A fire wall is a program that filters and manages what information can and cannot be taken out or put into your local system, thus offering significant protection from virus and intrusion attacks. While we will not go into details about what is needed—that is the worry for your technical people—*ask about the fire-wall protection your agency uses.* If appropriate, circulate information about it and ask for in-service training, notes in periodic in-house newsletters, E-mail nags, and other internal communications. If your agency does not have a security system or service, find out why and advocate for one if necessary.

A FINAL RATTLESNAKE ALERT: Sometimes you will find URLs that only contain numbers, such as

http://123.45.678.90.

This is the Internet protocol (IP) address discussed in Chapter 2. Entering it will produce the same results as typing in the alphabetic URL. Numeric URLs are fine most of the time, but groups that do not want to be easily identified will use this type of URL to mask their true identity. Remember the Wild West metaphor? The Web has rip-off artists, frauds, hate groups, and assorted criminals who do not follow the NASW *Code of Ethics* in any respect. A numeric URL is a dead giveaway for potential trouble, so beware!

Your Next Worry: E-Money

As of this writing, bankcard transactions on the Web are becoming safer. The issue is the level of trust. Most commercial websites now have "secured" bank transactions where you can enter in your bankcard numbers and be as safe as when you give your charge card to that waiter or store clerk. What you need to worry about is just *how safe is this secured website?* There is no easy gauge for this, so let the buyer beware. At minimum, ask yourself if you are trading with a reputable firm and if policies such as refunds and merchandise returns are acceptable for you and the client.

We help clients with their money in some practice areas. For example, some social workers function as public guardians for people who need help and supervision with money. A social worker working in a nursing home or other confined setting may often help the clients by making small purchases that otherwise would not be possible.

OPINION: At minimum, we suggest that all financial transactions over the Web, at least when related to clients, be thoroughly documented *on paper* and that the NASW *Code of Ethics* be consulted when policies for doing this are crafted by the agency.

Bless That Floppy Disk Drive!

What if you really need to save confidential records of Web activities? If you spend a surfing session with an individual client, for example, you may want to save the results for later discussion. A simple solution is to keep your Bookmarks/Favorites lists saved to a floppy disk rather than leaving the list (actually a file) on the machine. This is especially a good idea when you have several people using the same computer. To do this in the IBM type of machine in Netscape,

- Put a formatted floppy disk in the computer's *A* drive (if it is the default).
- Click on the Bookmarks button.
- Choose the Edit Bookmarks feature.
- Choose the Edit choice and then the Select All feature.
- Choose the Edit and then the Copy choice.
- Go to the File choice in the upper left corner of the browser.
- Choose the Save As choice.
- Select the floppy drive.
- Give the file a helpful name.[14]

---

[14] If you are using different bookmark files for different tasks, such as having a specific file for each individual client, then create a file name system that is memorable. Just be certain that the bookmark file ends with the *.htm* suffix and the name/client connection cannot be intuitively guessed by someone else. The same applies for the Favorites files for Explorer.

- Click the OK button.
- Close the Bookmarks window.

Now delete the bookmarks from the browser's Bookmark file. Usually this means going out of the browser to the file manager and following the file tree from Netscape to Users to a named file until you get to the "bookmark.htm" file that can now be deleted.

To use the bookmarks now on the floppy drive,

- Go to the File pull-down menu in the upper left corner of the browser.
- Choose the Open Page choice.
- Click the Choose File button and then select the floppy drive with the book-mark file.
- Click on the file containing the bookmarks (whatever name you have given it).
- Choose and click the bookmarked website you want to visit.

  In Internet Explorer,

- Get your cursor into the website you want to record.
- Right-click the mouse and choose Add To Favorites.
- Click on the Create In button.
- Select the Links folder.
- Click the OK button.

  Now, in your windows program, not your browser,

- Find the Links file.
- Copy it to a formatted disk in the floppy drive.
- Delete the files in the Links folder on your main drive.

  When you want to use the floppy disk list of your links, then

- Put the formatted disk into the floppy drive.
- Click on the File pull-down menu in your top left screen.
- Choose the Open option.
- Choose the Browse choice.
- Select the floppy drive.
- Click on the file you want. This will take you to the URL you saved.

  If you are using a Macintosh computer (directions for Netscape only),[15]

- Put your preformatted floppy disk in the drive.
- From the Mail feature, select the Window.
- Select the Bookmark choice.
- Choose File and then Save As.
- Go to the desktop/disk and select the Untitled: choice.
- Give the file a name that you will remember.
- Choose the Save choice.

---

[15] Unfortunately, this may not be possible on some Macintosh Machines as some now no longer have disk drives.

To summon the bookmarks from the disk,

- Turn off the browser.
- Insert the disk into the drive.
- Click on the disk icon.
- Double-click on the bookmark file you want to use.

These methods are actually much easier to use once you have practiced them a little bit. They will help you conveniently keep track of your browsing records, and you can even keep separate client systems on different floppy disks. The point is simple: If you keep your records on a floppy disk, you have a much greater degree of security than if you simply leave the bookmarks on the computer. Unfortunately, you must do all of this on the same browser because the files are not generally interchangeable. Naturally, you do need to keep that floppy disk safely tucked away in a secure place! Treat the Favorites or Bookmark disk with the same care and attention you accord to other confidential materials such as telephone logs, case notes, and files on clients.

Lock the Door and Put out the Cat

We have saved the best security technique for last: Lock up your computer when you leave. If you are in a workplace setting where you can physically lock up and isolate the machine by closing and locking a door, then do it! If this is not possible because you share resources, be certain that all of your browsing records are removed from the machine when you are done, and then lock up that floppy disk just as carefully as the case files. Never reveal your password, and change it often, perhaps once every two months or so. When you do, be certain it is not a word in the dictionary, a name, or anything guessable. Include a few numbers in it, too! If you are at a public workstation, be sure no one is looking over your shoulder when you log in. If your computer actually has a real lock and key built into it, use it! These simple, cheap, and timely habits may do as much for ensuring your security as using the most expensive security system available.

Summary

We have covered only the basics. Regardless of the browser you use and all of the security features it has (many of which we have not described), you have ever-present dangers that can occur within your own office or anywhere else on the planet. At present, there are few codes, rules, or policy interpretations that clearly specify the boundaries for professional practice with client systems on the Web. At minimum, it is important to manage all records of Web sessions by deleting them or keeping them in a secure place. Given the potential harm that can arise from breaches of confidentiality, we have every obligation to assure clients that all possible precautions have been taken and to fairly warn them of potential risks. A telephone log or open case file on your desk could pose the same danger. We just have a new dimension to worry about, but one that is larger by several orders of magnitude. Most people regard the Web as rather harmless, and a great deal of it is. Yet many types of transactions that would get you dragged into a court of law elsewhere remain quite unregulated on the Internet. Until our profession decides on the specific limits and boundaries for using the Web in practice and until policies and routines are developed, play it safe.

Exercise 3A
Security and Confidentiality for Your Issue

- This is a paper exercise. You do not need to use a computer.
- It is similar to Exercise 2B: The Paper Web, but more focused.
- The purpose of this exercise is to sharpen your thinking on specific security and confidentiality problems that your chosen issue may hold.
- This work will carry over into the next exercise.

DIRECTIONS

A. Write the one area, topic, and issues that crystallized your issue in Exercises 2A and 2B. Again, write this information *in the center* of the following diagram.[16]

Example

If your area of interest is "research," the topic is "program evaluation," and the issue is "My Cousin's House," an actual shelter-providing agency, then you would write this in the *italicized center part* of the diagram.

Area: _____

Confidentiality: _____

Security: _____

Area: _____   Area: _____

Confidentiality: _____   Confidentiality: _____

Security: _____   Security: _____

Area: _____

Area: _____   *Topic* _____   Area: _____

Confidentiality: _____   *Issue:* _____   Confidentiality: _____

Security: _____   Confidentiality: _____   Security: _____

Security: _____

Area: _____   Area: _____

Confidentiality: _____   Confidentiality: _____

Security: _____   Security: _____

Area: _____

Confidentiality: _____

Security: _____

---

[16] If you know how and if your instructor approves it, you can draw a systems diagram such as an "eco-map" instead of the one in this exercise. If you do, then adapt steps B, C, and D to it.

B. Write the eight other areas in the diagram around the central area.

Example

Now write the other areas—practice, field, policy and services, social and economic justice, populations at risk, diversity, HBSE, values and ethics—in the places around the circle.

C. Think of a *confidentiality issue* for each of the surrounding areas *and* your central issue. Write them down on the diagram. Use a few words to crystallize the issue.

Example

If you are conducting the agency evaluation from the example given in **A**, the "practice" area might contain "Confidentiality: No computerized name lists accessible."

D. Repeat this process for identifying *security issues.*

Example

The "practice" area might contain "Security: No easy office computer access."

Note: Do the most comprehensive diagram you can. Some of the areas may not have readily identifiable security and confidentiality issues, but others will.

SUMMING IT UP

Look over your work and answer the following questions in one or two paragraphs.

1. What are the major confidentiality issues for the areas?

2. What are the major security issues for the areas?

Exercise 3B
Security Assessment

■ This is a computer exercise. You will need a Web-connected computer.

■ The purpose of this exercise is to sharpen your awareness and understanding of security and confidentiality issues and conflicts that may be related to your issue or similar issues.

DIRECTIONS

Review the work you did in Exercise 3A. Specifically review your major confidentiality and security findings for the two paragraphs in Summing It Up.

Read through the list of websites below and select the three that may most likely be related to your issue or suggest similar security and confidentiality issues. Visit each and thoroughly examine its contents in terms of what it suggests for your own issue by examining the questions below.

For each website report:

A. What are the confidentiality issues and ideas this website suggests for *your* issue?

B. What are the security issues and ideas this website suggests for *your* issue?

C. What *conclusions* do you have about your issue and what this website presents?

List of websites:

American Arab Anti Discrimination Committee http://www.adc.org

American Civil Liberties Union http://www.aclu.org

Anti-Defamation League http://www.adl.org

Gay and Lesbian Alliance Against Defamation http://www.glaad.org

Japanese American Citizens League http://jacl.org

National Association for the Advancement of Colored People http://www.naacp.org

National Congress of American Indians http://www.ncai.org

National Council of La Raza http://www.nclr.org

1. Website chosen: _____

    A. What are the confidentiality issues and ideas this website suggests for *your* issue?

    B. What are the security issues and ideas this website suggests for *your* issue?

    C. What *conclusions* do you have about your issue and what this website presents?

2. Website chosen: _____

   A. What are the confidentiality issues and ideas this website suggests for *your* issue?

   B. What are the security issues and ideas this website suggests for *your* issue?

   C. What *conclusions* do you have about your issue and what this website presents?

3. Website chosen: _____

   A. What are the confidentiality issues and ideas this website suggests for *your* issue?

   B. What are the security issues and ideas this website suggests for *your* issue?

   C. What *conclusions* do you have about your issue and what this website presents?

Exercise 3C
Tracing URLs

- This is a computer exercise. You will need a Web-connected computer.
- The purpose of this exercise is to help you develop skills for tracing URL origins and ownership.
- This exercise is not connected with any of the nine content areas. It is a skill you need.

DIRECTIONS

Choose any single website from this chapter's exercises (or another with your instructor's permission) and do the following.

A. Find out about the source for the website:

- Get the website on the browser.

If using the Netscape Navigator,

- Go to the View pull-down menu located in the upper left corner of the window and select the Page Info choice.

If using the Microsoft Internet Explorer,

- Go to the File pull-down menu located in the upper left corner of the window and select the Properties choice. The URL and its security profile, if any, will be in the General and Security file folders. Unfortunately, Explorer provides less information so you cannot easily find posting dates.

- Read the available information about the webpage and record:

  The location for the page. *This is its actual URL.* Jot it down on paper.

  The modification dates, if any.

  The security parameters, if any.

- Briefly summarize what you found.

B. Visit the Network Solutions InterNIC website. InterNIC is the organization that manages and assigns URLs for all domains except *.gov* and *.mil.*

The URL is: http://internic.net

Instructions are at: http://www.networksolutions.com/cgi-bin/whois/whois

NOTE: The Whois search only looks for second-level domain names. To use Whois, cut off the server-name part of the URL (the *www* part) and type in the middle part of the URL (subdomain) and the final domain. (Refer to Chapter 2, Figure 2–3.)

EXAMPLE: www.unknown.net is entered as: "unknown.net" (without quotation marks).

(If you are curious, try entering your own last name followed by a comma, a space, and then your first name! You may be surprised at the results!)

- If you are trying to trace a numeric URL (one that consists of an Internet protocol number such as 123.45 . . . etc.), visit the American Registry of Internet Numbers instead. The URL is: http://whois.arin.net/whois/arinwhois.html

- Enter the IP number you want to trace into the Whois search engine.

- Enter the URL you want to trace into the Whois search engine or IP number in the ARIN search engine and submit your request.

  NOTE: Some websites "guest" on sponsoring servers. Others use ISPs that are commercial firms. As a result, do not be upset if you get no results or results that make no sense.

- Briefly summarize what you found:

C. What can you find out about the sponsoring firm or organization?

- If you have a result that gives you the name of the sponsoring organization or provider, preferably the organization and not the ISP (they are only a conduit), look up this firm on the Web through any of the following resource websites:

  Internet Yellow Page Directories:

  Netscape Netsearch: http://home.netscape.com/netcenter/yellowpages.html

  Excite: http://yellowpages.zip2.com

  LookSmart: http://yp.bellsouth.com

- Briefly summarize what you found:

SUMMING IT UP

What conclusions can you draw from this work?

Write a paragraph that summarizes your work, and draw at least one conclusion from it.

Questions for Discussion

What are the specific policies one should recommend to protect confidentiality and Web issues?

The writers take a very "anti-cookie" stand. What are the merits of a "pro-cookie" viewpoint?

Should the profession form and take a specific stance toward hate groups and others that seek to harm people and organizations?

References

Barrett, D., & Lamb, L. (1998). *Bandits on the information superhighway (what you need to know)*. Sebastapol, CA: O'Reilly and Associates, Inc.

Blankenhorn, D. (1998, June). Web wars: Personal marketing breeds privacy concerns. *Datamation*. [On-line].
Available:
http://datamation.com/PlugIn/issues/1998/june/06web.html

Butterfield, W. (in press). Human services and the information economy. *Journal of Computers in Human Services*, 15 (2/3).

Electronic Frontier Foundation. (1998). *Cracking Des: Secrets of encryption research, wiretap politics, & chip design*. Sebastapol, CA: O'Reilly and Associates, Inc.

National Association of Social Workers. (No date). *Code of ethics*. Washington, DC: Author.

National Association of Social Workers. (1997). *NASW speaks* (4th ed.). Washington, DC: Author.

Stein, L. (1998). *Web security: A step-by-step reference guide*. Reading, MA: Addison-Wesley.

Edupage Citations

Investor's Business Daily. (3 October 1997). *Porn found on 25% of corporate computers.* [Reported in Edupage, October 7, 1997].

New York Times (31 October 1998). Hactivists say: "The revolution will be digitized." [Reported in Edupage, November 1, 1998].

Additional Readings

Cheswick, W. (2000). *Fire Walls and Internet security : Repelling the wily hacker* (2nd ed.). Reading, MA: Addison-Wesley.

Gelman, R. (1998). *Protecting yourself on-line: The definitive resource on safety, freedom, & privacy in cyberspace—An electronic frontier foundation guide*. San Francisco, CA: Harper Edge.

Additional Websites

Health Care Financial Administration
Policy on Security
http://www.hcfa.gov/security/isecplcy.htm

Johnson, J. (1995)
The information highway from hell: A worst-case scenario
Computer Professionals for Social Responsibility
http://www.cpsr.org/cpsr/nii/hell.html

Quittner, J. (August 25, 1997)
Invasion of privacy. *Time Magazine, 150* (8). [On Line].
Available:
http://cgi.pathfinder.com/time/magazine/1997/dom/970825/nation.invasion_of_p.html

PART II

USING THE WEB

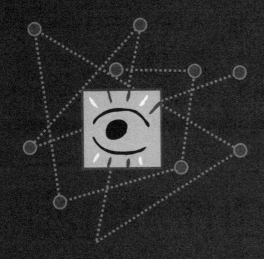

CHAPTER 4

Basic Searching for Information

Some of the things you can do with readily at-hand resources . . .

. . . Find out more about populations at risk.

. . . Enjoy diversity on an unimagined scale.

. . . Explore extensive resources with clients.

. . . Find out facts and information about foundations and agencies.

. . . Look up research for various practice-related topics.

CHAPTER OVERVIEW

New information is constantly being added to the Web, but keeping track of it is humanly impossible. In addition, we often need information that is peripheral to or unrelated to social work. This chapter covers

- Finding Information
- Finding Webpages: Using Known URLs
- Finding Webpages: Guessing URLs
- Finding Webpages: Following Links
- Finding Webpages: Following WebRings
- Finding Webpages: Using Meta-Lists

If possible, go through this chapter while at your computer! It really helps!

FINDING INFORMATION

Mr. Waters

You are working with an older man in adult day care. Mr. Waters has coped very well with advancing Parkinson's disease for thirteen years. One of the ways he copes is by keeping informed about the latest medical research on the disease. He and his family use this information to help make decisions on what new medications and treatments might be worth investigating. He was among the first pallidotomy surgery recipients in the United States, thanks to his own perseverance and his family support. This brain surgery alleviated some of the major symptoms, and he literally ran—slowly—down the corridor after the procedure. He regularly scours newsletters and medical materials for emerging information on Parkinson's disease.

He has found a printed URL in one of the several Parkinson's-related newsletters he regularly reads. He is not computer literate, and his family does not have easy access to the Web. He wants to know more about what this website has to offer and has asked you to help him.

Now that you have mastered some of the basics and learned some dimensions for safe practice, we can move on to how you find resources on the Web. Newbies (folks very new to the Internet) often complain, "I could not find anything on the Web." The opposite happens, too. "I found a hundred thousand websites, but the first few were not any good and the rest were worse." While this is often true for the novice, you can usually find highly specific information with a little effort if you know how and where to look. This is a genuine skill, and it can be mastered with a little practice. Anyone can "surf" the Web, but it takes real ability to find what you want without getting completely distracted, frustrated, or lost!

Before we start, we must provide a word on searching for that one "mother of all websites" you want to find. We sometimes hope that there is one website out there with all the information on a subject. This mythical website can direct us to all emerging information, provide exhaustive current links, and, in short, hold comprehensive resources that will meet all of our information needs. This can be compared with the search for the Holy Grail and can be just as elusive a crusade. Would you expect the same from a single book or journal article? Of course not. The Web has exploded into existence within such a short time, and you can find very similar websites that have little knowledge of—or linkages with—each other. As a result, forget the search for *the* website. Instead, concentrate on finding several to use and choose from. Even if you use all of the strategies described in this chapter and the next, you may still miss important sites. There are no guarantees!

FINDING WEBPAGES: USING KNOWN URLS

The easiest way by far to find great websites is to simply write down the published URLs for them when you see or hear about them. Services, programs, agencies, companies, and individuals are publishing URLs for their webpages more and more in newsletters, directories, brochures, news articles, and other paper print

FIGURE 4-1 Printed URLs are becoming as common as phone numbers.

(Figure 4-1). Radio and television commercials and public service announcements often provide URLs, too. Take a close look at the labels in the supermarket the next time you go shopping. You can even find URLs on billboards and on the backs of trucks. In short, URLs are becoming very common in our world, just as telephone numbers did many decades ago.

Develop the habit of jotting down promising URLs when you find them. You can add them to specific Bookmark/Favorites files for later use, or simply write them down in a paper notebook. Just be sure you copy the complete URL accurately, paying attention to characters and capitalization. This is how Mr. Waters learned about a website in the opening case. The webpage was for *The National Parkinson's Foundation, Inc.*, and the URL was simply printed in a newsletter (Figure 4-2). This site obviously holds a lot of promise. Facts, library resources, research activities, grants and funding, conferences, and support groups can be found here. In many cases, one well-developed website like this one might be all you need for a specific topic or task.

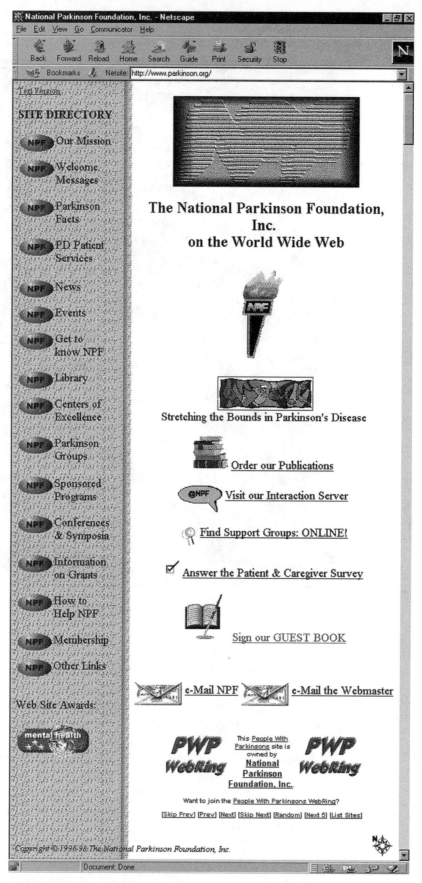

FIGURE 4-2 Note the many resources available from this single website. (Used by permission of the National Parkinson Foundation, Inc.)

Advantages and Disadvantages

The advantage to this approach is that you will almost always get *something,* even if it is not exactly what you expected. Agencies, companies, and services generally publicize only *stable* websites. They have gone to a lot of trouble setting them up and then advertising them, so chances are very good that the URL will work. When an organization has printed and distributed ten thousand brochures with its website prominently displayed, it is not going to change its URL for a long, long time. The disadvantage is that the website may be less than desired and may hold limited and useless information that is supposed to spark your imagination. This may not be very satisfying. More often than not, you will probably be pleased or at least find a link to something more useful.[1]

While published URLs are usually fairly stable and reliable, this is not always the case. One of the more common problems with this approach is that organizations, especially the nonprofits we generally work with, often change servers when a sponsor becomes available or when they buy a server of their own. When this happens, the webweaver will usually leave a "forwarding address" type of message at the old website and, if you are lucky, provide at least the new URL plus a hyperlink to it. Just as in the case of the post office, forward messages do not last forever. If you do get a forwarding message, be certain to bookmark it or write it down immediately as the old URL will likely disappear within a few months.

TIP: Keep a running Post-it note in your wallet, purse, or small notebook, and get in the habit of carefully writing URLs on it when you find them. Do not count on your memory! Surf the websites later on, and record them in your Bookmark/Favorites files if they are helpful.

FINDING WEBPAGES: GUESSING URLS

What if Mr. Waters was curious but did not have any brochure or newsletter? Try guessing! Learning to guess what a workable URL could be for a given issue, product, agency, organization, or service is not very hard. This strategy can actually work quite well with a little practice. This is because of how URLs are often structured. Many organizations, especially commercial firms, government offices, and service agencies, try to have very transparent and memorable URLs. These URLs are fairly predictable because they try to incorporate recognizable key words or abbreviations, and the domains are often obvious. This makes guessing the URL possible. We have used this strategy with some success, although it is not well described in the literature (Notess, 1997). We really like it![2]

---

[1]   One exception is the *.com* (commercial) domain. Competitive firms seldom link to each other, so do not expect many links to rival companies and products if you are looking up a commercial site. Sadly enough, this also applies to some nonprofit organizations as well.

[2]   There actually is a search engine website for guessing URLs. "Amnesi" can provide numerous potential URLs from fragments. The URL is
      http://www.amnesi.com

How to Guess

Let's imagine that you are working with Mr. Waters and do not have any URLs for Parkinson's disease issues. Begin by guessing what a typical Parkinson's URL might look like. Remember the common conventions for URL structures from Chapter 2? We could guess the following:

■ Most websites begin with the common server name *www.* As a result, make *www* the first part of your guess.

■ The next part, the subdomain, is often a key word such as a formal name or recognizable abbreviation. Several key words, such as *parkinson, parkinsonsdisease,* or *parkinsons,* might work.

■ The last three characters usually provide the domain. You only have six domains to use. Try 'em all!

We can construct six different *guess URLs* based on this strategy. We start by using the *www,* then add *parkinsons* as a subdomain, and finally add each domain. This results in the following guesses:

http://www.parkinsons.org

A nonprofit organization connected with some dimension of Parkinson's disease would certainly consider this a possible URL because it is very transparent and direct.

http://www.parkinsons.com

This could be the URL for a commercial firm dealing with Parkinson's disease issues, such as a pharmaceutical firm, a physician's group, or similar entity.[3] A commercial firm might also donate space on its server for a nonprofit agency.

http://www.parkinsons.net

This could easily be a net-based discussion or support group.

http://www.parkinsons.edu

A university research center or teaching hospital might use this as the easiest way for you to find their website.

http://www.parkinsons.gov

A government agency distributing the latest research about Parkinson's disease might use such a URL.[4]

http://www.parkinsons.mil

Never underestimate the military! In addition to connecting lots of installations, these sites also include veterans' hospitals, clinics, research organizations, and many other often surprising sites.

---

[3] It could also be a nonprofit organization or agency that is using a donated commercial organization's server instead of having one of its own. Developing commercial sponsorship is a time-honored community organization approach, is it not? Remember: Not all *.com* sites are directly trying to sell you something.

[4] Government office sites are often "alphabet soups" of acronyms made up of the first letters of the agency. For example, the URL for Health and Human Services is

www.hhs.gov

The Social Security Administration is

www.ssa.gov

This is a fairly reliable assumption for many federal public-governmental agencies and organizations. As a result, the *.gov* domain is often predictable for guessing at the national level.

Naturally, we could also substitute different key words for the subdomain into the same structure. This would give six more URLs per key word, such as

www.parkinsonsdisease.org

but let's just start with the ones already mentioned. We tried these six guessed URLs.[5] What we discovered follows the URL we tried.

http://www.parkinsons.org

The Mulligan Foundation is dedicated to providing a variety of information and resources for (you guessed it!) Parkinson's disease.

http://www.parkinsons.com

This URL led to *NetHealth*, an information service providing a "gateway" with a long menu of various health-related problems. Parkinson's disease was listed, and a short page of links was available.

http://www.parkinsons.net

This produced a net-based organization called *Parkinson's Network*. Like the Mulligan Foundation, this website held a wide variety of information and resources.

http://www.parkinsons.edu, .gov, and .mil

None of these remaining URLs worked. The "No DNS" message told us that there was probably nothing at these possible sites. *No DNS* is the abbreviation for *no domain server*, further supporting the probability that nothing was there when we conducted the test. (Remember, though, you could get the "No DNS" message if a site's server was turned off.)

Three useful websites out of six is not a bad beginning! Looking further, we reviewed each of these three working websites and discovered that (1) half of the guessed URLs actually led to a real website, (2) all of these working websites were related to Parkinson's disease, and (3) when analyzed for contents, these three websites provided:

- Three sources for large quantities of general information about Parkinson's disease
- Two different professionally written articles on exercise, including graphic how-to illustrations
- One professionally written and reviewed scholarly article on Parkinson's disease and sleep disorders
- Two action and advocacy groups on Parkinson's disease issues
- One Parkinson's disease newsletter/newspaper website
- Four international Parkinson's disease organizations and links to their websites
- Five national and state-level Parkinson's disease foundations with accompanying links
- One live on-line chat for supporting victims of Parkinson's disease and their families

---

5 This example and its accompanying Web-based search were conducted on May 14, 1998. All of the sites with active resources may have considerably changed by the time you read this, and some of the URLs that were not developed may have evolved.

- One *WebRing* on families with Parkinson's disease
- One short, annotated *meta-list* of specific Parkinson's disease websites.

Only two of the immediate links from the three guessed websites were dead. Only four of the immediate links were redundant. All together, this guess approach produced *twenty-one different immediate links* on Parkinson's disease that you and Mr. Waters could follow up. Pretty impressive for a little guesswork, is it not?

Advantages and Disadvantages

We strongly recommend the guessing approach, especially if you are looking for mainstream websites. The advantages are that it takes very little time, it is fairly easy, and it can really be a lot of fun! (Sometimes your guesses will really surprise and amuse you! Guesses can be way off the mark, too, and lead you to some profoundly weird websites!) The main disadvantage we know about is that you can never be sure you have found that "mother of all websites" for your topic because what you did find might not have significant links to other important sites.[6] Also, this approach only works when you have a pretty specific and commonly recognized key word such as *parkinsons* or an abbreviation that is easily recognized. Finally, you may miss some pretty good websites simply because they were not the first to register the guessable URL and had to settle for something less.

TIP: Practice guessing. It is a good exercise in critical thinking and can be a very quick and efficient way to find some URLs. Try guessing before you resort to any search engine if you can!

FINDING WEBPAGES: FOLLOWING LINKS

Most websites provide links to other websites. After all, this is often one of the main purposes for having a website in the first place! While the initial website you visit may not be helpful, *scour it for more external links* and follow them! These are sometimes obviously labeled "Links," but they can be subtly titled "Other places to visit," or "Our favorites," or "More places to visit," and so on. In addition, other external links can be hidden elsewhere in the website such as in the graphics. Look for these when you look over the webpage because they may lead you to more useful information.

TIP: Always search each webpage in its entirety for links. Some may be misti-tled, embedded in graphics, or poorly identified, but most websites will have them.

Let's go back to the National Parkinson Foundation, Inc., website (Figure 4-2) from Mr. Waters' newsletter. We found a button marked Other Links in the lower

---

[6] For example, one of the three websites gave the name, phone number, and "snail-mail" address for The American Parkinson's Disease Association but not the URL:

www.apdaparkinson.com

We looked it up and discovered that this new website contained a wealth of information, including advocacy information, specific sources for fellowships and grants, a locator for support groups by state, and a similar information and referral locator by state. The guessing strategy completely missed this!

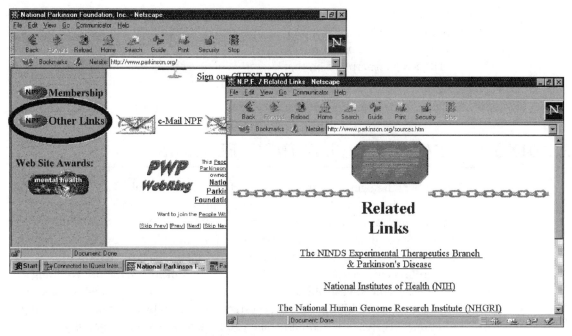

FIGURE 4-3 Always look for additional links. They are not always as clearly marked as this example. (Used by permission of the National Parkinson Foundation, Inc.)

left corner of the homepage. Clicking on Other Links took us to a short list of additional external resources Figure 4-3. This is an example of resource links provided by the webpage's author, and it is *typical of many practice-related websites.* Once you have jumped off of a known webpage to external links, you may not have to look much further.

Remember, however, that resource webpages (e.g., "Visit Our Super Links") *may not contain all of the external links within the website.* This website was no exception. There were several other external resource links on this website that were not on the Other Links webpage. Exploring around produced the following: One additional link, in the news section, was a simple interactive quiz. Three external links were available from the library section, and seven on-line connections to "Centers of Excellence" were available, too. In total, eleven additional links were available within this site beyond the identifiable Other Links webpage. There is nothing inherently wrong about this approach, especially in larger websites providing several types of information.

Why is this common? Often this simply cannot be avoided. Web designers usually do not intentionally hide their links. The problem arises as sites evolve and become more sophisticated. Organizing most of the links into a coherent list can be a daunting task, and there are always links that do not easily fit anywhere—taxonomic angst. As a result, always assume that additional hidden links may be available somewhere else in a website.

Advantages and Disadvantages

The advantages of this "explore for more links" approach is that there are very good chances of finding additional resources once you have found the homepage. Additional links are almost *de rigueur* these days; that is, it is unfashionable *not* to have them. Do remember the disadvantages of being limited to the bias of the website's authors or sponsors and the common practice of putting links elsewhere in the website. Finally, site maintenance can be an issue, too. If the site is not regularly maintained by the webweaver, then many links, obvious or hidden, may be out of date or no longer functional.

TIP: Keep a sharp eye on that cursor! Whenever it changes from the *arrow* to the *hand*, you have probably found a hidden link.

FINDING WEBPAGES: FOLLOWING WEBRINGS

Remember when guessing the URL turned up something called a WebRing? These specialized links, formally called *WebRings*, allow you to go to a host of related websites. You can find WebRings by specifically looking for them, but you can also stumble across them accidentally, so it is important to know how to recognize them when you wander into them. First things first: What are WebRings?

WebRings are *closed circles* of websites that are linked together by WebRing software. Seventeen-year-old college student Sage Weil invented them (Starseed, Inc., 1999). The WebRing website is currently operated by Starseed, Inc. Starting out at one website will eventually take you back to where you began if you keep following the Next Site choice. (We get to navigation in a little bit.) You can also skip around in most WebRings and randomly access member websites. WebRings vary considerably in size, ranging from a handful of related sites within one to groups numbering in the hundreds. The minimum number that Starseed, Inc., will support is a WebRing of five members. Starseed, Inc., provides the software free of charge.

The actual WebRings are created by "owners" who are usually the webweavers for specific websites. They get other websites to voluntarily agree to be linked together into a WebRing. All websites within a WebRing are voluntary because it is impossible to be a member without knowing it. This is because you have to include the WebRing software somewhere in your individual website if you want to participate. While the WebRing is technically "owned" by a single website, every site in it is owned and operated by the individual webweavers. The WebRing "owner" acts more like a manager. The advantage is that member sites can join in with minimal programming and administrative tangles. This arrangement is very appealing to groups with the same interests.

The number of WebRings is rather staggering. According to Starseed, Inc., on April 15, 1998, there were 46,330 different WebRings linking a total of 534,370 individual websites (Starseed, Inc., 1999). While this certainly does not approach the millions of sites actually available on the Web, it is not trivial either. WebRings should thus be taken as a very serious source for information on many topics and issues. It is safe to assume that you can probably find a WebRing for almost any given topic. The real advantage to WebRings is that, unlike search engines that may bury good websites within a million useless ones, or the ever-illusive "meta-list" (next section), WebRings usually provide wonderfully convenient lists of topically relevant sites.

Recognizing WebRings

Let's assume that Mr. Waters and you accidentally found a WebRing. How did you know it was a WebRing in the first place?

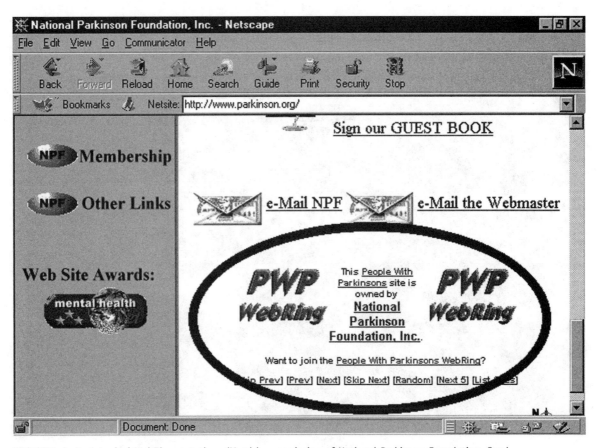

FIGURE 4-4 A typical WebRing notation. (Used by permission of National Parkinson Foundation, Inc.)

In general, WebRing navigation is fairly obvious. It is usually found at the bottom of the website's homepage (Figure 4-4). Most WebRings are clearly marked because the members want you to know that they are part of a specific WebRing. (A website can be a member of several WebRings, by the way.) Each website's navigation style and graphics will vary, but most WebRing markers typically look like the one in the figure.

The National Parkinson's Foundation is clearly a recognizable member of the "People With Parkinsons" WebRing because it is so labeled. Note the specific navigation cues: Skip Previous, Previous, Next, Skip Next, Random, Next 5, and List Sites. These cues are common in WebRings—and a direct giveaway that you are in one. Exact navigation choices may vary, and not all sites are as obvious. Sometimes the navigation is more obscure, and the fact that a site is part of a WebRing may not always be directly stated. The point is that *when you see these options, you are in a WebRing whether or not it is clearly marked.*

While you may accidentally stumble onto WebRings, lists of them are available, too. For example, the WebRing homepage (Figure 4-5) URL

> **http://webring.com**
>
> or
>
> **http://www.webring.com**

will take you to a rich inventory of various WebRings on many subjects. You can even search for specific topics because the website has its own search utility.

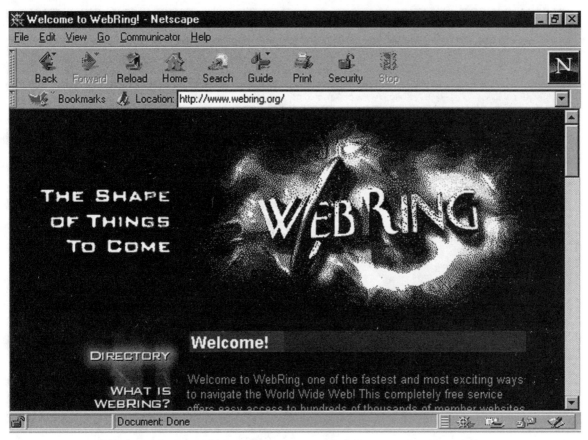

FIGURE 4-5 The WebRing Homepage. (Used by permission of WebRing.)

Using the Search Utility:

There are two ways to look for resources at the WebRing website: (1) Use the internal search utility for a specific term or key word, or (2) explore the subject directory that is provided. Let's examine the search utility first.

Just like the Find feature in your browser, the WebRing website has an internal search engine that will help you to find specific information within the website.[7] This is called the *key word* approach. First, type a specific key word or two into the white box. Now select how you want the search utility to look for the words if you are using two or more of them. Selecting Any Word gives you WebRings having any of multiple key words in the site's database and yields the largest number of places to look. Using the All Words choice gives WebRings with all key words in any order. The Exact Phrase choice only brings up WebRings with the exact key words, in order, and usually yields the smallest number of WebRings to choose from. You should also tell the search utility where to look. The search program can look for key words that the WebRing's owner has listed along with key words in the WebRing's title. It also looks

---

[7]   Additional characteristics and features for search engines are taken up in the next chapter.

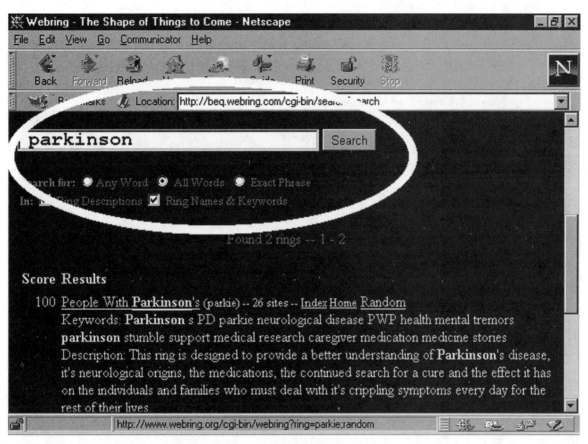

FIGURE 4-6 The WebRing search utility. (Used by permission of WebRing.)

inside the descriptive paragraphs that the owner has provided. Checking both gives you the maximum number possible.[8]

Entering the key word "parkinson" into the search utility (Figure 4-6) and pressing the return key results in once again finding the "People With Parkinson's" WebRing. This listing would be very helpful had we not discovered it through accidental guessing. Reading the description written by the WebRing's owner usually gives enough information to make a decision on whether or not to proceed exploring the WebRing further. We can explore it by looking at the title of the WebRing, the index, the homepage of the owner website, or a member website at random. We recommend looking at the Index webpage first. The Index page not only lists the actual websites in the WebRing but also provides brief descriptions of their contents, giving you enough information to decide if you want to continue with it or not.

---

[8] There is an important trade-off in how you set the choices. If you cast a broad net by trying for the maximum number of possible WebRings, your odds of finding *something* useful are the best, but you will also find many WebRings that are not very helpful. This will cost you time. We recommend looking for the largest number of rings in general, especially when you are looking for a wide range of resource information. The actual results will probably be a fairly manageable number of possible sites, often less than fifty. If you have to read through the descriptions for several hundred sites, though, you obviously should narrow the search.

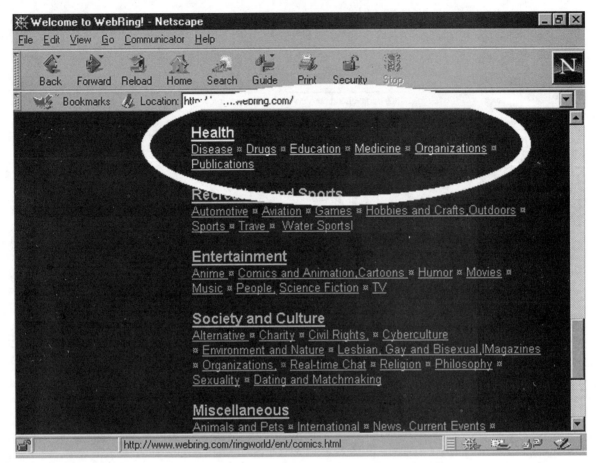

FIGURE 4-7 Some categories on the WebRing website. (Used by permission of WebRing.)

The Category/Directory Approach

If you did not find something in your key word search or if you want more WebRings to choose from, try looking for similar WebRings that might have some connection to your needs but a different name. The WebRing homepage shows a categorical directory (Figure 4-7) for various lists of WebRings. Lists of WebRings for the arts and humanities, business and economy, computers, Internet, health, recreation and sports, entertainment, society and culture, and miscellaneous subjects are available. You may find closely related WebRings that you did not think about because the words you wanted, such as "parkinsons," were not included.

Parkinson's disease is a medical condition, so the WebRing Health directory should be promising. It further lists six different divisions: disease, drugs, education, medicine, organizations, and publications. Now comes the hard part. Just what do you need, and are you willing to take the time to look for it? In your work with Mr. Waters, let's presume you both are simply curious about resources at this point. You and he could now explore each of the six divisions in the Health directory if you wanted to take the extra time.

When we conducted our own search, the third choice (Education) paid off. The Health Education list held a WebRing entitled "Medical Education Ring." We found a Parkinson's disease related ring entitled "Parkinson's Disease and Stroke Teaching Presentations" (Figure 4-8). Bingo! Another WebRing with Parkinson's information and a complete tutorial! The message is quite clear: Whether you

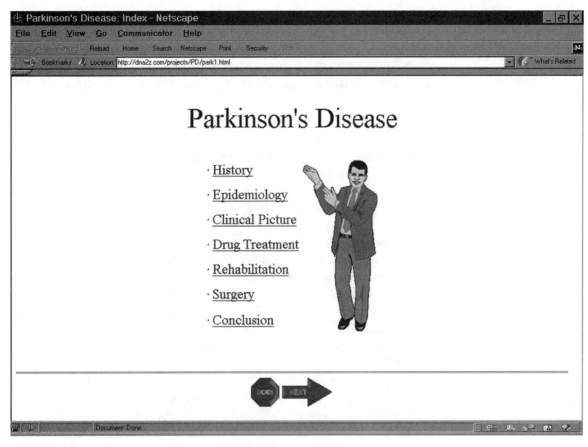

FIGURE 4-8 A website from a WebRing. (Used by permission of Yali Friedman.)

accidentally encounter a WebRing or directly look for one, you may find excellent resources once you find one!

We have described WebRings because they are becoming common and your chances of encountering them are good. There are other similar types of software programs that link websites together. If you want to investigate this alternative, go to another "ring" website, called "Bomis" (rhymes with Thomas). The URL is

http://www.bomis.com

Once you have found a possible WebRing, the next step is to see what is really available. Remember: What you think it may be about can turn out to be vastly different when you enter the ring. Specific topics for webpages can be found by calling up the WebRing's index and using the Find feature to look for a specific topic. This works easily when the website has been accurately titled.

TIP: When evaluating WebRings, click on the Index choice. This gives a list of all of the current member websites in the WebRing. You can make more informed choices when you know its members. "By their links ye shall know them."

Advantages and Disadvantages

You need to know more about several advantages and disadvantages. WebRings have value because they link related sites together without requiring the individual webweavers to do much maintenance. This makes them very popular, and their use is increasing. WebRings can also give you a very good grasp of the nature of a topic. While the first few sites may be interesting but not especially relevant, eventually you may find a website in a WebRing with the exact information you are looking for, making the whole process most worthwhile. Again, first look through the Index. The Index can also provide a wide "snapshot" of what contents you could expect to find elsewhere on the Web. However, beware of the following problems.

WebRings are often euphemistically titled, misnamed, or not intuitively named, so look at the actual WebRing rather than relying on accuracy in its title. It is often very difficult to accurately title a WebRing if it contains a lot of diverse sites and even has antagonistic members.

The mission, scope, and nature of the ring are determined by its ring manager. The ring will often reflect the personal tastes, values, and interests of this one member or website. As a result, *some rings can be quite biased and narrow.*

WebRings often resemble coalitions where *the only common thread between some very different websites is the subject.* As a result, the quality and nature of the websites can vary tremendously within a single WebRing, so pay attention to what you are viewing. You may find some very strange combinations! Highly personal webpages, offbeat alternative sites, and mainstream "establishment" organizations may all be linked together one after another. Just because a webweaver has decided that it is in their interest to be part of a WebRing does not mean they completely endorse all of the other member websites within it.

WebRings, even the really big ones with hundreds of member websites, are deceptively small in comparison with what is really available on the Web. Thus, while WebRings may give you a reasonable overview, they are certainly not comprehensive!

Finally, WebRings vary tremendously in issues, and their diversity is extraordinary. Some are very useful, while others may be abysmal, offensive, and just plain strange. WebRings reflect many dimensions of "human behavior in the electronic environment." Some are totally against every principle our profession holds. Hate groups use them. Some are extremely offensive to specific populations at risk or diverse groups. Others have a little something to offend everyone. Beware, especially when working directly with clients.

TIP: Look for WebRings, especially when you are on unfamiliar ground. While the authors think that meta-lists offer more efficient possibilities for finding resources, WebRings can be interesting and worthwhile. WebRings are much more likely to have up-to-date information than printed lists, because they are usually updated more often.

FINDING WEBPAGES: USING META-LISTS

While most websites have links to other websites, these are often on the paltry side. In addition, it often looks like every website you visit is linking to everyone else whether they are using WebRing software or not. There are, however, websites dedicated solely to providing huge lists of links for specific areas of interest. Kind souls volunteer to maintain these lists, and some of the lists can be truly vast. We call these websites **meta-lists** because they try to give a *meta* or larger view of a subject. They are analogous to compiled bibliographies, and they can be extremely useful if you find them.

You will find other terms for *meta-lists.* Information Gateway sometimes is used and is reasonably synonymous. Clearinghouse is often applied, too, and the two clearinghouses at the end of this chapter, Argus and The Mining Company, can supply many different lists of thousands of subjects. Resource Center and variations can be found as well. Another term for emerging lists is "channels." Many search engines now provide large "meta-lists" with this title. Remember: The Web is so new that agreement on terms has not evolved. *What is important is to specifically look for these large compiled lists around subjects or issues, be they called information gateways, resource centers, clearinghouses, channels, meta-lists, or whatever else.*

Just how big does a list have to be in order to be a meta-list? We do not really have a definitive answer to this nifty tautology. Perhaps a cutoff of fifty URLs or more is a good place to make a practical definition, unless the subject is so narrow that it does not have that many websites in total. Creating a list of fifty or more links is a significant undertaking and involves a much more serious commitment than simply compiling a list of a few common URLs that are found around a given issue. Keeping such a list updated and accurate also shows genuine commitment.

What will a meta-list do for you? A useful meta-list attempts to provide a reasonably comprehensive listing of the most significant sites around a given subject. Better ones provide active links *and* short descriptions of what you will find if you follow the link. Obviously, accurate abstracts can save you a great deal of time! Larger meta-lists, especially those compiled by professional librarians, can be reasonably comprehensive. "One-stop shopping" for URLs is sometimes possible with a good meta-list.

Some meta-lists even provide website ratings according to some scale or standard for measurement. This, too, can save considerable time if the rating system is professionally acceptable because someone else has searched and abstracted these resources for you and evaluated them. *As a result, a well-crafted and maintained meta-list may work better than using the search tool approach described in the next chapter because you will not have to look through tons of irrelevant URLs.*

Do you remember that we found one website with a meta-list when guessing URLs for Parkinson's disease? This website (Figure 4-9), in the authors' opinion, is a good example of what a smaller, well-crafted meta-list provides. Note that it is maintained by an individual, Jeffrey S. Kaye, and that his credentials are available. Also note that this site has different categories, such as medical links in one area and advocacy-related resources in another. This makes navigation easier.

Clicking on the Other Links choice brings up the screens shown in Figure 4-10. Note that each of the resources has a brief description/abstract. In this example, each of these websites was also linked, eliminating tedious typing of the new URLs.

Other resources for Parkinson's disease can certainly be found. The key point is to remember that there are often specific webpages with extensive resources that have been intentionally created for reference.

How do you find meta-lists? Good question. Here is a poor answer: The problem is that while there are thousands of meta-lists, you often encounter them by accident, just as in the case of WebRings. To make matters worse, there are no central databases such as the ones WebRing and Bomis maintain, to help you locate them. One good source for meta-lists is the Argus Clearinghouse. You can find carefully reviewed listings of meta-lists, but just remember there are countless other lists out there, too. The URL for the Argus Clearinghouse is

www.clearinghouse.net/index.html

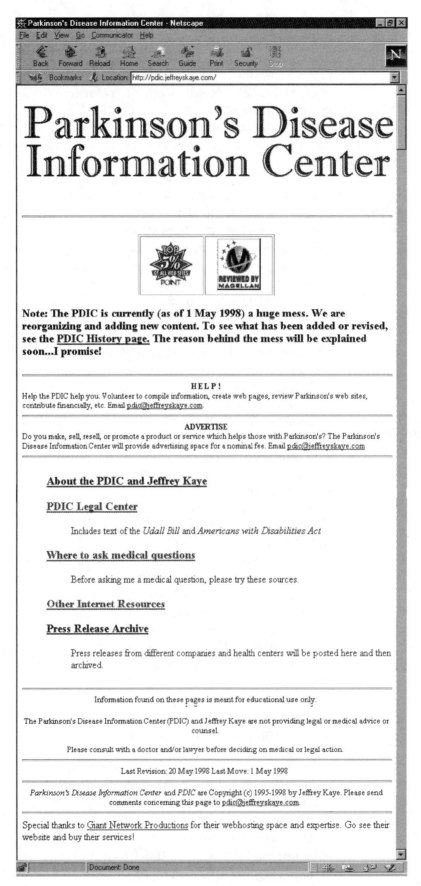

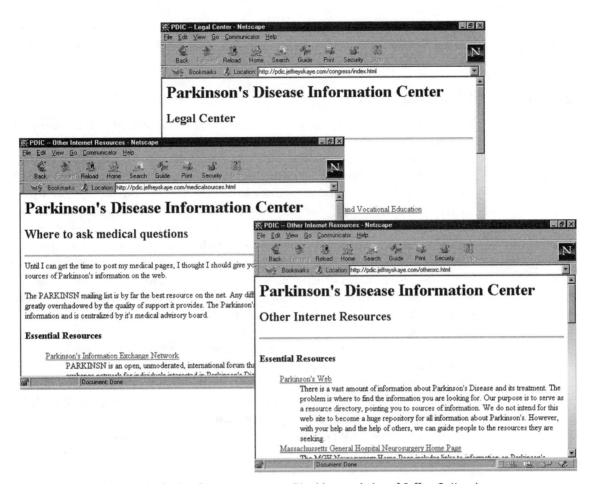

FIGURE 4-10 Always probe further for more resources. (Used by permission of Jeffrey S. Kaye.)

The Mining Company also provides lists. The URLs are

http://www.miningco.com and http://about.com

Both of these resources can provide extensive lists of URLs. They can also be viewed as hierarchic directories, a search tool discussed in the next chapter. What about specific meta-lists for social work? We have provided a short list of possible places to visit at the back of this chapter. Do remember that there is no high ground. Smaller teaching colleges and universities can put out lists that are as sophisticated as those from the larger research-dominant universities. The authors have the following suggestions to find more.

Consumers sometimes develop and maintain extensive lists. When a person or a loved one has a specific disease, for example, families and friends often want to learn as much about it as possible. In any given population, there are probably consumers or collateral relatives and friends who are willing to create and maintain webpages. Someone is bound to keep a meta-list somewhere!

Asking the members of a listserv may be very helpful, or following links from websites may reveal one. Sending an E-mail request to the webweavers at especially relevant websites is also a possibility. Library resource sites and professional reference services can be *very* helpful in locating meta-lists.

In the authors' experience, resource lists from *mainstream* organizations may be less comprehensive. These meta-lists, while often quite good, may be more biased than consumer-driven ones because *establishment* organizations may not list websites they do not endorse or approve of. Controversial, alternative viewpoint, or antithetical websites are thus often excluded. Commercial for-profit organizations also are often quite limited in their links. They rarely help you find their competition!

Advantages and Disadvantages

The real advantage of meta-lists is that they can provide reasonably good resources for a given topic. This saves time. *A well-organized meta-list will be faster than any other method for finding resources on the Web.*

Meta-lists have disadvantages as well, and it is important to remember them. As already mentioned, good meta-lists can be very hard to find. In addition, they are not always up-to-date, especially when maintained by volunteers. A lot of new webpages with great resources can emerge overnight on the Web. If these are not regularly discovered and updated into the meta-list, then you will miss them entirely. As a result, *meta-lists may not be completely current.*[9] If you absolutely need hot-from-the-server URLs, then you need to use a key word type of search engine, which is described in the next chapter. When you do find a website that a meta-list should include, E-mail the list's manager about the new resource. This courtesy is genuinely appreciated!

Finally, you are still limited by the talents and world view of the people creating the meta-list. This is no different than the case of smaller lists or WebRings. What may be relevant for you may be trivial for them, so it is possible that their meta-list may be useless for your purposes. You cannot do much about this other than keep your eyes open for another meta-list.

Spread the wealth! When you find a great meta-list for a subject, make a note of it and pass the URL along. It may help a small circle of friends or a much larger group. You never know.

BEST TIP: We have saved the best tip for last: Ask a librarian! They are really great at finding resources on the Web!

Summary

We have discussed five different strategies for finding Web resources. First, looking for obvious published URLs is very helpful. When contacting an agency or organization, *ask if they have a website.* They are often quite pleased to share their URL with you. If they do not have one, chances are good that they are considering one in the near future and your request is a helpful advocacy for the technology. Next, guessing is a serious strategy that can really pay off if you have a pretty distinct key word that is easily recognizable. Following the provided links for most webpages is also a good strategy for finding resources. Just be sure you do not rely only on the Our Links section of the website. WebRings can provide excellent resources. Finally, meta-lists, especially if they are well maintained and reasonably unbiased, can truly provide stunning resources. Each of these specific techniques has distinct advantages and disadvantages. When none of these approaches help, it is time to use a search tool.

---

[9]   Meta-lists generally are far more accurate than printed lists of URLs. This is because it may take a publisher a year or longer to print and distribute a paper list. URLs change during this time. Websites emerge and disappear. A frequently maintained meta-list will be far more up-to-date with fewer dead links.

Exercise 4A
Guessing URLs

- This is a computer exercise. You will need a Web-connected computer.
- The purpose of this exercise is to sharpen your guessing abilities for discovering Websites.
- This work will carry over into the next exercise.

DIRECTIONS

A. Look over the "key words" from Exercise 2C. From them, choose three key words that you think are reasonably specific, unambiguous, and likely to produce good guessing results. The words do not have to be related to each other. Provide a short reason for your choosing each one.

The three key words are

1._____ because _____

2._____ because _____

3._____ because _____

B. Use each of the three words, one at a time, in the format given in the example and following. Type them into the browser's Open Page (Navigator) or Open (Explorer) box and click on the Open or OK button. Refer to Chapter 2, Figure 2–4 if you need to.

Report your results, if any, on the line next to the "guessed" URL.

Example

Key word 1 : *housing*_____

Tried: Result:

www. *housing*_____ .org   Project Sentinel, N. Calif., advocacy

www. *housing*_____ .net   No result

www. *housing*_____ .com   No result

www. *housing*_____ .edu   No result

www. *housing*_____ .gov   No result

www. *housing*_____ .mil   No result

(In this example, we found one website specializing in rights and responsibilities, dispute resolution, and discrimination investigations.)

Key word 1 : _____

Tried: Result:

www. _____ .org   _____

www. _____ .net   _____

www. _____ .com   _____

www. _____ .edu   _____

www. _____ .gov   _____

www. _____ .mil   _____

Key word 2 : _____

Tried: Result:

www. _____ .org   _____

www. _____ .net   _____

www. _____ .com   _____

www. _____ .edu   _____

www. _____ .gov   _____

www. _____ .mil   _____

Key word 3 : _____

Tried: Result:

www. _____ .org   _____

www. _____ .net   _____

www. _____ .com   _____

www. _____ .edu   _____

www. _____ .gov   _____

www. _____ .mil   _____

C. How many total "hits" did you find?

How many relevant "hits" did you find?

SUMMING IT UP

What conclusions can you draw from the "guessing" strategy?

Write one paragraph that describes your conclusions.

Exercise 4B
Follow the Links

- This is a computer exercise. You will need a Web-connected computer.
- The purpose of this exercise is to sharpen your awareness of the "following links" technique.

DIRECTIONS

A. Look over the results from Exercise 4A.

If you found one or more relevant websites in terms of your issue, visit the website again or the most promising one that has additional "links" available.

NOTE: If you did not get a result from "guessing" (unlikely, but it happens), then go to any of the meta-lists in Exercise 4D *or* in the references at the end of the chapter and *follow one until you have located a promising website* that comes close to your issue and has additional resource links available. Begin the Summing It Up section of this exercise from this new website, not from the meta-list itself.

Remember:

"Links" is a general term. Look for "Resources" or "More Places to Visit" or other similar concepts, not just the word "Links."

B. Scan the links available from the "guessed" or "meta-list–found" website.

Record the URL, name, and number of links available.[10]

Choose and go to the most promising website in terms of your issue.

Again look to see, if an additional list is available. If so:

Record the number of links available up to fifty.

Again choose and go to the most promising website in terms of your issue.

Record the number of links again, up to fifty.

First website:

URL: _____ Name: _____

Number of links: _____

Second website:

URL: _____ Name: _____

Number of links: _____

---

[10] Some lists can number in the hundreds, so stop at fifty if you have to! If by chance the website has an internal search engine instead of a list of links, then enter the best key word from Exercise 4A and continue on.

Third website:

URL: _____ Name: _____

Number of links: _____

Determine the total for the three websites you have visited.

Total links: _____

SUMMING IT UP

What conclusions can you draw from the "following links" strategy?

Write one paragraph that describes your conclusions.

Exercise 4C
WebRings

■ This is a computer exercise. You will need a Web-connected computer.

■ The purpose of this exercise is to sharpen your understanding of WebRings.

DIRECTIONS

A. Look over Exercise 2C, and review your "Guessing URLs" work if it is available. From them, choose three key words that you think are reasonably specific, unambiguous, and likely to produce good guessing results. The words do not have to be related to each other. Switch to new key words if they produced poor results. Provide a short reason for your choosing each one. If you are repeating the same key words from earlier exercises, simply reproduce what you wrote before. (This makes it easier for the instructor.)

The three (same/new) key words are

1._____ because _____

2._____ because _____

3._____ because _____

B. Go to the WebRing website: http://Webring.com

■ Choose one of the three key words and enter it into the search engine in the WebRing website. (Refer Figure 4-6 if needed.)

■ Press the Search button and examine the results.

■ Look through the list of potential WebRings (if any) and choose the one that looks the most promising for your issue.

■ Repeat this for the other two key words.

■ Look at the descriptions for all of the WebRing(s) you have found from the key words and *choose the one WebRing that suggests the best potential for your issue.*

NOTE: If you do not turn up any relevant WebRings, then go to the WebRing homepage and explore the categories (Health, Recreation and Sports, Entertainment, etc.). Refer to Figure 4-7 if needed.

C. Get the description of the WebRing you want onto your screen and select the Index choice. Read through the first fifty descriptions of member sites (or more if you like. Some of these lists are huge, and some are shorter.). Write a summary of what you saw on the Index and its relevance to your issue.

Example

Practice: You are working with clients in an adult day care center who are interested in African American genealogy and family research.

WebRing name: *The African American Genealogy Ring* Number of websites: <u>61</u>

SUMMARY

This WebRing contains many personal websites where people share and discuss their family research and accomplishments. It may be very helpful when researching specific family names and areas. In addition, there are several resource websites with databases, such as "African American Census Schedules On-Line" for Alabama from 1886. I also found resources for . . .

WebRing name: _____

Number of websites: _____

Summary:

SUMMING IT UP

What conclusions can you draw from the "WebRing" strategy?

Write one paragraph that describes your conclusions.

Exercise 4D
Meta-Lists

- This is a computer exercise. You will need a Web-connected computer.
- The purpose of this exercise is to sharpen your ability to recognize meta-lists and to become familiar with a few of the more specialized ones.

DIRECTIONS

Visit one of the meta-lists in each of the following nine areas. Surf one of the websites from the list, but not in depth or this will take forever! Some may be so large that they have a "site map" or "site index" tool built into them, and these are quite handy. Briefly describe what you found in one or two sentences.

Practice

Caregivers

http://www.caregiver911.com/html/general_links.html

or

Pat McClendon's Clinical Social Work Webpages

http://www.Clinical SocialWork.com

_____

_____

Field/Agencies

Elder Care and Child Care

http://www.eldercare.com

or

United Ways . . .

http://www.unitedway.org/localway/uwson web.html

_____

_____

_____

Policy and Services

Disability/Social Security

http://www.idsi.net/tri/ssa.htm

or

Welfare Reform

http://www.aoa.dhhs.gov/network/welfarereform.html

_____

_____

_____

Social and Economic Justice

Civil Rights

http://www.law.cornell.edu/topics/civil_rights.html

or

Social and Economic Development

http://caster.ssw.upenn.edu/~restes/praxis.html

_____

_____

_____

Populations At Risk

AIDS

http://www.smartlink.net/~martinjh

or

Mental Health

http://www.moodswing.org/links.html

_____

_____

_____

Diversity

Native Americans
http://indy4.fdl.cc.mn.us/~isk/linkpage.html
or
Deaf Culture
www.deaflibrary.org

_____

_____

_____

Human Behavior in the Social Environment

Older Adults
http://www.ageofreason.com/homepage.htm
or
Grief
http://www.webhealing.com/links.html

_____

_____

_____

Values and Ethics

Bioethics
http://www.asbh.org
or
Family Law
http://www.trentlaw.com/

_____

_____

_____

Research

Qualitative Research
http://www.nova.edu/ssss/QR/web.html
or
Social Research Centers
http://www.ukans.edu/cwis/units/coms2/po/index.html

_____

_____

_____

SUMMING IT UP

What conclusions can you draw from the "meta-list" strategy?

Write one paragraph that describes your conclusions.

Questions for Discussion

Will URLs become as common as phone numbers in the future?

What motivates people to create WebRings and meta-lists?

What should you look for when analyzing a WebRing's or meta-list's biases and values?

References

Notess, G. (1997). Internet search techniques and strategies. *ONLINE*, July. [On-line]. Available: http://209.43.34.82/onlinemag/JulOL97/net7.html

Starseed, Inc. (1999). WebRing website. [On-line]. Available: http://webring.com

Additional Readings

Hahn, H. (1999). Harley Hahn's Internet and Web yellow pages. New York, NY: Osborne-McGraw-Hill.

Polly, J. (1998). The Internet kids and family yellow pages. New York, NY: McGraw-Hill Companies.

Additional Websites

Summers, E. (1998) *College and Research Libraries NewsNet*, March 1998, Vol. 59, No. 3 Gateways to social work/welfare on the Net Practice wisdom to go http://www.ala.org/acrl/resmar98.html

Prominent Clearinghouses

Argus http://www.clearinghouse.net/

The Mining Company http://www.miningco.com

Rings and Trains

Bomis Rings http://www.bomis.com

WebRing http://webring.com

Meta-Lists:[11]

Baccalaureate Social Work Directors (BPD) http://www.rit.edu/~694www/bpd.htm

Ball State University http://www.bsu.edu/csh/socwk/WEBRSC.HTM

Bigna, S. (1999). (Shirely's List) Social Work Web Resources http://www.uindy.edu/~kml/resources/socialwork/index.html

Colorado State University http://www.colostate.edu/Depts/SocWork/WEB%20links.html

Computer Use in Social Services Network (CUSSNet) http://www.uta.edu/cussn/cussn.html

Columbia University Social Work Library http://www.columbia.edu/cu/libraries/indiv/socwk/

George Warren Brown School of Social Work http://gwbweb.wustl.edu/websites.html

Grassroots—Andrews University http://www.andrews.edu/SOWK/grassroots.htm

Murray, M. Resource List for Social Workers Web Site http://129.82.209.104/webstuff.htm

The New Social Worker http://www.socialworker.com/websites.htm

Social Work Search (Thomas Cleereman) http://www.socialworksearch.com

SWAN (Social Work Access Network) http://www.sc.edu/swan

University of California Berkeley http://hav54.socwel.berkeley.edu/SocialWelfare/index.htm

University of Michigan Library http://www.lib.umich.edu/libhome/rrs/selector/swpage.html

Vernon, R., and O'Shea, D. (1999) Meta-Lists for Social Work (Listing of websites with fifty or more resources each) http://socwork.uindy.edu/links/meta1.htm

---

[11] These websites provide jumping-off places to find resources. There are many more. Some of these websites will also take you to more specialized meta-lists in social work. This list is not comprehensive in any way, and we have only included the more general websites. Our apologies are extended to colleagues we may have unitentionally overlooked.

CHAPTER 5

Directories and Search Engines

Some of the things you can do with search engines and directories . . .

. . . Create lists of URLs about a subject or topic.

. . . Find the latest information about emerging practice issues.

. . . Locate highly specific types of resources.

. . . Save a lot of time!

CHAPTER OVERVIEW

New information is constantly being added to the Web. Keeping track of it is impossible. In addition, we often need information that is peripheral or unrelated to social work and have to search for things we do not understand very well. When you do not know a good URL and can not find a webpage with relevant links, when your guessing is not working, and no meta-lists are in sight, do not worry! There is *still* a good chance you can find what you need by using a search engine or a compiled directory of resources. You may already be familiar with some of the more popular ones such as Yahoo!, Excite, LookSmart, Lycos, and an ever-ballooning field of others. These and a few others automatically appear on a menu when you click the Search button in both the Navigator or Explorer browsers. Clicking will summon menus for powerful search engines that scour the Web looking for everything under the sun! This chapter covers ways to choose and use them along with many others. You need to acquire this skill. This chapter covers

- ■ Search Tools
- ■ Just What Are Search Tools?
- ■ The Types of Search Tools
- ■ Choosing Search Tools
- ■ Using Search Tools

If possible, go through this chapter while at your computer! It really helps!

SEARCH TOOLS

Emma Lazarus Centers, Inc.

You are the planner for Emma Lazarus Center, Inc., an agency with a seventy-year history of helping immigrants and refugees.[1] The agency offers a host of services in five different neighborhoods within your city. Each neighborhood has distinct ethnic or national characteristics such as those of central and eastern European, Middle Eastern, Asian, and Hispanic residents. Services include legal help with residency status, citizenship, advocacy for entitlement services, drop-in centers for teens and other youths, and a wide variety of programs and classes to help families make workable transitions into life in the United States.

About 80 percent of the world's refugees are women and children. Based on a review of contact records, the agency clearly tends to serve male heads of families to a larger degree. Moreover, the agency does not have policies or positions on a number of feminist-related issues such as equitable employment, children's rights, female circumcision, education for women, cultural conflicts over domestic violence, and women's vulnerability through isolation. This gap is becoming apparent; problems and value conflicts between the centers and neighborhood residents are developing. For example, when the teen-services programs began to include family-planning referrals, the men from a local religious organization were outraged. A similar problem arose in one community when a woman clearly needed shelter from an abusive husband. She was in danger for her life, and Emma Lazarus, Inc., directly paid for her relocation and shelter for several months. Her ethnic association was furious, called a press conference, and threatened to boycott the agency. The community now regards the woman as an outcast and the agency as a source of trouble.

The executive director wants your department to study and describe the salient issues related to providing services to women from various cultures. This research will be used for briefing the board of directors as part of a "policy retreat" scheduled later this month.

While the methods for finding good websites described in the last chapter can be very effective, there are times when you need to use a **search engine** or **hierarchic directory** to find resources. First, just what are we talking about? The generic term *search engine* commonly refers to *two different types of compiled databases.* These **databases** essentially are huge lists of URLs and information about them. The lists can easily number in the millions, especially for the larger commercial search websites. The way that the lists are compiled and maintained determines if they are created by an active search engine program that scans the Web or compiled into a hierarchic directory from contributions webweavers have sent in. These differences are important, and we examine them in a few pages. Both are known as **search tools**. If you have never tried using a search tool before, an example will be helpful.

---

[1] Immigrants generally have voluntarily become residents of a new country. Refugees have been forced to relocate.

FIGURE 5-1 Search buttons for Navigator and Explorer.

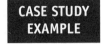

CASE STUDY EXAMPLE As a worker at the Emma Lazarus Center, you could start the computer, connect to the Web with the browser, and then bring up a search tool by choosing from several that are automatically available, or, instead, enter the URL for a specific search website you want. Once in the website, you would then enter a key word such as *refugees* or click on a category such as *World events* and, after a few more interactions, get a list of related URLs. You could then choose from the URLs on the list and visit as many web-sites as available or desired. This is very similar to how you use the Subject Search feature in most modern library catalogs.

The easiest way to access the major commercial search tools is to click on the Search button at the top of the browser (Figure 5-1). Clicking on the button will bring up a large menu of popular search tools such as Excite, Lycos, InfoSeek, Yahoo, HotBot, AltaVista, and others. While it is convenient and tempting to use this feature, DO NOT BE DECEIVED! There are *thousands of other search tools* on the Web. Some may be far more useful than the commercial ones the browser automatically brings up. The general-purpose commercial search websites often have excellent and rather comprehensive resources, but more narrowly focused search-dedicated websites often have databases that may be more tailored to your needs and easier to use. As a result, you need to be able to use and access both the large commercial search tools and the more specialized ones and know when to choose between different types.

On the positive side, with the incredible mass of information available on the Web today and its continued explosive expansion, the chances of finding very useful and relevant websites on women, immigration, and refugees—and almost any-thing else—are extremely high. On the negative side, search tools can be extremely frustrating to use. If you do not carefully plan your search, use the appropriate tool, and select the best key words or categories, you may find absolutely nothing or get deluged with thousands of worthless webpages called **false drops,** such as one with the message: "Hi, I'm Bob. Isn't the plight of refugees just awful? Click here to see pictures from my spring vacation in Lower Devil Fish."

We call this the "avalanche or desert" outcome, and either can be a waste of your time. Choosing and using search tools is an acquired skill you need to develop if you are going to use the Web in social work.

JUST WHAT ARE SEARCH TOOLS?

Search tools are computer programs that create and maintain *databases*. These databases usually are lists of URLs, the titles of the homepages for them, and short descriptions or the first few sentences of what you will find at the specific websites.

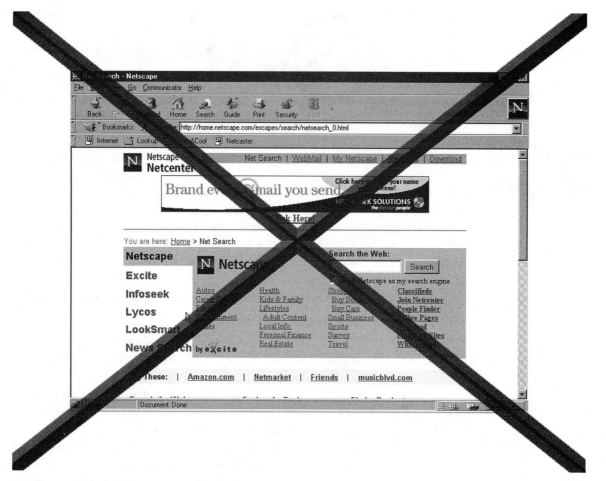

FIGURE 5-2 Mr. Search Menu is *not* your friend.

Simply put, *a search tool is just a giant list of goodies on the Web and not much else.* The *not much else* part is where things get complex.

JUST DO NOT DO THIS, OK? The *worst* way to choose a search tool (incredibly stupid idea 142B) is to simply choose one of the more popular websites at random from the Navigator or the Explorer search menus and blithely enter a key word or two without paying attention to the type of search you need or what the tool will do for you. We think this point needs repeating: Simply choosing a search tool at random and entering the first thought that comes to mind is a really dumb idea. While many search tools look almost the same and work with similar commands, the differences are staggering. In short, "Mr. Search Menu is *not* your friend." Get the point? Let's understand why.

If a "search-tool-challenged" social worker simply brought up a few of the major websites from the website shown in Figure 5-2 and entered the key word *refugee,* the results might be surprising. An actual search with the key word *refugee*[2] produced the following (Figure 5-3):

■ 22 links from LookSmart

■ 172 links from Yahoo!

---

[2] These data are from an actual search conducted by the writers on 29 June 1998.

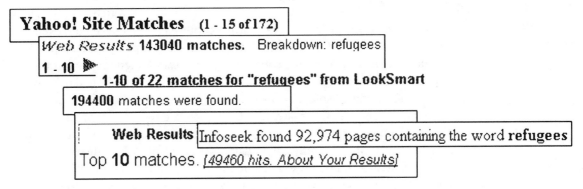

FIGURE 5-3 Tremendous variation!

- 49,460 links from Excite!
- 92,974 links from InfoSeek
- 143,030 links from HotBot
- 194,400 links from AltaVista

Quite a variation in raw numbers, is it not? Here is the scary part: What if the worker *only* used the *LookSmart* search engine? They would conclude that there were only twenty-two URLs available. If they only consulted the *AltaVista* search engine, they would conclude the opposite: almost two hundred thousand! Desert or avalanche, remember? Without a direct knowledge of the type of search tool in use and the type of search being conducted, credibly analyzing any results would be hopeless.

To make matters worse, *none* of the lists of URLs generated by these different search tools—and these are among the best—usually have even the faintest resemblance to each other! Moreover, conducting the same search at another time or day—even with the same search tool—would produce still different results. Why?

Remember the Wild West metaphor from Chapter 1? The Web appears to be nice and orderly only because the browser makes it look that way. Instead, there is chaos. Thousands of webpages are added each day. Others are modified or removed. The nature of what is actually available is always changing and growing. As a result, no two search efforts ever produce identical results, even in the same database. The people who create search tools cope with this mess in several ways.

Search tool (and browser) designers impose their own logic onto the Web. Every search tool imposes its own unique sense of order, but this leads to different results because each search tool's design is unique. The tool you choose will impose its own logic on the Web, but it is an artificial logic! Strange and weird results often follow, deserts appear where there should be abundance, and the resulting lists from different search tools seldom resemble each other. At the heart, the search programs that drive the tools are often fundamentally different. Active search tools such as search engines are "artificial intelligence" computer programs that use "algorithms" or mathematical procedures for detecting stuff and making sense out of it. While we do not go into details—like sausage, do not ask to see the kitchen—do remember that some of this programming is not very reliable or stable. The artificial intelligence programs in the search engine computer programs are just that, artificial and not very smart. While these computer programs are actually quite clever, they are no match for human thought. As a result, search engines are elegant but not infallible. A lot of extraneous stuff can filter through a loose algorithm, and some really great URLs can easily get buried or never even discovered.

Most of the database(s) the search tool consults—any type of search tool—are substantially created by computer software, *not by human beings!* Remember those algorithms we just mentioned? People may later modify the resulting database, or it may instead be crafted solely by the computer without benefit of any human attention and stashed away for later use. Thus, there are two very different forms of databases: completely robot-generated ones and those that have some human intervention or mediation. Humanly edited databases are smaller than their robotic counterparts because human resources are more limited. Humanly edited databases tend to be less comprehensive but more relevant. The robot-made counterparts are apt to be far more thorough but less organized and loaded with nonrelevant URLs.

No two search tools analyze the same website in the same way. Some examine every smidgen of a new website, webpage by webpage from the opening URL to the last html command. Others only examine the URL, perhaps the title, and maybe the first hundred words or so of just the homepage. This directly affects the size and scope of the resulting database. A "review everything" type of tool, also known as **full-text indexing,** generates a more thorough list of resources because it is reviewing so much more information than its "review a little" counterpart. Yet the "review everything" search tools are likely to catalog—and give you—a lot more useless information because the resulting database is huge and redundant. The smaller databases from the "review a little" search tools may be more relevant and easier to consult but not very comprehensive. In a rather oversimplified way, "review everything" tools are likely to find great URLs and then bury them. "Review a little" search tools are more user friendly but can completely miss some really excellent websites.

Search tools, especially the more sophisticated robotic ones, often give probability estimates of how relevant the URL may be in terms of the key words you have used. Estimates such as "99 percent reliable" and similar indices are quite common. These ratings are usually determined by frequencies and word counts that are artifacts from how much of the website was reviewed in the first place plus the nature of the algorithms in use and the key word you put in. You should not take the ratings too seriously. They are helpful but limited.

Many search tool providers are vying for your attention in this capitalist world. This is especially true for the familiar "free" search tools you automatically access from your browser. The corporate sponsors are not providing all this free service just to be nice. They are trying to establish market share. Most of the larger commercial search websites want you to become a loyal customer and make their website your homepage. As a result, not only are search tools different, but there is intense competition between the commercial firms that own them. This leads to little cooperation between them, if any. Do not expect this to change much until the end of Western civilization.

Finally, be not deceived; no search tool is capable of searching the entire Web. Period. While some of the really large ones such as AltaVista and HotBot dredge through a pretty respectable chunk of the Web, they are still only seeing a sample of what is available at any given time. Worse yet, they do not know what they have missed because they missed it in the first place so they do not know what they have missed because they missed it in the first place so they do not know . . . and you will not know either! (Nasty little tautology, is it not?) You cannot do anything about this.

From this comes A BASIC RULE OF SEARCH: If it is *really* important, never rely on only one search tool. Ever.

Are you asking yourself "Why bother"? There are millions of webpages on our planet right now, and thousands are added every day. It would be humanly impossible for us to coherently organize them all into a universal database that everyone could use. Given human behavior and diversity, agreement on what such a database should contain and how it would be organized would be impossible anyway, or at least pretty strange. As a result, *search tools provide a vital service* by constantly looking for new websites, inventorying them, and adding this new information to huge databases that you can access.

Back when the Web was young (not very far back, by the way), the search options were Yahoo!, WebCrawler, Lycos, and little else. Those days are long gone. Now literally *thousands of different search tools* range from big general-purpose programs to highly specialized ones, and the state of the art continues to evolve. No two are exactly alike. Yesterday's thriller quickly becomes forgotten. Standardization remains an oxymoron. The tools themselves are elegant pieces of computer programming, perhaps resembling baroque concertos, but still only in their infancy. While this may improve as the Web matures, we want to stress that *it is highly unlikely for search tools to yield complete, comprehensive, and useful results without a great deal of planning, practice, intuitive thinking, and—we hate to admit it—luck!*

Wait! It gets worse! You have to know what type of tool to choose as well!

THE TYPES OF SEARCH TOOLS

There are perhaps six different varieties of search tools available today.[3] Learning how to recognize each one and use it correctly is vital for conducting searches that are efficient, thorough, and manageable in length. First, there are two *very different* ways search tools look for URLs to add to their databases. Some—the *key word search engines—actively search* the Web looking for new stuff. Others—the *hierarchic directories—passively wait* for people to register or list their websites. This is a crucial difference that ultimately colors and molds the nature of the resulting information. Learning the differences is well worth the effort because it will help you learn which search tools to use, why, and when.

RULE: Always read the description of what the search tool actually does. This information is usually available from the About Us, More Information, or FAQ (Frequently Asked Questions) types of links on the homepage.

Key Word Search Engines

Key word search engines are turned on regularly every few days or so; they search the Web for new URLs that were not there before; and they then process the results and update the database. They do this by looking for and following new links. When they get to a new website, they review it and categorically enter data from it into their databases. Some of the larger search engines run continuously, so the databases are updated very frequently, at least once a week. These search

---

[3] Much of this section is grounded on Habib and Balliot's studies (July 24, 1998).

engines tend to build incredibly large databases, and the contents are often extremely current. These are called **key word search** engines.

In brief, these search engines are based on artificial intelligence (AI) computer programs called **spiders,** although **robots** and **crawlers** are terms you may encounter, too. These programs isolate and define key concepts and subjects by the most frequently appearing words. The programs omit basic words (the, at, and, too, etc.), and look for unusual words, generally nouns. These discovered words are examined in terms of frequency counts, syntax, and other information by the program's algorithms. This has to be done by the computer, because it would be humanly impossible for anyone to do it millions of times in a day. (Would *you* want to personally review a hundred thousand URLs on *refugees,* one at a time?) *Unusual words that are high in frequency are recorded and often become key words in the search engine's database.* Most search engines use key words that already are within their existing databases and integrate new discoveries with the older terms. You know you are probably in a key-word-type search engine when you have to manually type in a key word and press some type of Search Now button. If you have chosen a key word that has been previously detected and recorded, you may be in luck!

ADVANTAGES AND DISADVANTAGES   Key word search engines have several advantages. They are the *most current* because the search for new websites is largely automated. They are usually the *most comprehensive* because they often use full-text indexing. The size of the databases can be astounding. They are very *good at finding highly specific and obscure terms* because of their key word creation abilities.

At least four disadvantages may be present as well. (1) The databases are vast and easily produce avalanches of useless "hits," especially when the key word is rather general. Listings of hundreds of thousands of URLs are not unusual. (2) If the term you want includes a common abbreviation such as *INS* (the Immigration and Naturalization Service of the United States Department of Justice), then you may get buried in a vast pile of stuff such as *ins*urance companies, plug-*ins* software vendors, and walk-*ins* reception centers at UFO landing sites. Be careful with key word search engines when you have "alphabet soup"! (3) The key word you use may be different from what the search engine decided was important. This is especially possible because a computer program—and not a human being—usually created the key word. (4) Even when you do have a human being somewhere in the loop, the chances are very good that this person is not a social worker and probably has a crummy grasp of what we do anyway. As a result, quality control can be abysmal.

TIP: When you have a very *precise, exact, and narrow concept* that can be succinctly described by one or two key words, the key word/active search types of engines can work quite well.

Hierarchic Directory (Searchable Databases)

Other search tools *passively wait* for people to submit new URLs to them. These wait to be contacted by the webweavers or host providers instead of actively searching the Web to find newly published websites. Once contacted, the search service may directly enter the URL with the key words provided from the submitter, or a human may review a new submission and decide if the website should be added to a database or not and what key words should be attached. These types of search tools usually put their results into large files that can be accessed by a hierarchic access program. The information can be organized and presented in categorical ways that can be broad to specific, such as *refugees, political refugees,* and *political refugees in the United States.*

You are probably using a **directory search** tool when you see lists of categories that are hotlinked, such as "Click here for education, entertainment, travel, etc." This is not always the case, though, because some of these tools have internal search abilities built in. This *internal search engine* feature is common in many types of databases including directory listings, so just because you can enter a key word does not always mean that you are in an active key word type of search engine at all. Instead, you may be in a passive directory search engine without knowing it.

The directory type of tool may be all you need if you have a specific subject or category you are looking for. This is especially true for the humanly edited ones. When website creators register their website in a directory-type database, they generally provide their own key words to help potential visitors find their site. Who else is better suited to suggest pertinent key words than the creators? The human editor for the database is also far more capable of discerning thought than any artificial intelligence program.

ADVANTAGES AND DISADVANTAGES   Hierarchic databases have several advantages. They are usually more accurately indexed because of human intervention, making key word usage more accurate and results far more relevant. Similar types of websites may be grouped together in any resulting list, forming a custom meta-list type of resource.

More hazards are present. These databases are far more limited in scope and smaller than those generated by machines because of the time required for humanly reviewing and editing them. The human dimension can produce categories that are rather biased, arbitrary, and inaccurate. Categories may be mixed, redundant, or virtually unusable. Poor organization is chronic in larger hierarchic databases because the information is so vast and seldom divisible into neat, coherent, mutually exclusive packages. Taxonomic angst strikes again. The lists of resources may vary to a high degree in terms of scope, currency, and size.

TIP: When you are searching for a resource that can be easily described as a category or an area of interest, especially one with a common unambiguous name, hierarchic directory databases are a good choice!

The differences between these two fundamental types of search tools produce a critical choice. A key word search engine will give you the most up-to-date list that can be found. It will be far more current than any directory-based search tool, meta-list, or other source because it *actively looks for new materials rather than waiting* to be given them. Yet great new URLs may be buried under a lot of superfluous twaddle. The directory type of tool will lag far behind, but it will probably be much more user-friendly and accurate. In addition, a database made up from people's voluntary contributions and human editing will be far smaller and make more intuitive sense.

Wait! There is still more to understand! There are different combinations of these two types of search tools!

Combination Directory and Key Word Search Tools

Combination directory/key word creations try to combine the best features of the key word engines and directory-based search tools. Some of these search tool/directory databases allow you to control which features you want to use, while others do not. **Coordinated search** tools link both the key word and directory features together in a combined manner that can be very productive. *Noncoordinated* sites do not. You need to read the instructions to find out which is the case. These search tools are becoming more common as the state of the art improves. Most of the larger general-purpose search tools such as Yahoo, Excite, and InfoSeek now allow you to enter key words, search through already compiled directories, or both. In addition, some of these commercial search websites actively search for new URLs and also accept submissions. The nature of how their databases are compiled and the distinction between the active key word search engines and the passive hierarchic directory tools is blurring.

Some of these combination search websites provide **concept search** abilities, too. Instead of simply looking for the literal key word you have entered, they will also look for related words. For example, if you were looking for "immigrant *policy,*" the program might also look for "immigrant *law,*" immigrant *statutes,*" and "immigrant *repatriation.*" Infoseek, Excite, and Yahoo! will do this for you, and many other websites are developing the ability.

Combination tools are more sophisticated than just the key word or directory types alone and have many advantages over the single-dimension types. Yet, they can be tricky to use and have all of the hazards of the first two. There is an additional problem. You usually do not know what database is being searched, especially at the larger commercial search websites. This phenomenon occurs because these websites often maintain multiple databases instead of just one. As a result, you cannot always be sure the key word you entered is being searched through all of the various databases. Nevertheless, these combination search tools can produce excellent results, especially if you pay attention to what you are searching for and how you are doing it. The finer points are discussed later in the chapter.

TIP: Combination tools can be a little harder to use until you get a sense of how they work. Once you do, however, you may find them very useful because they can be more comprehensive yet precise.

Multiengines

There is a fourth category for search engines, called **multiengines, meta-engines,** or **meta-search engines.** These are "all of the above" in nature; they search *more than one engine at a time* and usually offer an integrated synthesis of results. They are also occasionally referred to as *multithread* engines. They are not search engines in the classic sense at all. They do not gather any information but instead access the databases of other search engines, compile that information, and present it in a hopefully user-friendly way. From the writers' experiences, these search engines can really hit the mark immediately or be way off! Try 'em!

ADVANTAGES AND DISADVANTAGES   There are some advantages provided by multiengines. They tend to be more tolerant of imprecise key words and search terms. (They use "looser" algorithms.) They can dredge up just as many links as the ones already discussed but often prioritize and present only the few that appear to be the most closely related to your search issue. You can search the databases for several search websites at once and then decide which ones to pursue further. You can avoid tediously entering the same commands over and over.

They do, however, have specific liabilities. They search for a "common denominator" type of key word or category. The results can be problematic, especially if the term or concept has no agreed-upon consensus about what it means. *Welfare,* for example, can mean many things to many people *and* computerized search programs! Another disadvantages is that multiengines often use data from only the more popular search engines and directories. As a result, you may be getting information that is compiled only from the more general-purpose databases. If this is the case, then the data will reflect popular tastes and interests but may not be of a scholarly or professional nature. This is akin to using the *Reader's Guide* in the library when you should be consulting a more professionally researched source.

In short, pay attention to the databases the multiengines are getting their information from. The number of multiengines is growing, and there are many available on the Web.

TIP: Multiengines can be great time-savers. If you are after a common subject that is likely to show up in several general-purpose search engines, you may find starting your search with them very helpful.

Specialized Search Engines and Directories

We promised thousands of search tools at the beginning of this chapter. We were not kidding. Myriads of specialized search-dedicated websites are available on many topics. In a sense, these resources are extensions of the meta-lists we discussed in Chapter 4. Perhaps the major difference at times is simply scale. For example, The Mining Company and Argus Clearinghouse websites described in the last chapter as meta-lists could certainly be categorized as directories in their own right. Some specialized search websites may incorporate actual key word search technologies and actively look for new websites. Others are of the hierarchic directory type. Combinations can be found, too. The range and variety are tremendous. We discuss a few in more detail in the next few pages, but for now do be aware that there often are many alternatives to the big commercial search websites.

ADVANTAGES AND DISADVANTAGES   The advantages of specialized search websites are multiple. Usually, they are humanly mediated, so the countless machine-generated false drops are often avoidable. Additionally, when specifically dedicated to an issue, problem area, or ideology, they often reflect the organizational culture of the interest group. Thus, agreement on key words and terms can be fairly straightforward. Another advantage is that since these are usually single focus or single purpose in nature, they can be fairly comprehensive.

They also have liabilities. They are limited to the values and talents of the creators and sponsors. As a result, they can be biased or severely limited in scope. They are also limited in resources by the nature of the webweaver(s) and sponsor(s). A search engine maintained voluntarily by an individual may be far more limited than one kept by a larger organization, although there certainly are delightful exceptions.

TIP: Specialized search engines and directories can be extremely helpful for specific tasks or types of resources needed. Be sure you bookmark them when you find them, because they are often hard to locate.

Internal Search Engines on Websites

Finally, there is a special type of search engine you often encounter, especially on larger supported sites that are designed to provide specific information or reference materials. *Internal search engines* can be built right into websites, and these can be the key word type, directory type, or both. They can range from very simple search programs, just like the Find utility described in Chapter 2, to ones that permit restricted and specialized searches. You can easily recognize them because they usually have a place for you to enter a key word and click a Search, Submit, or similar command. (The WebRing internal search engine illustrated in Chapter 4 is a typical example.)

ADVANTAGES AND DISADVANTAGES   These internal search engines are invaluable, especially in large, complex websites where the specific resources you are searching for are not obvious or intuitively available.

Two hazards are sometimes present. (1) Most internal search engines are rather dumb and will only clumsily look for a key word or two. This produces the false impression that nothing is in the website when in reality it may hold worthwhile materials, but you inadvertently chose the wrong key word. (2) You usually cannot tell just what kind of search engine is at work, and the webweavers often fail to provide this information.

TIP: When using an internal search engine on a website, be certain to use several key words because the search feature may be far more limited than apparent. They are helpful, but they are no match for the large custom-designed search utilities found in actual search-dedicated websites.

CHOOSING SEARCH TOOLS

So far, we have briefly discussed active, passive, combined, multiple, specialized, and internal types of search tools. Which is best? To choose a "good" search engine—one that will give you relevant URLs within a fairly short time in a useful format—you need a very clear understanding of your information needs. *Just what kind of website are you after in the first place?* This sounds pretty basic, but the exact properties, boundaries, and characteristics of what you are looking for should determine the search tool you choose.

What Are You Looking For?

Consider the following list of questions for researching immigrants and refugees:[4]

- Are you seeking a broad overview of a subject to later narrow it (i.e., *refugees* and then *Serbians*)?
- Do you want websites for a very narrowly defined topic (i.e., *older married women's roles in Sunni Muslim families.*)?

[4] This section is modeled after a website designed by Ms. Debbie Abilock at The Nueva School in Hillsborough, Calif. The questions mirror a general search guide that is referenced at the end of this chapter. An interactive version can be found at the Brooks/Cole-Wadsworth website: http://socialwork.wadsworth.com/vernonlynch/student

- Do you need encyclopedia-type information (i.e., *history of Bangladesh*)?

- Are you looking for very specific legal information (i.e., *naturalization laws and statutes*)?

- Do you need balanced scientific information that is scholarly and reliable (i.e., *doctoral dissertations on women, migration and assimilation*)?

- Are mathematical or statistical procedures important? For example, do you want to perform a multiple regression analysis on refugee-related statistics from your agency?

- Can you state your search needs best in a phrase or sentence using natural language (i.e., *How can we help women immigrants and refugees?*)?

- Would a proper name of a person or place help (i.e., *Yassir Arafat* or *North Yemen*)?

- Are you especially interested in one geographic region such as a state, nation, or continent?

- Do you only want specific Internet domain URLs (i.e., education (.edu) or government (.gov) websites)?

- Are you looking for nontext materials such as pictures or recorded sounds (i.e., public domain photos of the evacuation of the United States Embassy in Saigon in 1975)?

- Do you need hard factual information or advice and opinions?

- Are you seeking materials suitable for children (i.e., a Croatian website with children's stories)?

- Are you looking for a specific list or on-line support group (i.e., one for Estonian immigrants or Sierra Leon refugees)?

- Are you looking for something in a language other than English (i.e., French websites for a Haitian family)?

- Do you just want to browse?

No two search tools are going to treat any of these information needs in the same way, and none will address them all. Paying attention to the nature of your information need or question will drastically influence how you choose and use a search engine or hierarchic directory.

Let's review some of the issues we have discussed so far. While most search tools *appear* to be similar, there is no overarching agreement on terms or hierarchies between them. While commands such as Search and Find may look the same, each individual tool uses a different approach, sets different priorities, and compiles information differently from the others. As a result, using the same key word or category in one search tool will produce different (sometimes drastically different!) results in another, because no two search tools or directories are constructed in the same way.

Moreover, the structures of the databases are different. The names for terms, categories, and subjects are not standardized. The way the programs retrieve information differs. Some search tool designers have stereotypical ideas about our profession and may be good at using terms like *welfare* as key words but not much else. Others are even less informed and sometimes have a wholly inaccurate idea about social workers or our needs. And when there is not a person behind the database, you are stuck with what a machine decided was important.

TABLE 5-1	THE BASIC SEARCH PROCESS	
STEP 1 **The "art" of search . . .**	**STEP 2** **Choose the search tools . . .**	**STEP 3** **Enter *controlled* keywords and analyze your results . . .**
Precisely define what you are looking for. Generate possible key words, including general-to-specific choices. List possible synonyms.	Key word Directory Combination Specialized Internal	Single, simple key words Words in combination Words with modifications **. . . then repeat as needed.**

USING SEARCH TOOLS

Because of the great variation in search tools and their users, you need to *learn how to create a targeted search.* The unskilled use of a search tool can yield hundreds of thousands of useless results! This learned skill separates the capable from the bewildered. The process, which is fairly simple, is diagrammed in Table 5-1.

Step 1: The "Art" of Search

The first step requires precisely defining what we are looking for. Most of us use a *linear search* pattern when we think about the information we need in practice. We move from general concepts to specific ideas out of habit and curiosity. Searching for a website is similar, like looking for a book in the library. You can generally "surf" to get a feel of what is available, or you can look for a highly specific and unique website. Maybe you want to generally browse a shelf to see what is there. Or maybe you are looking for a very precise collection of books on one topic by a specific author. The following steps are helpful in finding what you need.

GENERAL-TO-SPECIFIC CHOICES   The art of search begins with determining just how general or specific you need to get. Let's continue with our refugee policy example. A very useful place to begin is to *determine how general-to-specific your need really is.* A search with few limitations such as using the single term *refugee* may dredge up countless URLs, few of which may be very useful. Moreover, plodding through a million crummy URLs gets tedious. Remember the data presented at the opening of this chapter? The largest number of hits was 194,400! Yuk! Again, when you generally search without precision, you will usually find tons of personal stuff such as "Don't you just hate what they are doing to refugees?"; thousands of commercial items such as "Smith and Jones, Attorneys at Law, Specializing in Immigration and Refugee Law;" and heaven knows what else. If you want to know about a specific geographical region, for example, then include it in the search process to make your search much less general and more targeted and precise.

TABLE 5-2	YOU NEED INFORMATION		
1. On refugees on a global basis	2. By a Geographical area such as Central Europe	3. By a specific nation-state or locale, such as Bosnia, Croatia, and Serbia	4. By specific cultural features, such as Muslim women within Bosnia
KEY WORDS Very general ←—————————————————————→ Very specific Broad Key Word(s) Narrow Key word(s) Categorical Terms Categorical Terms			
Refugees	Central Europe, refugee	Bosnia, refugee	Muslim, women, refugees, Bosnia

GUIDELINES FOR KEY WORDS   When looking for a large number of websites, use the more general key words when you start your search. This may result in far too many URLs to choose from; but some search tools prioritize, and the first few may be all you need. (The cream sometimes rises to the top.)

Do remember that most search tools prioritize—list the most likely URLs to be relevant first—by the number of times the key word appears in the website. Never depend on a computer program to do your thinking for you. Carefully check how accurate the assessments appear to be by looking at the first few URLs and any descriptions. If these accurately reflect what you are looking for, then continue exploring your results. If not, disregard them and try a new combination of key words. (Crud can rise to the top, too.)

If you are after highly specific and specialized information, then gravitate toward your more precise key words. We could diagram general-to-specific needs and key word choice as shown in Table 5-2.

1. Determine just how general to specific your information needs are *prior to search!* The more precise, the better! *Then* choose and adjust your key word(s) or the categories you want to find.

2. Remember that key words or categories will have different meanings in different search engines because of variation in how the databases are constructed and the lack of common agreement on terms. (The database about *refugees* in one engine may hold very different contents from another.) As a result, *list various synonyms and similar terms for your key words or categories, and be prepared to use them.* In our example, information about *refugees* could easily be storied in search engine databases under alternative terms such as *shelter, asylum, sanctuary, haven, displaced, resettled,* or *repatriation.* REMEMBER: A search engine that is not humanly reviewed will not be capable of discerning judgment. It will simply pick out key words it mathematically thinks are important.

3. Generate alternatives for key words or categories, and be ready to use them! Never rely on just one! *Drag out that thesaurus!*

4. Be prepared to include several key words together when searching. The more key words you use together, the more likely you will find exactly what you need without getting buried under millions of useless URLs.

Perhaps you and your supervisor at Emma Lazarus Centers want to find common issues for Muslim refugee women from the Central Europe region because a large immigrant community from this region uses your services. Just using the term *women* will produce a useless avalanche in any search database. Combining the possible key words—such as *Central European refugee women*—may work much better. Even more targeted phrases—such as *Bosnian Muslim refugee women*—may produce fewer but even more useful URLs.

REMEMBER: A short list of directly relevant URLs is often all you need. Four or five relevant URLs may lead to additional links, WebRings, or useful meta-lists.

Generate as many key words and patterns for using them as possible *prior to search,* and categorize them in term of how general to precise they are. The nature of your requirements and curiosities will determine where to begin. If one key word does not work well, then substitute another; just pitch the old one over the side and try a new one that is closely related.

Follow these steps and you will usually get far better results than simply choosing a random search engine and entering the first word that comes to mind. Yet without knowing the characteristics of each search engine, you may still get buried in an avalanche of information or find none when something should be there. This brings us to the next part of the search process: choosing the precise type of search tool you need.

Step 2: Choose the Search Tool(s)

THE EASY PART: CHOOSING A SEARCH TOOL   Clicking on the Search buttons for either Netscape or Internet Explorer will summon up a menu for the more popular search engines (see Figure 5-1 at the beginning of this chapter or the Directory and Search Engine Guide at the end). If, instead, you want to use a more specialized search engine, then enter its URL and bring it up.

THE NOT-SO-EASY PART: CHOOSING A SEARCH TOOL   Just how do you choose a specific tool out of the thousands available? We have some suggestions that may be helpful. At the outset, it is important to remember that the state of the art for search tools is constantly evolving, and the search engines and directories are continually changing. We recommend the following:

Learn a Few Very Well   Rather than trying many different types of engines, learn only a handful at first. Most search engines, directories, and combinations visually look and operate the same. In fact, it is hard to tell them apart anymore. You type in key words or click on a category and away you go. Yet each search tool can actually be quite different. As a result, learn one of each type. Learn them in depth by reading all of the instructions and descriptions and then playing with various choices and settings. We suggest the following, based on the work of Habib and Balliot (June 24, 1998).[5]

---

[5]   A large question-structured table is listed at the back of this chapter, and it is also available on-line at the Brooks Cole/Wadsworth website for this text. It has quite a few search engines and directories to choose from. We suggest you do not use it until you have done all of the exercises for this chapter.

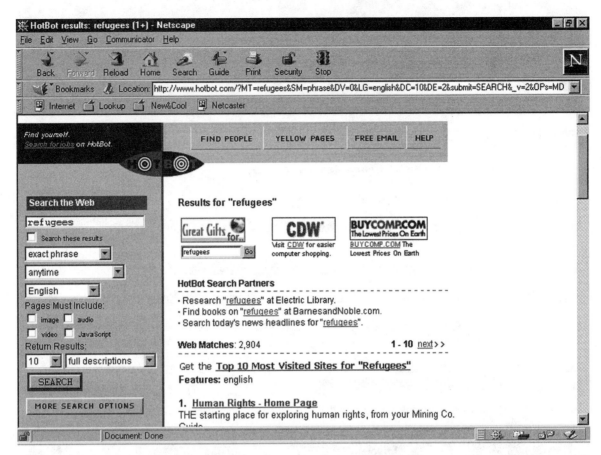

FIGURE 5-4 HotBot, an active search engine. (Copyright © 1994–99 Wired Digital, Inc. All rights reserved.)

- Key word search engines

  http://www.hotbot.com

  HotBot's (Figure 5-4) database is vast, and it is continually upgraded every few weeks. It is fairly easy to learn. You can control many aspects of the search, such as how the key words will be used (e.g., as an exact phrase or all of the words), the time the URL was entered into the database (e.g., within the last week to any time), or the language (e.g., any language or choose from several). Try it for very specific key words.

- Hierarchic directories

  http://www.yahoo.com

  Yahoo! (Figure 5-5) offers a vast assemblage of URLs that are organized into the largest subject search inventory on the Web. Its categories and links are well organized and clearly presented.

- Combination

  http://www.excite.com

  Excite (Figure 5-6) is very good at concept searches and literal key words. Concept searching is the default. It supports automatic stemming (use of the word's root) and sorting by site.

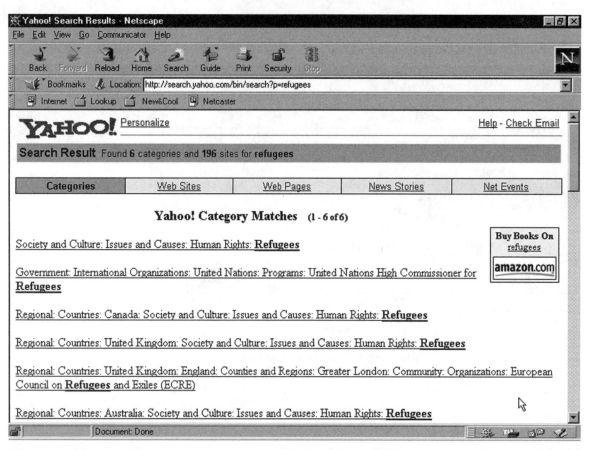

FIGURE 5-5 Yahoo!, a hierarchic directory. (Reprinted with permission for Yahoo! Inc., © copyright 1999. www.yahoo.com)

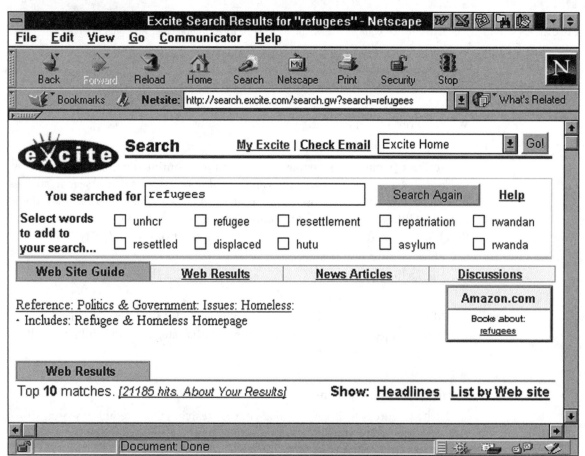

FIGURE 5-6 Excite, a combination with concept search. (Excite is a trademark of Excite, Inc. and may be registered in various jurisdictions. Excite Screen display copyright 1995–1999 Excite, Inc.)

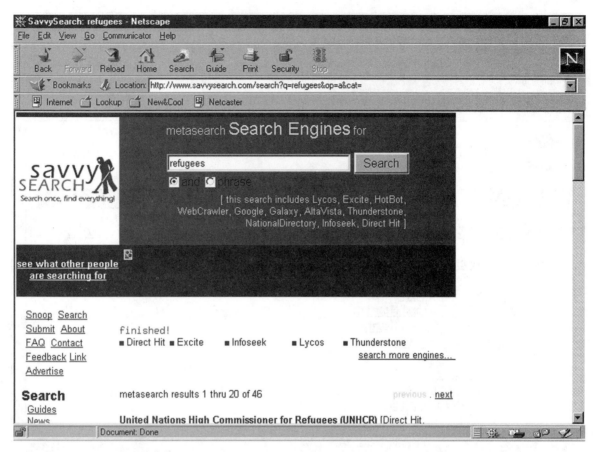

FIGURE 5-7 SavvySearch, a Multiengine with over two hundred databases. (© 1999 Savvy Search Limited.)

- Multiengines

  http://www.savvysearch.com

  SavvySearch (Figure 5-7) will look through databases such as Go To, Snap, Yahoo!, Magellan, eBlast, PlanetSearch, Open Directory, Mining Co., and Look-Smart. It claims to have consultative abilities with over two hundred search-related databases. It will also consult DejaNews, a database of discussion groups, under the Usenet News choice on the homepage.

- Specialized search engines

  http://search.cnet.com/Real/0,29,,0200.html

  C|net A–Z (Figure 5-8) is one of the specialized search engines. Go to www.search.com and *click on the line that says* "Specialty Searches—More than 100 different ways to search the Web A–Z List." You will find a menu page with many specialized search engines, directories, tools, and many other nifty utilities.

  You may have noticed that we are not providing details about any of these search tools. The reason is simple: Search tools constantly change and evolve. The graphics frequently change as designers strive to make them prettier. The way they gather and organize data is constantly changing. You need to regularly read the descriptions and updates for them to use them well.

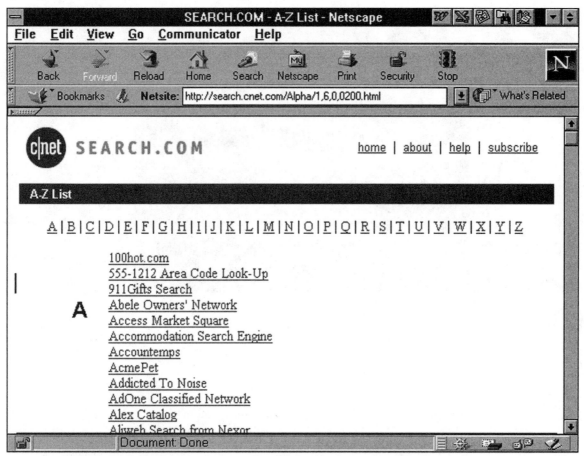

Reprinted with permission from CNET, Inc. © Copyright 1995-8. www.cnet.com

FIGURE 5-8 Special search tools on C|Net.

A "Fuzzy Rule" Next, here is a "fuzzy rule" that will help you out. (The reason this rule is "fuzzy" is that it does not work all of the time, although we have found it helpful as a guide when beginning to search.)

- The *more specific* and precise your search need (e.g., facts about a specific ethnic group of refugees), the more you may find *key word* search engines helpful. Since these engines actively search the Web, they will also include the most current URLs.

- The *more general* and categorical your needs (e.g., legal rights of all immigrants), the more the *hierarchic directory databases* may help.

- The combination search engines that use both key word and directory features are somewhere in the middle. When in them, try using the more unusual key word first.

WAIT! THERE ARE MORE! What about the other thousands we promised? Just as in the case of the meta-lists from the previous chapter, individuals and organizations sometimes build specialized engines around specific issues and interests.[6] These are often located on individual websites and resemble meta-lists with added

---

6 When you access a large meta-list and use the Find feature from the Edit pull-down menu, you are essentially using it as a search tool.

search engine capabilities. Perhaps the distinction blurs. The basic point to remember is that specialized search tools range from rather crude and limited affairs to truly massive and comprehensive websites. This is especially true for institutionally supported ones where employed staff labor to constantly maintain them. For example:

- How about a searchable database that might have refugee stories from *The New York Times?* Go to

  www.nytimes.com/auth/login?Tag=/&uri=/search/daily

- Want the latest political information on many issues including immigration? Try Capa Search:

  www.capa-news.org

- Want maps? Try MapQuest:

  www.mapquest.com

- Researching the philosophy of welfare and migrants for that policy paper? Try Hippias:

  hippias.evansville.edu

- Something in social work? Dr. Gary Holden's "World Wide Web for Social Workers" has a vast directory. It started out as a meta-list and just kept growing!

  www.nyu.edu/socialwork/wwwrsw

These are just a few examples of the many specialized engines and directories that are emerging. How do you find more? We suggest that you (1) ask yourself, "Who might be interested in the topic?" Ask yourself this question again and again. Governmental agencies such as the United Nations High Commission on Refugees, nongovernmental organizations such as the International Red Crescent or International Red Cross, various embassies, and certainly a lot of academic political scientists are possibly relevant in the case study at the beginning of this chapter. Any of these potential sources might support a website with a specialized search engine/hierarchic directory. (2) As in the case of meta-lists, ask around on listservs and other forums on issues that you want to research. Usually you will get recommendations if any specialized search engines are available. (3) Search for search engines with a search engine! Try the key words "specialized search engine" in some of the larger commercial search engines such as HotBot and AltaVista. You will find so many that you will probably want to put another limiting key word in! (4) Use compiled listings of search engines where selected search engines are already available and ready to go! Here are several for starters:

- All In One: www.albany.net/allinone/   This convenient website allows you to choose different tools for separate tasks such as looking for people or researching publications. You use the tools one at a time.

- C|net's search.com: www.search.com   Click on their A–Z List to see what is available.

- Beaucoup: www.beaucoup.com   This website claims to have over twelve hundred tools, directories, and indices across the world.

- 1000 Search Engines at

  http://www.aid4promotion.com/english/search_engines_search.html

has just that!

If there is not a "mother of all search tool lists," these just listed are serious kissing cousins! The quality of individual specialized search engines ranges from the excellent to the abysmal, and the quantity from the immense to the skimpy. Specialized search engines also vary considerably in their sophistication. Be certain to look for information on how the engine works and who is behind it.

DO REMEMBER: A specialized search engine around an especially well-developed topic may sometimes be the only search engine you need! This is very helpful when you have only a general grasp of the issues and concepts within the topic or area. If you find one, it may save you a lot of time in comparison with the larger popular engines. Moreover, specialized engines may have a larger percentage of relevant entries in their databases because they are often humanly edited and maintained.

Finally, consider using the internal search engines when available. Many websites, especially larger ones with several objectives and databases, offer internal searching abilities. This is no small task. The webweaver has to build in a search engine that runs well without causing problems. Most do this by using prewritten or "canned" programs designed to add on internal search engine capabilities. There is quite a range of sophistication in these programs. Some are not really much better than the Find feature in the browser. They just do a multiple Find search on all of the website's pages. Others can get very complex and sophisticated. The trade-off is that the more sophisticated the engine, the more space it takes up on the website's server. As a result, internal search engines are quite common but range from marginally useful to excellent. Since you do not know what the program is actually doing, you cannot easily judge how well the search engine works. We suggest that you try several synonyms whenever you are using an internal search engine.

Step 3: Enter Controlled Key Words and Analyze Your Results

Remember we mentioned that combining several key words together is generally better than just using only one? Let's pursue this as we learn how to get more refined results. Some search engines and directories are very simple to use, because they provide few choices and limited flexibility. All you do in these instances is click on an available directory or enter a key word or two and press a Search, Submit, or Go Find It type of button. These engines are very easy to use and fairly self-explanatory. The advantage to them is their ease and speed. The disadvantage—a big one—is that you have no control over what the engine is really looking for or how it goes about it. Based on the key words you have used, you may be right on target within its database, but you may be kilometers away. You will never know. It is a "black box" experience.

Other search engines are more complex, but far more controllable. These allow you to conduct more sophisticated searches beyond merely typing in a key word or two and entering it. These engines allow you to place various restraints on the key words you are using and can be a great help for avoiding the avalanche while still getting the best results from the database. There are five common ways to limit your search: capitalization, quotation marks, wild cards, automated delimiters, and logical or Boolean operators. Additional methods can include the use of positives or negatives, parenthetical groupings, or combinations of any of these.

RULE: Read each search tool's instructions before proceeding, because some will not handle all of the following strategies or perform in the exact way described.

Let's presume that you have decided to conduct a preliminary search on refugees and feminist issues as a starting point. Using the Simple Search feature on AltaVista, www.altavista.com, one of the larger and more comprehensive of the popular search engines, we try the following.[7]

First, we decide on our key words. In the example, we use *refugee* and *feminist*, although a more exhaustive search might incorporate other possible key words such as *immigrants, feminism,* or *women's issues.* A search for

feminist refugee

with just a space between the words and nothing else revealed 152,160 **hits.** Quite an avalanche.

CAPITALIZATION   Using *Capital Letters at the beginning of the Key Word* instead of just lowercase often has a direct effect on the search. Capital letters usually make most engines look only *for the exact word as typed* and not the word embedded in other words. It is very handy when you want only results for the exact key word as specified.

Feminist Refugee

produced 133,210 hits, which is still an avalanche but less than using nothing! Capitalizing eliminated other words like *feminism* and *refugees.*

The advantage to using capitals is that you can really cut to the heart of the matter. The disadvantage is that the exact words you have specified may be too narrow, giving you nothing, or too broad, still giving an avalanche as just described. You may need to try several ways to capitalize key words when you use them in combination, such as *Feminist refugee* or *feminist Refugee.*

QUOTATION MARKS   Search tools often handle quotation marks in a very precise way: When you put two or more key words within quotation marks, the tool treats all of the key words within as a single term or phrase. The engine also looks for the key words solely in the *exact order* you have enclosed them in the quotation marks. In a sense, quotation marks constrain the key words to a literal phrase. For example,

"feminist refugee"

produced only *three URLs in the AltaVista search engine at the same time!* Quite a dramatic difference! This is because it was literally searching for only this exact combination.

The advantage to putting key words in quotation marks is that you can severely limit the search. The disadvantage is that you may be putting the wrong words into the quote or placing them in the wrong order. A good strategy when using quotation marks is to try several combinations. The payoff with enclosing key words in quotation marks is that the search will literally be limited to solely the terms you specify. If you have an exact subject, this can really cut through the clutter! This is especially helpful in the key word search engines, because their databases are so vast.

You can often combine *capitals and quotation marks* to further restrain the search, depending on the individual search engine. We used

"Feminist Refugee"

in our test and got *only one hit* on the day we tried it. We found a researched article on the exact subject plus its bibliography. Not a bad beginning, and it sure beats wading through tons of useless URLs from the great beyond!

---

[7]   These data are from an actual search conducted by the writers on 8 July 1998.

WILD CARDS   Some engines will use different symbols, such as "*" or "?" that are called *wild cards*. These generally have the opposite effect of capitalization. These force the engine to include all words that have the key word *or its root*. It is known as *automatic stemming*. Using the term *refug** if the engine uses asterisks as wild cards will considerably broaden the search by looking for terms such as *refuge, refugee, refugees,* and so on.

> **femin* refug***

produced 1,209,830 hits. Yikes! This is a big avalanche in this case, but sometimes you want to broaden your key word's range.

The advantage to using wild cards (a form of *stemming*) is that you can control just how much you want the engine to look for. The root *refug** will find more hits than *refuge** and still more than *refugee**. (When we conducted this test, the results were 984,200; 554,240; and 313,590 respectively.) The disadvantage: You will need to get out your snowshoes if you are not careful!

AUTOMATED DELIMITERS   Some of the more sophisticated search engines have automated ways to narrow your search. The AltaVista website, for example, includes several ways to constrain searches. You can control for language by clicking on the "Search the Web for documents in . . ." choice. This limits the search to one of about twenty-five available languages from Chinese to Swedish. Limiting the search to languages you understand can be a great help! Many other search engines and directories offer these abilities to some degree.

Being able to automatically set parameters can give precision and control to the search process. The disadvantage is that searching is still a "black box" experience. Unless you have detailed knowledge of how the limits are set, you will not really have the foggiest clue about what the program is actually doing for you, but this approach is certainly convenient and pretty reliable if you use several different key words. Comb the "Why you should use . . ." or "FAQ" or "About using . . ." webpages within search tool websites for the specific information you need.

LOGICAL OR BOOLEAN OPERATORS   Conditional operators, also called Boolean operators, put *conditions onto the key words* so you can narrow the search and delete an awful lot of superfluous avalanche stuff that would hide your results. Terms that specify conditional relationships between two or more key words force the search engine to list only materials that exactly fit the conditions you have asked for. The common operators are AND, OR, NOT, and NEAR. Most of the search engines that can handle logical operators usually recognize them when the OPERATORS ARE TYPED IN CAPITAL LETTERS. In the simple search version of AltaVista, these produced the following:

> **feminist AND refugee**

produced 742,260 hits. AND is an extremely helpful operator because it controls the relationship between two key words. When AND is inserted, the engine only dredges up URLs where both words occur together next to each other. Unlike quotes, the words may be reversed when found, but they will be next to each other. As a result, this combination would retrieve URLs such as "*feminist refugee* theory for . . ." and "*refugee feminist* poetry from. . . ." AND works best when at least one of the key words is fairly specific.

> **feminist OR refugee**

produced 475,870 hits. OR substitutes two key words for each other. You can use it to search on more than one key word, such as "refugees OR immigrants." If this command detects either key word or both, it will list the URL for you. OR is also very handy when you are searching for abbreviations. For example, working with "nongovernmental organizations" is common in practice with refugees. The term is so common in this area of practice that it is often abbreviated "ngo." A search constructed with

> **"nongovernmental organizations" OR ngo**

might work very well. (Note that we have put the fully spelled version in quotation marks to force the search to look only for this term as an exact phrase.)

> **feminist NOT refugee**

produced 439,250 hits. NOT, like OR, controls the relationship between two key words by making substitutions, but more precise ones. If NOT is used between two key words, it lists the URL only if the other word is not present. For example, the command

> **"female genital mutilation" NOT "female circumcision"**

only lists mutilation-described URLs.

> **feminist NEAR refugee**

produced 367,670 hits. NEAR is a "looser" form of AND. It pairs up words that are—or at least should be—in close proximity to each other. For example,

> **starvation NEAR migration**

would retrieve a URL titled

> **Refugee *starvation* issues with child *migration***

The search engine is set to look for the two words within a specific proximity to each other. Generally the NEAR default is ten words. Some search engines will allow you to set the proximity range, such as

> **starvation NEAR/5 migration**

a five-word range. Read through the search engine's technical information to find the range.

Positive/Negative

Some search engines have different or additional protocols for entering and using logical operators. For example, some substitute + for AND and – for NOT. These have similar effects but are not exactly equivalent. Adding a + in front of a key word will force the search to make certain that this term is included. The – ensures its exclusion. Some engines allow you to use both Boolean operators and plus/minus signs together. Just be certain that there are no spaces between the plus or minus sign and the key word. *Learn the specific steps and command structure for the specific engine you have chosen.* Usually the Help section or "FAQ" in the engine's webpage will give the necessary instructions.

Parenthetical Grouping ()

A few search engines allow you to use parentheses to enclose several key words together in almost an algebraic way. This is equivalent to using quotation marks, but on a higher level. The number of items you can enclose as a unit varies with the search tool, so you have to read its instructions to correctly apply this constraint. It can be a very powerful way to get exactly what you are looking for, but it takes practice.

Combining Search Parameters

Combining several logical operators is also possible in some (but not all) search engines, and some will allow the other tricks as well. For example, you could create a fairly narrow search such as

> **(nongovernmen* organiz* OR "Ngo") NEAR "Female Genital mutilat*"**

if you wanted to locate or identify specific websites that deal with this specific issue. Learning how to use logical/Boolean operators takes practice but is well worth the effort!

To summarize, the art of search includes figuring out just how general to specific your search should be, generating alternative key words in case you need them, and carefully using them in a controlled manner so you have a good idea of what the program is actually doing with them. This is paramount before beginning your search! Once you begin, learn the characteristics of the search engine(s) you have chosen, including how they search and the type of databases they consult. When possible, specific search-related commands such as automated delimiters and Boolean operators can be of great help. What happens when you get that list of URLs you have asked for?

Depending on the characteristics of the engine(s) you have chosen, the key words you have used, and any conditional operators you have selected, you should now have a list of specific URLs plus some descriptions for each one. The list may be very brief or number in the hundreds of thousands. Every URL from the top down may directly have what you need or simply make no sense at all. The task now is to analyze the results and use them or decide to search again.

If you are happy with the apparent results you see, then simply click on the URLs you want to visit and start your research. If you have far too many hits to choose from, then try the first few, perhaps the first ten. If most of these are irrelevant, then search again with a new, more narrowly defined key word or rework the search with any available logical operators the engine can handle. You can also try another search engine. You also may get a list of further lists, especially in the case of directory search engines such as Yahoo! Taking our own advice on "Who else might be interested in the topic?", we chose Yahoo!'s "Government" category, entered the key word *refugees* and came up with two subdirectories: "Government Law" and "Government: International Organizations" as starting places.

REMEMBER: You can usually click on the "Back to the List" type of button if you do not like what you find. If you find you do not especially like any of the categories or subjects or their contents, then reenter a different key word or search parameter or change search engines.

You may occasionally get a message telling you that nothing was found. When this happens, you need to switch and reenter your search categories and key words accordingly. Use a more generalized key word. Also check your spelling, typing, and case because you may have made a mistake entering your key words. REMEMBER: There is no general consensus on key words or subjects between search engines at this time, and there may not be any for some time to come, if ever. Yet the Web is so vast, even now, that *something* should be out there!

Exercise 5A:
Dueling Search Tools

- This is a computer exercise. You will need a Web-connected computer.
- The purpose of this exercise is to sharpen your familiarity and comparative skills with search engines and hierarchic directories.
- This work carries over into other exercises.

DIRECTIONS

A. Look over Exercise 2C: Key Words, and review your other related work if it is available. From this, *choose three key words that you think are reasonably specific, unambiguous, and likely to produce good search results.* The words do not have to be related to each other. Generate new key words if the old ones produced poor results. Provide a short reason for your choosing each one. If you are repeating the same key words from earlier exercises, simply reproduce what you wrote before (to make it easier for the instructor).

The three (same/new) key words are

1. _____ because _____

2. _____ because _____

3. _____ because _____

B. Go to the HotBot website:

http://hotbot.com

HotBot is an *active search engine* with vast resources.

- Choose the first key word and enter it into the search engine in the website. You simply have to type it in the white entry box just below the red Search The Web label on the left side of the window.
- Do not set any other parameters in the boxes below the entry box.
- Click on the Search button and examine the results.
- Record the number of Web matches.
- Look at the descriptions for the first ten websites and compute the percentage of how many appear relevant or not in terms of your issue. If you have less than ten websites, then compute the percentage from the number that you do have.

(Use the first ten from the "raw" or default list, not the "Top 10 Most Visited Sites for. . . ." Not all search engines provide this type of service.)

- Repeat this process for the other two key words.

Key word(s) #1: _____

Number of Web matches: _____

Percentage of relevant hits: _____ %

Key word(s) #2: _____

Number of Web matches: _____

Percentage of relevant hits: _____ %.

Key word(s) #3: _____

Number of Web matches: _____

Percentage of relevant hits: _____ %

Determine which one set of the three key words produced the best results in terms of the percentage of relevant hits.[8]

Best key word(s): _____

C. Go to the Yahoo! website:

http://www.yahoo.com

Yahoo! is an *active hierarchic directory* with vast resources.

■ Enter the *same best key word(s)* from Exercise 2C in the white entry box to the left of the Search button.

■ Record the number of categories and websites: (Total websites for all categories).

Number of categories: _____ Number of websites _____

■ Scroll through the results, looking at the categories, and select the one category that most closely addresses your issue.[9]

■ Examine the first ten site matches, and compute the percentage of relevant hits for your issue. If you have less than ten websites, then compute the percentage from the number that you do have.

Percentage of relevant hits: _____ %

D. Go to Excite:

http://www.excite.com

Excite is a *coordinated search tool with concept-searching ability.*

■ Again enter the *same best key word(s)* in the white entry box to the left of the Search button.

■ Record the number of categories and websites:

Number of categories: _____ number of Websites _____

---

[8]   In the unlikely event that none of the key words produced anything of value, return to your key word exercise and generate new ones. Keep trying until you get a positive result.

[9]   If you only have one category, then simply use it. If you have no result—exceptionally rare—repeat this exercise starting with step **B.**

■ Scroll through the results, looking at the categories, and select the one that most closely addresses your issue.[10]

■ Examine the first ten site matches, and compute the percentage of relevant hits for your issue. If you have less than ten websites, then compute the percentage from the number that you do have.

Percentage of relevant hits: _____ %

E. Compare the results from each type of search tool—the search engine, the directory, and the combination with the concept-search ability—and answer the following questions with one or two sentences.

1. What were the apparent advantages of HotBot compared with the other two?

_____

_____

2. What were the apparent advantages of Yahoo! compared with the other two?

_____

_____

3. What were the apparent advantages of Excite compared with the other two?

_____

_____

4. Which tool—the search engine (HotBot), the hierarchic directory (Yahoo!), or the concept-search combination engine (Excite)—was the best tool of choice *in this instance* and why?

Write a brief paragraph of three to five sentences.

---

[10] If you only have one category, then simply use it. If you have no result—exceptionally rare—repeat this exercise starting with step **B**.

Exercise 5B
Search Skills

- This is a computer exercise. You will need a Web-connected computer.
- The purpose of this exercise is to sharpen your skills at setting parameters for search.
- This work carries over into other exercises.

DIRECTIONS

A. Look over the results from Exercise 5A: Dueling Search Tools and select the very best key word from all that you have tried.

Sharpen this key word by adding another word that is related to it. The word should clarify the first and make it more precise.

Example:

asian	*hmong*
Key word	Added word

My words are

_____	_____
Key word	Added word

B. Go to the AltaVista website:

http://altavista.com

AltaVista is an active search engine with vast resources.

Set the Language Box to any single language you can read and would like to use. (This is a form of an automated delimiter, described in the chapter text.)

Now enter the key words into the white entry box to the left of the Search button. Use each of the different conditional operator procedures that follow and record the raw number of hits and the percentage of relevant hits for the first ten websites that are listed. If you have less than ten websites, then compute the percentage from the number that you do have.

Use the *asian* and *hmong examples* below the line as a *model* for the words *you* choose.

1. Just the two words alone in lowercase, separated by one space:

   _____ Number of hits: _____ Relevant: _____%

   asian hmong

2. Capitalization:

   _____ Number of hits: _____ Relevant: _____%

   Asian Hmong

3. Quotation marks:

   _____ Number of hits: _____ Relevant: _____%

   "asian hmong"

4. Wild cards (AltaVista uses the star: * Just try one * for starters.):

_____ Number of hits: _____ Relevant: _____%

    asia* hmong

5. AND:

_____ Number of hits: _____ Relevant: _____%

    asian AND hmong

6. OR:

_____ Number of hits: _____ Relevant: _____%

    asian OR hmong

7. NOT:

_____ Number of hits: _____ Relevant: _____%

    asian NOT hmong

8. NEAR:

_____ Number of hits: _____ Relevant: _____%

    asian NEAR hmong

9. +/−

_____ Number of hits: _____ Relevant: _____%

    +asian −hmong

10. The _grand tour de force:_ Use any three of the preceding methods in combination:

_____ Number of hits: _____ Relevant: _____%

    +asia* NEAR Hmong

REMEMBER:

- There are no "best" delimiters per se.
- Each has its specific value.
- Not all search tools permit their use or allow as many as AltaVista.

C. Complete the following sentence:

Anyone using delimiters should know that. . . .

Exercise 5C
Multiengines

- This is a computer exercise. You will need a Web-connected computer.
- The purpose of this exercise is to sharpen your awareness and understanding of multiengines.

DIRECTIONS

A. Look over exercise 2C: Key Words and review your other related work if it is available. The key words you used in Exercises 5A and 5B will work fine. Choose the key word or words that you think will give you the most direct search results in terms of your issue.

Key words chosen: _____

B. Visit each of the following multisearch engines. Read through the "About . . . ," "FAQ," and "Why you should use . . ." information sheets to gain a sense of how they work and what they do.

Enter your key word or words into them and compare your results. Some of these will conduct several searches with different engine and directory combinations and sequences. Others will not tell you what they do.

Record how many hits in total you get.

Surf the list(s) and assess how relevant the websites listed are to your issue. Do this to get a sense of what the engine is producing, but do not surf in detail or you will be at this forever!

Decide how convenient the multiengine is to use and what makes this so. Use a short sentence for each.

When/for what purpose would you use this multiengine? Use a short sentence for each.

SavvySearch: www.savvysearch.com

Number of hits: _____

Relevance: _____

Convenience: _____

Useful for: _____

Mamma: www.mamma.com

Number of hits: _____

Relevance: _____

Convenience: _____

Useful for: _____

MetaCrawler: www.metacrawler.com

Number of hits: _____

Relevance: _____

Convenience: _____

Useful for: _____

Ask Jeeves: www.askjeeves.com

Number of hits: _____

Relevance: _____

Convenience: _____

Useful for: _____

Dogpile: www.dogpile.com

Number of hits: _____

Relevance: _____

Convenience: _____

Useful for: _____

C. Complete the following sentence:

Anyone using multiengines should know that. . . .

Exercise 5D
Specialized Search Tools

■ This is a computer exercise. You will need a Web-connected computer.

■ The purpose of this exercise is to sharpen your awareness and understanding of specialized search engines, hierarchic directories, and other available databases.

DIRECTIONS

A. Visit one of the specialized search tools in each of the nine curriculum areas.

Briefly answer the question or respond to the statement in a sentence or number if appropriate.

Practice

You notice peculiar white patches of skin on one of the children in a family during a home visit. Is it ringworm?

http://www.drgreene.com (Large database on health)

or

If you do not get that grant proposal for your employment training program delivered by tomorrow, you are toast! It is 4:30 PM. Where is the nearest FedEx drop-off box to where you are sitting right now?

http://www.fedex.com/us (FedEx locations throughout the world!)

Field/Agencies

As an HMO case management supervisor in Seattle, you must approve all treatment-related travel expenses. A worker submits a reimbursement form claiming 60 miles (98 km) for transporting a client both ways between Berea and Lexington, Kentucky. Should you OK the claim or have a discussion with the employee? What is the actual mileage, round trip?

http://www.indo.com/distance/ (mileage computer)

or

You are going to represent your agency at a conference next month and need information on hotlines for domestic violence, sexual assault, women's careers, sexual harassment, women's health, and breast cancer. Find one resource.

http://www.ir-net.com (Information & Referral Resource Network)

Policy and Services

Your executive director wants to see the website for the agency's congressperson. She is curious about whether they have introduced any new legislation that might be described on their website

http://www.votesmartusa.com

or

As a board member for a local housing council in rural Texas, you need to find out the implications of welfare reform for the agency's funding base. Find one implication.

www.welfareinfo.org (Welfare Information Network Clearinghouse)

Social and Economic Justice

A refugee family has brought 250,000 Slovakian Koruna in small denominations with them. How much is this worth in United States currency?

http://www.xe.net/currency (The Universal Currency Converter)

or

You need to brush up on your conflict resolution awareness and skills. Find a resource website.

www.igc.org/igc/issues/sj (Institute for Global Communications)

Populations At Risk:

Just what government-based information is available on refugees? Name one type of form or category.

http://lib-www.ucr.edu/govinfo.html (Infomine)

or

You need to find a scholarly article on infants and vaccinations. Provide the title, author, and source.

http://wwwindex.nlm.nih.gov/index/nlmindex.html (National Library of Medicine)

Diversity

You are working in a settlement house (yes, we still have them!) in a community with many families from Nepal. What languages should your agency be aware of? Find three.

http://www.samilan.com (South Asian Milan)

or

What dimensions to program planning might a Native Hawaiian bring to your agency?

http://www.cr.nps.gov/aad/nacd/ (Native American Consultation Database)

Human Behavior in the Social Environment

What resources can you find for better understanding the treatment choices for a diagnosed mental health disorder? Provide one website.

http://mentalhelp.net (Mental Health Net)

or

You want to have a computer in your agency's waiting room that has games on it that are suitable for children. Find one game and describe it.

http://www.yahooligans.com (Child-related database)

Values and Ethics

You are a coordinator in a shelter for domestic violence victims and want to find basic legal information about divorce and child custody for a client. Find one citation and include its source.

http://www.law.cornell.edu (Legal Information Institute, Cornell University)

or

You are researching a paper on the philosophical dimensions of the "Right to Life" movement as part of a family practice seminar. Find one website or source citation.

http://hippias.evansville.edu (Philosophy search engine)

Research

You need to research alcohol prevention models for a formative program evaluation in your agency. Find one paper that describes this and give its name, the authors, and citation.

http://ericir.syr.edu/ (Ask ERIC, and follow the Search prompts.)

or

You have good categorical data on recidivism for the last five years. Can you analyze it using linear regression?

http://www.maths.usyd.edu.au:8000/MathSearch.html (MathSearch)

_____

_____

B. Complete the following sentence:

Anyone using specialized search tools should know that. . . .

Summary

We would never discover the vast resources the Web holds without search tools. Yet choosing and using them is a skill. Plan your search ahead of time. Answer that basic question: "Just what am I after in the first place?" Answer it clearly, unambiguously, and first! Then brainstorm for key words and categories. What synonyms and similar concepts may help? Decide how general to specific your search needs to be. The more precise and specific a key word is, the more likely it will bring you helpful results. When your search is really important, use more than one search engine and always use several key words. Do not depend on just one engine or key word! Always read the description of the search engine, what it does, and how it works. This task includes becoming familiar with the search options it offers, the restrictions it will apply for you, what it really reviews (whole text or only part), and its rules for operations. Remember that the active key word search databases are often different from the passive directory types. Pay attention to specific names, titles, and capitalization. "Bosnia" will get you a very different list of URLs than "bosnia."

Be prepared to conduct several searches, even when staying within the same search engine. Different key word combinations can sometimes produce surprisingly different results. Be flexible. The search strategy that worked so well in one engine may produce useless twaddle in the next. You can also get very different results using the same search engine at a later time, because the algorithms are often fragile and new pages will have emerged. There is nothing you can do about it but to keep trying!

NEVER FORGET: Search engines are not very bright. They are idiosyncratic and often reflect the creator's vision of the Web instead of how it actually is: order artificially imposed on chaos by people who do not agree on what is important in the first place! AND DO REMEMBER: Those nice folks who create search engines are seldom real social workers!

Questions for Discussion

When most people generally surf, how effective are they?

What kinds of websites would you want a search engine to look for if it was specifically for social workers?

What categories would you suggest for a large hierarchic directory for our profession?

References

Abilock, D. (June 13, 1998). Choose the best engine for your purpose. Hillsborough, CA: The Nueva School. [On-line]. Available: http://www.nueva.pvt.k12.ca.us/~debbie/library/research/adviceengine.html

Habib, D., & Balliot, R. (July 24, 1998). How to search the World Wide Web: A tutorial for beginners and Nonexperts. [On-line]. Available: http://www.ultranet.com/~egrlib/tutor.htm

Additional Readings

Glossbrenner, A., & Glossbrenner, E. (1998). *Search engines for the World Wide Web: Visual quickstart guide series.* Reading, MA: Addison-Wesley Publishing Co.

Gould, C. (1998). *Searching smart on the World Wide Web: Tools and techniques for getting quality results.* Berkeley, CA: Library Solutions Press.

Maze, S., Moxley, D., & Smith, D. (1998). *Authoritative guide to Web search engines.* New York, NY: Neal-Schuman Net-Guide Series.

Additional Websites

Amnesi http://www.amnesi.com/

Search Engine Watch http://searchenginewatch.com/

The Spider's Apprentice http://www.monash.com/spidap.html

Types of Search Engines http://library.usm.maine.edu/guides/engines2.html

Selected Webpages Discussed in This Chapter

All In One www.albany.net/allinone/

Beaucoup http://www.beaucoup.com

Capa Search http://www.capa-news.org/voters/search.html

Cleereman, T. *Social Work Search Engine* http://www.socialworksearch.com

C|net http://www.search.com

Hippias http://hippias.evansville.edu

Holden, G. *World Wide Web Resources for Social Workers* www.nyu.edu/socialwork/wwwrsw

MapQuest http://www.mapquest.com

The New York Times www.nytimes.com

1000 Search Engines http://www.aid4promotion.com/english/search_engines_search.html

Directory and Search Engine Guide

- This guide offers suggested places to start a search by posing various types of questions and needs.
- These search tools are generally excellent, but other perfectly fine ones are available too!
- There is no preference in the presented order of the tools.
- These resources may have changed.
- You can access an interactive hotlist of these resources at: http://socialwork.wadsworth.com/vernonlynch/student

INFORMATION YOU NEED	SEARCH TOOLS TO TRY
You want an overview by subjects or categories to be able to narrow it. **Example:** You want to research "child welfare policy," but do not know what direction (e.g., income maintenance, protective services, family services, etc.) you want to pursue in depth just yet	Yahoo! www.yahoo.com Excite www.excite.com Infoseek www.infoseek.go.com
Fast access to relevant hits and an option to refine: An idea of what is in each document before you go to each page would be helpful. **Example:** You need to know more about a new surgical procedure for Parkinson's disease, but not information about other dimensions such as policy, support groups, etc.	HotBot www.hotbot.com AltaVista www.altavista.com
Just what is available on the Internet for a topic? **Example:** You want a broad snapshot of many sites that relate to Krohn's disease and are willing to have many irrelevant ones just to get a notion of what is out there.	Metacrawler www.go2.net SavvySearch www.savvysearch.com Mamma www.mamma.com Ask Jeeves www.askjeeves.com
You want quality, evaluated sites suitable for general (nonacademic) use that are reliable. **Example:** You need sites on general substance abuse issues for clients to view.	Magellan magellan.excite.com Lycos-Point Option point.lycos.com WebCrawler www.webcrawler.com
You need to do a specific search on a very narrowly defined topic. **Example:** You want to search relevant webpages for funding sources for adoption programs with African American children and youth.	AltaVista www.altavista.com Lycos www.lycos.com HotBot www.hotbot.com
Encyclopedia-type information. **Example:** You want to read general articles on the Internet.	Free Encyclopedia of Internet http://clever.net/cam/encyclopedia.html

INFORMATION YOU NEED—(Continued)	SEARCH TOOLS TO TRY—(Continued)
Common key words in a phrase need to be included in the search. **Example:** You have key words such as: schizophrenia, manic depression, bipolar, borderline personality, and similar terms for mental health disorders.	AltaVista www.altavista.com Lycos www.lycos.com Infoseek www.infoseek.go.com Mamma www.mamma.com
Web pages in or about a programming language. **Example:** You are crafting a webpage for your agency and need to look up a specific reference for JAVASCRIPT or html.	AltaVista www.altavista.com HotBot www.hotbot.com All-In-One www.albany.net/allinone/
You need balanced scientific information from verified sources for an academic research project. **Example:** You want hard incidence statistics for AIDS in Hispanic communities by state or region.	AltaVista www.altavista.com Lycos www.lycos.com Magellan magellan.excite.com All-In-One www.albany.net/allinone/
Mathematics or statistics information, university-level. **Example:** You need help negotiating a multiple regression procedure for your BSW or MSW research project, or you are in trouble.	MathSearch http://www.maths.usyd.edu.au:8000/ MathSearch.html
You can describe a topic in a sentence using natural language. **Example:** "Find lawyer for people with immigration problems."	Ask Jeeves www.askjeeves.com Infoseek www.infoseek.go.com WebCrawler www.webcrawler.com
Information based on a proper name. **Example:** Who was Mary McDowell?	HotBot www.hotbot.com AltaVista www.altavista.com Infoseek www.infoseek.go.com LookSmart www.looksmart.com
You want webpages for a geographic region. **Example:** You want to research European approaches to income maintenance.	HotBot www.hotbot.com Yahoo! www.yahoo.com Excite www.excite.com

INFORMATION YOU NEED—(Continued)	SEARCH TOOLS TO TRY—(Continued)
Webpages from a specific Internet domain. **Example:** You only want governmental (.gov) websites for a discussion of Americans with Disabilities Act (ADA) policy interpretations and issues.	Metacrawler www.go2.net HotBot www.hotbot.com All-In-One www.albany.net/allinone/
Images or sounds: Photos, art, designs, logos, videos, music, noises, media type (JAVA, VRML) or file extensions (.gif, .jpg). **Example:** You are creating a webpage for your agency and need several public-domain photographs of children.	Lycos-Pict. & Sounds www.lycos.com/ picturethis/ AltaVista image.altavista.com SavvySearch www.savvysearch.com
You want specific legal information. **Example:** You need legal information for an advocacy project you are working on.	CataLaw www.CataLaw.com LawCrawler lawcrawler.findlaw.com
Advice and opinions. **Example:** You want opinions from Usenet posts on sentencing alternatives for domestic violence perpetrators.	DejaNews www.dejanews.com Lycos www.lycos.com reference.COM
To browse: You want to simply browse categories. **Example:** You will be attending a social work conference in another city or country and want to see various attractions or look for special events.	LookSmart www.looksmart.com Yahoo! www.yahoo.com Magellan magellan.excite.com Excite www.excite.com Infoseek www.infoseek.go.com
Sites just for kids. **Example:** You want to put a group of child-relevant websites on a terminal to occupy children in your agency's waiting room.	Yahooligans! www.yahooligans.com A2Z a2z.lycos.com/Just_For_Kids/ OneKey www.onekey.com
Concepts for describing a topic without knowing its exact name. **Example:** You want to find out more about specific medications for treating depression but do not know the pharmaceutical terms.	Excite www.excite.com Yahoo! www.yahoo.com InfoSeek www.infoseek.com

INFORMATION YOU NEED—(Continued)	SEARCH TOOLS TO TRY—(Continued)
Finding lists. **Example:** You have a client who is a caregiver for an Alzheimer's victim. You are looking for an on-line support group.	Lizst www.lizst.com Tile.net title.net/lists DejaNews www.dejanews.com reference.COM www.reference.com
Information available in many languages. **Example:** You are working with a Haitian family that only speaks French.	AltaVista www.altavista.com HotBot www.hotbot.com SavvySearch www.savvysearch.com EuroSeek www.euroseek.net (allows searches outside of the English language)

Guide created by Ms. Dawn O'Shea, Dr. Robert Vernon, and Dr. Darlene Lynch. This guide is based on one created by Ms. Debbie Abilock (June 13, 1998).

CHAPTER 6

Evaluating and Using Web Information

Some of the things you must keep in mind when using information found on the Web . . .

. . . You are on your own when it comes to telling the cybertreasures from the cybertrash.

. . . You have to critically evaluate *all* Web information *before* you use it.

. . . You must evaluate Web information in the light of social work values.

CHAPTER OVERVIEW

Meanwhile, back in the Wild, Wild West, the Web is a virtual gold mine of information. Yet there are mountain lions hiding in some of the caves in which you are prospecting. Ignoring these "big kitties" could result in fatal professional wounds. The social work profession stresses building relationships in a noncritical, nonjudgmental manner with our clients. Approaching the Web in a similar manner is very dangerous. You must be a tough and thorough critic if you are going to successfully evaluate what you find. This chapter teaches you several mechanisms to do so:

- Evaluating Information
- Analyzing the Domain
- Determining Sponsorship
- Determining Authorship
- Determining Currency
- Determining Scope
- Determining Accuracy
- Determining Objectivity

If possible, go through this chapter while at your computer! It really helps!

EVALUATING INFORMATION

CASE STUDY   The Slankowski Family

You are working the graveyard shift in a church-based shelter for the homeless that is operated by an interdenominational church council in your county. Staffed by church volunteers for years, the shelter is operated out of a church basement. Earlier in the year, the church council decided it needed a professional social worker to oversee this shelter program. You have just started this job and have decided to do a week of the graveyard shift to see how things operate during the night. There are no real records or even lists of resources for shelter residents since the shelter has focused upon "sheets and eats" and not case management. The council hopes to change this. So do you.

At around midnight, the Slankowski family appears out of nowhere pounding on the shelter door. The family consists of Marian Slankowski, age forty; her sister Sophie, who has Down's syndrome, age forty-four; and their aunt, Florence Slankowski, a very frail, elderly woman in her late eighties. Marian Slankowski tells you she and her family have no electricity in their apartment and the electric space heater they use to keep warm is not working. The temperatures have plummeted to well below zero this evening, and all three women are so cold they refuse to take off their coats. Marian shows you four unpaid electric bills, but she does not seem to understand why her electricity was turned off.

Three months ago, Marian was laid off from her job at a small local factory where she had worked on an assembly line for three years. Her boss told her she could not collect unemployment compensation because she had not worked at her job long enough. After interviewing Marian, her sister, and their frail aunt, you strongly wonder if Marian is cognitively impaired. Sophie just smiled and had difficulty answering your questions. She acts very shy. You had difficulty communicating with Florence Slankowski as well since Marian tended to answer the questions you addressed to her. When you finished getting the intake information you needed, Marian shouted to her aunt telling her that they would be staying at the shelter. You suspect that Florence did not hear much of what you said.

The family quickly devours the sandwiches and milk you offer them out of the kitchen. Marian tells you the family has spent all of its savings and has been living off of the aunt's small social security check. This pays the rent. The little that is left over goes to buy food for the three. There is no money for electric bills.

After you get the family settled down for the night in the shelter, you decide to see what kinds of resources you can find for this family. Since it is the middle of the night and you do not even have a list of the county's resources, you open up your laptop computer, plug it into the phone jack, summon your ISP, and begin searching for resources for this family. Your primary goal is to prevent this family from becoming permanently homeless. You have also been trying to do some research on-line about homelessness and housing programs. You are hoping to prepare a report to the church council with some recommendations on shelter changes and operations.

Your task in this case is twofold. You need to find the information to help this particular family and to prepare your council report. You would hope to find information on homelessness, unemployment, cognitive disabilities, and geriatrics. You will also have to evaluate this information *on your own* before you use it.

If you went to the library and searched for information in the professional literature, you would have some assurance that what you found had been evaluated by others. Librarians use time-tested mechanisms to evaluate their holdings. Editors also take steps to ensure that what they publish in their journals or newspapers contains accurate information. The "Get it first, but get it right" ethic is a standard. Librarians and journalists know that personal and institutional reputations can be enhanced or destroyed based on the accuracy of information. Unlike these information professionals, a webweaver or website sponsor can be anyone with any agenda. You cannot count on their being invested in information accuracy.

WARNING: Any webweaver can post anything on a website, and some do. The normal safeguards for information published in professional journals or libraries do not exist on the Web!

Do not jeopardize your reputation as a social worker by professionally using Web information you have not evaluated. As a social worker, your credibility, your job evaluation, or even that raise and promotion could rest on whether or not you competently evaluate the Web information you use. The Slankowski family deserves such, and the *Code of Ethics* demands it.

ANALYZING THE DOMAIN

You learned about website URLs in Chapter 2. In most cases, the URL indicates the *domain* of the website. The domain tells you if the website is a governmental unit, a university or research institute, a commercial company, or a nonprofit organization. Generally, governmental and educational institutions post information that is the most reliable. While individuals and even commercial companies frequently post helpful information, they are more likely to have an ax to grind or something to sell, which strongly influences the quality of the information that they post. Nonprofit organizations can also post very biased information. You can never assume that all nonprofit organizations are guided by the same values as social work. You should remain skeptical of what is posted on nonprofit websites until you do a little investigation.

Governmental Websites:

Government-sponsored websites[1] are the repository of some of the most valid and reliable information. Contrary to popular belief that "you cannot trust the government," these websites consistently offer accurate and objective information. The public nature of administrative units results in many checks and balances. These work quite effectively in ensuring that inaccurate information and misinformation are weeded out before being posted. You want to know when you are looking at a government website because of the usual high quality and reliability.

---

[1] This section describes government issues for the United States only. Information for Canada is available at InfoCanada:

http://www.info-canada.com/index.html

The writers are not able to provide expert comments for Canadian Government websites or other countries at this time.

TABLE 6-1	EXAMPLES OF FEDERAL GOVERNMENT URLs
U.S. Census Bureau	www.census.gov
Department of Health and Human Services	www.hhs.gov
Department of Energy	www.doe.gov
Department of Labor	www.dol.gov
The Library of Congress	www.loc.gov
The White House	www.whitehouse.gov

TABLE 6-2	EXAMPLES OF FEDERAL DEPARTMENT AND CONTRACTED WEBSITES	
FEDERAL GOVERNMENT DEPARTMENT		**FEDERALLY CONTRACTED WEBSITES**
National Institutes of Health http://www.nih.gov		Knowledge Exchange Network (KEN) http://www.mentalhealth.org
Substance Abuse and Mental Health Services Administration www.samhsa.gov/cmhs/cmhs.htm		National Resource Center on Homelessness and Mental Illness www.prainc.com/nrc/index.html

FEDERAL WEBSITES (.gov) AND OFFICIAL CONTRACTORS *Federal government websites* can be recognized by the *.gov*[2] in their URLs. Examples are provided in Table 6-1. Some *federally contracted websites* have URLs with the *.org* or even the *.com* domain. In these situations, you will always find the contracted website linked to the appropriate federal department's webpage (see Table 6-2). If you find yourself on an *.org* or *.com* website that claims to be affiliated with a governmental unit, follow the link back to the governmental department's webpage. Once there, make sure the *.gov* website has a link to the contracted .org- or .com-based website. If no such link from the government website exists, do not assume that this is an official government website or one endorsed through contract. *This mutual reciprocity is critical.*

TIP: Mutual linkages (each website directly links with the other) provide the basic way to check for the relationship between government and nongovernmental contractors. IF mutuality cannot be verified, beware!

When you are at a governmental website, it is important to remember that the website should alert you to a contractor or recommended website by presenting you with a disclaimer statement (Figure 6-1) or notice that you are leaving the official website. While generally credible, contracted websites require closer scrutiny.

---

[2] Military websites generally have similar conventions and features as the *.gov* information provided here.

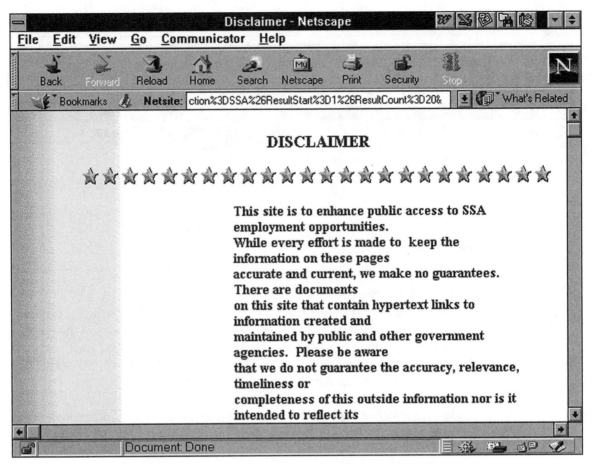

FIGURE 6-1 A typical disclaimer notice.

TIP: You know when you have moved from an *official* federal website to a *contractor* when the domain in the URL located in the browsers Address Box automatically changes from the *.gov* to another domain. This usually applies for other levels of government as well.

STATE, COUNTY, AND CITY WEBSITES   Official *state websites*, whether run by the state or contracted out, have considerable variation in them. Some are quite comprehensive, while others give comparatively scant information. Some are almost exclusively run by the state, while others are almost entirely managed by contractors.

Many non-federal-governmental units have adopted a different URL convention. Understanding this convention will help you to spot smaller government-sponsored URLs. The information at state-municipal websites is generally quite reliable, so you want to know when you are really accessing an official government-sponsored website.

The convention for states is as follows:[3]

■   Begin with the server name *www.*

■   Add the subdomain *.state.*

---

[3]   Exceptions to this convention are Guam, Puerto Rico, and the Virgin Islands. Refer to Exercise 6A for these URLs.

FIGURE 6-2 A typical state-level URL following the convention.

- Add the postal state abbreviation. Example: *.il* for Illinois.
- End with *.us*.

EXAMPLE: By convention, Illinois (Figure 6-2) would be

http://www.state.il.us

If you access the state homepage, you can then look for the particular departmental unit, such as the Department of Public Aid. The names vary. Many states provide information about state and county social services on-line. Such information is very helpful when making referrals, since it usually gives you the most up-to-date information regarding benefits and eligibility. In addition, when contracted, these websites are generally credible.

With the Slankowski case, you would want to know if Marian Slankowski had been accurately informed by her employer regarding her right to unemployment benefits. While there is considerable variation in unemployment compensation because it is state-administered, three years could establish a possible claim.

If the shelter was located in the state of Illinois, you could type in the Illinois government URL using the state URL convention, as in the preceding example. (This is similar to the guessing strategy from Chapter 4.) Once you accessed the homepage, you would want to verify that it is indeed the correct website and proceed to look for more information. Always peruse the website's complete contents to verify that it is a legitimate state website.

Many *city and county government websites* (Table 6-3) follow a similar conventional URL format[4] to that for states. For a city,

- Start with the *www* server name.
- Add the subdomain *.ci* for city.
- Add the name of the city such as *indianapolis*.
- Add the postal state abbreviation. Example: *.in* for Indiana.
- End with *.us*.

For county governments, just substitute *.co* for *.ci* and substitute the name of the county instead of the city.

---

[4] Using this convention is voluntary, and many smaller cities and counties that do not have their own server do not follow it. In addition, there are often no conventional agreements for abbreviating local names. Each city or county has chosen its own abbreviation or has elected to use the entire name. Chicago, for instance, uses *Chi*, while Seattle uses *Seattle*.

TABLE 6-3	EXAMPLES OF CITY AND COUNTY GOVERNMENT URLs		
CITY GOVERNMENT	**URL**	**COUNTY GOVERNMENT**	**URL**
Indianapolis, Indiana	www.ci.indianapolis.in.us.	DuPage County, Illinois	www.co.dupage.il.us
Stillwater, Minnesota	www.ci.stillwater.mn.us	Fairfax County, Virginia	www.co.fairfax.va.us
New York, New York	www.ci.nyc.ny.us	Galveston County, Texas	www.co.galveston.tx.us
Mobile, Alabama	www.ci.mobile.al.us	Multnomah County, Oregon	www.co.multnomah.or.us

CASE STUDY EXAMPLE

In the state of Illinois website, you find a link to the Department of Employment Security. This could be the state department office that handles unemployment compensation. Sure enough, the Illinois Department of Employment Security administers unemployment compensation. This webpage gives information on the state's unemployment compensation program. By searching the employment security website, you find out that Marian should qualify.

From the website, you also find out where the local employment security office is and its phone number. You save the information on a disk so that you can make a print copy. You decide that you will ask her more about how her employment ended because she may indeed have benefits she has earned.

You can use this information with considerable confidence in working with the Slankowski family since this is a government-sponsored website. Your evaluation of the information does not have to be extensive. The most important assessment at this stage is whether or not it is a government-sponsored website. While this is easy to determine from the kinds of information posted at the website, you also are confident since you know the conventional way in which most state URLs are constructed.

TIP: Government websites and URLs are occasionally satirized or exploited. Phony federal websites are usually easy to spot since they do not end in the .gov domain. Mutuality in links is a second clue. Since smaller units may or may not follow the conventions described or may use a private server, always check to be certain you have not wandered into some disgruntled taxpayer's revenge!

Educational Websites: .edu

Like the government websites and their immediate official contractors, educational institutions also generally post more reliable information, although these warrant more caution. *Any* institution can obtain the *.edu* domain for its URL simply by calling itself "educational" and requesting one. There is currently no reliable mechanism for checking on the appropriateness of any institution calling itself "educational."

In general, public and private universities, colleges, high schools, and even elementary schools and preschools take care to present accurate information on their websites. Well-known educational institutions do not want to damage their public image by being associated with false, misleading, or inaccurate information. Of course, there are fewer checks and balances in place in educational institutions, and errors or misinformation is sometimes posted, even if inadvertently. Most educational institutions appreciate being notified of such an error and provide information on how to easily contact their webweaver. There are significant exceptions to this.

WATCH FOR THE TILDE   Most colleges and universities permit faculty, staff, and students to put up their own personal webpages using the university's server. Universities pride themselves in cherishing academic freedom so that even if a faculty member or a student posts misinformation, the university will, in most cases, not challenge this personal posting.

What you need to understand when evaluating an educational website's information is that *a university may not sanction the posted information.* Do not automatically assume that all information posted by a university's server is quality information. Bogus university websites are occasionally posted on the Web, sometimes as pranks and sometimes for legitimate reasons.[5]

There are fewer conventions for flagging personal information on educational websites, but one is often reliable. Generally, the *tilde* (~) signifies that you are moving from the official realm of the website to the personal realm. A fictitious example of such a website (also shown in Figure 6-3) follows:

http://www.sidewater.edu/socialwork/~vinch/homeless.html

TIP: If you need to verity information and find the tilde (~) in a URL, E-mail the website owner for information about the person's background and relationship to the institution. Also ask about their purpose in posting the information.

CASE STUDY EXAMPLE

Searching for homelessness information for the Slankowski family and for yourself as a new employee of a homeless shelter, you come upon a website with an .edu domain. This website for The Bay Area Homelessness Program (http://:thecity.sfsu.edu/~stewartd/welcome.html) is guesting on the San Francisco State University's server. Before using this information, you contact the webweaver about the background of D. Stewart, whom the university is allowing to put up this information. Since contact information is available, you E-mail the program for information on D. Stewart and for information on the author of the educational materials posted on this website. These educational materials include simulated exercises designed to teach others about homelessness. This might come in handy since the church council asked you to begin representing the shelter in the community by making community presentations about homelessness. You bookmark this website and would, of course, get permission from the author before using these materials.

---

[5]   For an example, visit the "University of Santa Anita" website:
http://147.129.1.10/library/lib2/AIDSFACTS.html
Designed by John R. Henderson at the Ithaca College Library to teach students how to evaluate websites, it is totally fictional but looks legitimate. Using the information about AIDS posted on this website in a class presentation or practice would make you look very foolish! While this website is intentionally obvious, there are many that are far more sly and subtle.

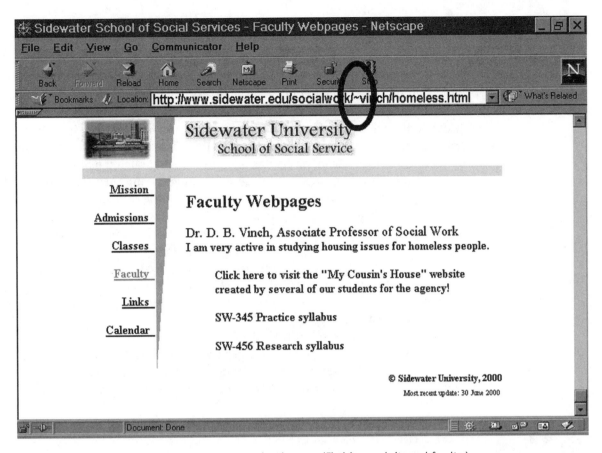

FIGURE 6-3 The tilde (~) usually means personal webpages. (Fictitious website and faculty.)

TIP: Educational institutions sometimes host websites for service organizations and for many populations at risk. In addition, you can often find superb research information. Just be certain to verify that it is provided by a reputable, *traceable* author.

Commercial Websites: .com

Countless businesses are bringing their commercial enterprises to the Web. Posting website information about themselves and their merchandise makes it easy for you to purchase their products or services. Using the Web to further a company's profit-making goal is to be expected. What complicates things is that *commercial websites can also post very reliable information as a public service.* Your task, when you find yourself at a commercial website, is to attempt to determine what is quality information and what is just product promotion.

For example, a company that sells medical supplies may post a research study on its website as a public service. This study may represent quality research at its very best with valuable information you can use, or it could be very slanted or mediocre research that is designed to sell a piece of medical equipment. You can be sure if a study slams a company's product the article is not going to be posted.

Reputable companies are usually very honest about presenting themselves as a business. You usually know as soon as you visit their website that they are a commercial enterprise that sells such and such. If you find you cannot tell what a commercial website is vending, be very cautious about using any information you gather there. Some websites intentionally pose as noncommercial websites providing considerable information about a particular topic. You may have to surf deeper into a website before realizing you are being hustled to make a purchase, such as to buy audiotapes or patent medicine. You also might get fooled by a company's intentional use of a deceptive website title. Some website titles are designed to look like nonprofits when nothing could be further from the truth.[6]

Complicating things further is the fact that nonprofit organizations, including social service agencies, often use a commercial ISP to host their website. When this is the case, a URL with a .com domain is often used even though the nonprofit website is not really selling anything but simply getting out information to the public on itself and its services. (They got a real deal!) If the content on the website does not readily let you know you are at a nonprofit website, look for a mission or purpose statement. Reading about the organization's purpose will usually make it clear whether this is a for-profit or not-for-profit website.

In addition, some commercial firms donate server space to nonprofit organizations as a public service. This is called *cause-related marketing*, and it is one way agencies can get server space at no cost, something that warms the hearts of most executive directors and comptrollers.

Complicating things even further is the fact that some commercial businesses do not use the .com domain in their URL but use .org instead. When looking at a URL with either the .com or .org domain, remember that you really can take nothing for granted. The domain represents only one clue. You must investigate further.

CASE STUDY EXAMPLE

You have decided that you need to begin building your personal library on homelessness. By searching on-line, you find a number of books on homelessness that are sold by book companies. These commercial websites, like Open Group Books (http://www.opengroup.com), allow you to search their book listings by topic. By searching under "homelessness," Open Group Books provided you, a potential customer, with a fairly extensive list. This book company clearly identifies itself as a commercial enterprise and discusses up front all their charges. The list of books on homelessness, including detailed bibliographic information, will come in handy, so you bookmark the website and save the bibliography on your disk. Providing you with books on your topic of interest is a public service provided by this book company and others. Of course, the company is also hoping you will purchase your books from them. This book company also has posted, again as public service information, how you can use the Library of Congress catalog system to do further research on homelessness.

While searching for homeless resources, you run across another website for an organization called "Homes for the Homeless" (www.HomesfortheHomeless.com). Note the .com URL. This large, private, nonprofit organization provides residential-based educational training for homeless families (you read the section "About Us") and uses .com even though it is far from a commercial website. Not exploring this website simply because it has a .com domain would eliminate a potential resource for your client if you were searching for a comprehensive residential and educational program for a homeless person in New York. It also would have eliminated your finding some very helpful reports.

---

[6]   Actual examples of these websites are not presented in this book because of liability reasons. There are plenty out there! If you have mastered the previous chapters, you can readily find 'em!

TIP: Beware of .com websites, but do not dismiss them! They can often hold excellent resources and may simply be the hosts for actual agencies. They also may provide excellent public services and resources.

Organizational Websites: .org

Service-oriented organizations—the ones that employ social workers—are more and more frequently using the Web as a means of carrying out their nonprofit missions. A website allows a human service agency or organization to market its services, educate the public on issues related to its mission, empower and advocate for its clients, and raise money. Nonprofits do, however, come in all different shapes and sizes. Some have missions that are in opposition to social work purposes.

You cannot assume that all websites using the .org domain have values similar to those that underlie the NASW *Code of Ethics.* With any .org website, you will need *to take a close look at its purpose (mission) to surmise its values.* These values shape an organization's decisions about what information to post and not post on its website and the way the information is to be pitched.

The size of a nonprofit organization is something to consider when assessing a website's information. Larger nonprofit organizations, especially those that are national or international in scope, generally have a bigger stake in maintaining their public image or reputation. These organizations are generally more likely to carefully scrutinize the information that they post on their websites. The volume of viewers at these large websites also results in their getting more feedback regarding the information they post. These larger nonprofits also have more resources available to them to put mechanisms or systems of checks and balances in place to ensure that what they post is quality information. So, if you were searching for homelessness statistics and found statistical data posted on the "National Coalition for the Homeless" website (http://nch.ari.net), you would expect that considerable effort went into ensuring that the information they posted was accurate. In fact, NCH is one of the largest national organizations dealing with homeless issues. A small agency would probably not have many checks and balances and may not update information as frequently.

CASE STUDY EXAMPLE	While surfing the Web for homelessness information, you encounter the "National Alliance to End Homelessness" (http://www.endhomelessness.org) and the "National Law Center on Homelessness and Poverty" (http://www.nlchp.org). Both of these nonprofit organizations have .org domains. Both provide information about their missions and are dedicated to ending homelessness. The Law Center also focuses upon protecting the legal rights of people who are homeless. These organizations have missions that are in keeping with social work values. By scanning the contents of the information both websites provide, you find that the information they post is consistent with their stated missions. Both of these websites could potentially help you improve your shelter's operation and financial resources.

TIP: Trust a national, well-known organization's information before you trust that of a small, unknown organization or agency. In the case of factual accuracy, bigger is generally better.

Network Websites: .net

The original intention of the .net domain was to create network-related websites for design, development, and support of the Web. The websites in this domain have become less distinct. While you can still find many network providers and associated firms, many commercial and nonprofit organizations now use this domain name, too. This is largely because of the many ISP hosts that have the .net domain name. As a result, treat .net URLs with *all* of the cautions already discussed.

DETERMINING SPONSORSHIP

A good place to begin the evaluation process is to take a close look at the **sponsor** of a website. Who are they, and what motivates them to invest the time and money to post and then maintain a website? Knowing something about the sponsor is a major clue for assessing the quality of a website's information. Sponsors come with a variety of agendas. Some are invested in providing factual information, some in interpreting facts, and still others in persuading you to think a certain way or to invest your money in their service or product. You will be accessing (and assessing) different kinds of information depending upon who the sponsor is and what their intent is in relation to their website.

Determine a Sponsor's Identity First!

The first thing you want to know about a client is their name. Who is this stranger, and how do they self-identify? Will they refer to themselves formally or informally? Do they present themselves to you as "Angie," "Angelina," "Angelina Morgan," "Ms. Angelina Morgan," or "Dr. Angelina Morgan: BSW, MSW, Ph.D., LCSW, ACSW"? Your first impression and feel for a new client come from their telling you their name. Likewise, your first task with a website is to determine who the sponsor of this website is and what they call themselves.

Government sponsors usually have fairly clear purposes or missions, often mandated by law. The information they post supports their mission. Often, their websites inform the public of the work of their particular department or unit and/or provide information addressing the needs of the public. Failure to service the public can result ultimately in censure from an executive, legislative, or judicial branch of government. Governmental departments are sensitive to how they are viewed by the public, as it should be in a participatory democracy like our own. Government sponsors also tend to stick to facts, because these have the least potential for offending any constituency. They are also invested in presenting themselves in a positive light to the public. This means they try to showcase the good work they do. If they refer to problems or failures, they do so mostly in terms of informing the public how they have corrected the problem. Of course, most sponsors, government or otherwise, try to put their best foot forward.

When a governmental unit sponsors a website, you will probably have some idea of their purpose and how they fit into the bigger scheme of things in your country. Your familiarity with the structure of your system of government (basic civics knowledge) orients you to the website. In the case of other organizational or institutional website sponsors, you may have little background knowledge about who they are and what they do. Your first task is to do a little investigative work to get a fix on the sponsor.

TIP: Always find out the sponsor *before* you get invested in reading the website's posted information. No sponsor? Don't bother.

CHECK THE HOMEPAGE'S TITLE   Website titles that tell you nothing are common. Many websites use titles that are nothing more than a series of letters. "AMI" does not tell you anything. Often, institutions use abbreviated versions of their names. Most will tell you on their main page what the abbreviation stands for. "AMI" stands for Aids Ministry of Illinois. It also stands for the Association for the Mentally Ill. You have to look for the words behind the letters to know who the sponsor is. This is not a deceptive practice and should not concern you unless you cannot find posted those words that tell you what the letters stand for.

You should expect—and demand—all website sponsors to operate with integrity and to be up front about who they are and what their purpose is. Reputable sponsors treat all visitors with respect and do not try to deceive with misleading titles.

TIP: When you encounter a misleading Web title, do *not* use any of their Web information. Any attempt to deceive or mislead bodes poorly for the quality of the information found at such a website.

GO FOR THE HOMEPAGE HEADER   The name of the institution or organization that is sponsoring a particular website is usually included somewhere in the header on the homepage (Figure 6-4) and on all other webpages if the website is well designed.

Remember that when you key in a URL with lots of "string" after the domain, you have probably accessed a webpage embedded deeply within the website. Some websites display information about their sponsor on every webpage of their website, but most do not. At best, they might have a logo on each webpage, but a logo may not really tell you much about their identity. The same situation occurs when

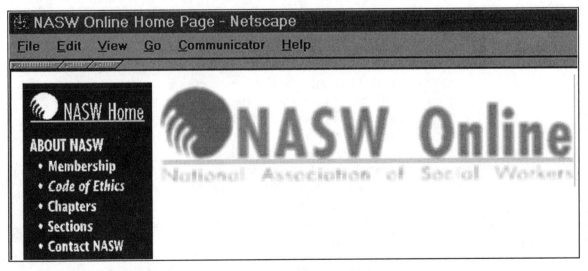

FIGURE 6-4 The National Association of Social Workers header clearly demonstrates sponsorship in the "About NASW" section. (Used by permission.)

you follow an external link from another website or link to a page from a list of hits prepared by a search engine. You can end up linked to an embedded page with no sponsorship information whatsoever. Always look for an internal link that takes you back to the homepage. This internal link is often labeled *Home* or *Main*. It is usually found in the footer, but it is sometimes in the header as well. If you have encountered a website with poor navigation (no link to the homepage can be found), see if you can remove some of the string after the domain name in the address and hit the Return key (this is described in Chapter 2).

TIP: When the name of the sponsor cannot be found on the homepage or on a direct link from it, beware! Search elsewhere for the information you are seeking. Just remember: Never take candy, even in the form of Web information, from a stranger!

PERSONAL WEBSITES   Not all websites are sponsored by organizations. Some websites are put on-line by individuals. Called "personal" or "vanity" webpages, such websites require considerable scrutiny on your part since the information they have posted has been selected by one individual serving as a jack of all trades: author, editor, and publisher. No system of checks and balances exists. You are dependent upon the expertise and integrity of this one individual—a total stranger who could be anyone. Yet, you can find excellent information on some personal homepages. What you need to be aware of is that there is a considerable range in quality. A personal homepage may be nothing more than an individual's personal soapbox with pictures of their pet mountain lion Fluffy, or it may be a place where a reputable researcher posts her latest findings that will not appear in print for a year or more.

CASE STUDY EXAMPLE

In searching for resources for the Slankowski family, you encounter a website entitled "Tederico's Page: Homelessness, Hitchhiking, Panhandling, and Homeless Programs" (http://4homeless.hypermart.net/). This personal homepage is designed and maintained by Tederico Latham. Mr. Latham's website is hosted by a commercial ISP that posts business websites for free in exchange for the right to post ads on these websites. This is an excellent website despite the distractions. It contains links related to homelessness, articles on homelessness and poverty, statistics, volunteer opportunities, a chat room for people who are homeless, personal stories about homelessness, and survival tips for people who are homeless. Tederico Latham, himself formerly homeless, uses his website to provide information for people who are homeless and also to advertise his Web design company (tastefully done and not the central focus of the website).

The audience that his website addresses is people who are actually homeless, and, to a lesser extent, those who work with them. He has tips on how to hitchhike safely and successfully, computer games to play while waiting for a shelter to open, and the locations of shelters and soup kitchens across the country. His website has much to offer, and, as a result, reputable, larger homeless organizations link to his page. You find a lead on free voice mail for people who are homeless. Marian Slankowski has told you that her phone is disconnected. She will need a place for potential employers to contact her, so this may come in handy.

You can just as easily find websites dedicated to eradicating people who are homeless, referring to them in derogatory terms. You can expect that any information such a website has posted will be hostile to all "street people" regardless of their circumstances. No need to read further. You are not going to find quality information here—at least not factual information.

Look for sponsor information posted on personal webpages. Many individual sponsors will state up front what motivated them to put up the information on their website as well as something about their background. Many websites contain information in the footer about how to contact the Web sponsor. If background information is not available, E-mail the sponsor and ask them to identify their purpose and background. Responsible sponsors will E-mail you back with the information you request. *If you get no response to such an inquiry, do not use the information.* You cannot evaluate the quality of the information posted without this information.

Another strategy is to use one of the "personal search" types of search engines, and then look up the InternNIC registration, too (see Chapter 3, Exercise 3D: Tracing URLs). Research the origin and perhaps the person putting the website up. If they claim to be a member of a national organization or group, see if they are listed on the group's website. Also evaluate the quality and nature of the links. Investigate who links to them.

TIP: As in the case of commercial websites, beware but do not dismiss personal websites out of hand. If you think the information is helpful, it is worth a few days' delay to verify its authenticity via E-mail. If you cannot contact the author or sponsor, then forget the website.

Read What a Sponsor Says about Its Purpose or Mission

Website titles or names may or may not tell you much. In an ideal cyberworld, website titles would be informative. For instance, you would expect a website with the title "The World Socialist Website" (http://www.wsws.org/index.shtml) to be an internationally based website supporting socialism. And, in fact, if you follow its internal link, "About ICFI," you will discover that this is the website sponsored by the International Committee for the Fourth International, which traces its roots to the world socialist organization established by Leon Trotsky in 1938. By the same token, "Libertarian.Org" (http://www.libertarian.org), another private group, presents an alternative viewpoint. Again, a clear link to the sponsor, FreeMarket.Net, is provided.

Some website titles, however, suggest one thing but in reality are something quite different. This can be caused by a simple difference in the use of language. For instance, when social workers see the word *entitlement*, we usually think of those programs such as contributory social security retirement benefits. Another individual or organization may see *entitlement* and think "welfare cheats" and "government free rides." Different spins on the same word or words used in a website's title can result in very different website content. So, just do not judge a website by its title. You have to investigate further.

Regardless of what a sponsor has chosen as its website title, read what the sponsor says about itself. You will encounter many websites that state their mission up front on the main page under the website title. Others will provide you with an internal link labeled *Mission, Purpose, About Us,* or *Read Me.* Always read this section *first,* unless you are already very familiar with the sponsor. It will give you information about its purpose and often its history and accomplishments. From this information, you can make a decision about whether or not it is even worth looking at the information posted.

After reading what a website has to say about itself, scan its content to ascertain whether or not the information actually posted supports its stated purpose. If the stated purpose or mission and the actual content conflict, you should be extremely leery about using any of the information. If it smells fishy, it probably is a red herring and an old one at that.

Missing sponsor information can be just poor Web design, or it may reflect an attempt to cover up the organization's real intent in posting information. You just have no way of knowing.

TIP: If no information about the website's purpose is posted, you have no alternative but to read though the *entire* website before you use any of its posted data. If you encounter a sponsoring organization that gives little or no information about itself, this should alert you to the possibility that this sponsor itself has less legitimacy.

The Secret Sales Pitch: Hidden Commercial Agendas

Many sponsors are on the Web to make a fast buck or to at least promote their products or services. Just like the salesperson you encounter when shopping, you cannot expect a commercial website to give you the whole truth and nothing but the truth. Yet, advertising on the Web is quite different from most printed advertising. In a journal, newspaper, or magazine, the advertising is easily distinguished from the factual information. The ad has its own flagged page or is boxed off in the printed material. There are no such conventional practices when it comes to the Web.

Ethical companies are up front about who they are and what they sell. Unfortunately, not all Web sponsors subscribe to ethical standards or even have them. Some profit-making enterprises have intentionally designed websites to look like altruistic, nonprofit organizations with lots of public service information. With such websites, you may find yourself many links into the website before you realize you have encountered a commercial enterprise that is trying to sell you a service, a product, or a viewpoint. When this occurs, you should be extremely cautious about using any of the information you find.

TIP: Deceptions seldom exist in isolation. Even if a commercial website lists research studies supporting their product, you have no way of knowing what studies they intentionally did not mention or how rigorous any posted research really was.

CASE STUDY EXAMPLE

Marian Slankowski talked about not having the money to buy her sister's medication. She showed you her sister's empty medication bottle, which was not a standard prescription bottle. When you asked for more information, Marian told you that their mother, who died last year, was ordering her sister's medication through the mail and that the medicine was supposed to "make Sophie smarter." Concerned that Marian's sister may be going without a medication she really needs, you search on-line and find a website claiming to be "cognitive research based." This research website looks like a nonprofit organization. However, it never refers to itself as such and does not list any board of directors. Deep into the website, you discover that the website is promoting a certain nutritional program through tapes, books, and vitamin supplements for sale on the website.

Beware when an "institute" or "foundation" does not appear to have any connection with mainstream research facilities or educational institutions. It may have chosen to call itself an "institute" even though nothing at the website indicates that it is engaged in research. If its articles only report the research of others that support the agenda, it may be because the website has an agenda of its own. Beware of incestuous scholarship where the same individuals write all of the available articles and books and only refer to each other.

CASE STUDY EXAMPLE

Check other sources. It is possible that Marian's mother put her daughter on this vitamin supplement hoping to improve her daughter's health and cognitive abilities. Other reputable nonprofit websites dedicated to promoting research and education in regard to Down's Syndrome such as "Downsnet"—

http://www.downsnet.org/library/dsnu/01/2/70/page04.asp

—warn against the exaggerated claims of nutritional regimes that have yet to be proven using standard research approaches.

TIP: If a website sponsor *looks* like a nonprofit organization, look for a statement that indicates this is the case. If it *states* it is a nonprofit organization, see if it lists the names of its board members and their affiliations.

Check the Sponsor's Choice of External Links

In addition to looking at a website's purpose and mission, you can tell a great deal about a sponsor by the external links. The sponsor's purpose and mission may still be disguised in their mission or purpose statement. If this is the case, the mission and purpose may become much clearer as you explore the website's external links. Web sponsors seldom want to link to other websites that contradict their purposes and values. If they do so, it is usually for educational purposes only and this is usually stated clearly prior to the viewer's following the link. If the external links lead to websites with specific identifiable agendas or values, assume that such values and agendas are supported by the sponsor as well. These may be more subtly disguised in their website's information but are probably there.

A good question to ask is: Where *isn't* this website linking to? If links to websites you would expect to find are nowhere to be found, this is another red flag that the website is not being up front about who it is and what its purposes are. It is most unusual when there really are no external links, because most authors at least provide a few by convention. Even when citing other researchers in the articles posted on the website, verify them! If you find that the links are all internal ones, do not trust the website.

DARLENE AND BOB'S RULE: By their links ye shall know them!

DETERMINING AUTHORSHIP

Closely tied to sponsorship is **authorship**. You need to know not only who is sponsoring a website but also who actually wrote the posted text. Differentiating between the two is important. In the case of a personal homepage, the sponsor and the author can be the same individual. When the sponsor is a nonprofit organization, a government agency, a business, or an educational institution, assume that the sponsor employs individuals with expertise in the relevant area to write the text for the website. Of course, there is no guarantee that this is the case. Sponsorship size, resources, and commitment to quality information are key in shaping the decisions a sponsor makes on whom they employ to author their text. Some sponsors have national reputations such that you can be quite confident of the expertise behind their posted text. You know that the U.S. Census Bureau is not employing stenographers and welders to make methodological decisions and then write about these decisions for posting on the website.

Some organizational sponsors tell you about the expertise of those who have authored their posted text. For example, the Urban Institute (http://www.urban.org), a large, nonprofit, bipartisan institute that conducts research and policy analysis related to large-scale social and economic problems, lists all staff by research area. When you visit this website you can get the names of all those working, for instance, on housing and community development research projects. The institute posts on-line the reports of research conducted under its auspices, including the names of the original authors and investigators. Internal links to additional information about the authors are also provided. *This is the ideal situation.* The website has made it easy for you to assess authorship. If you have already determined that the sponsor—for example, the Urban Institute—is reputable, you can feel confident that the information posted about their authors is trustworthy.

What you will more commonly encounter at a website is a lack of author information. For instance, at the *Regional Task Force for the Homeless* website (http://www.electriciti.com/homeless/home.htm), you can find a list of *"Myths About Homelessness"* with no author listed. Reading about this sponsoring organization, you find they are a partnership of government authorities, private agency providers, community groups, and advocacy groups for the homeless in San Diego County. Serving as a clearinghouse of information on homelessness, this sponsor has developed a centralized system for collecting, analyzing, and disseminating information on homelessness. This certainly appears to be a legitimate sponsor with considerable expertise in issues relating to homelessness. However, if you have never heard of this sponsoring organization because you work in St. Anthony, Newfoundland, what you know about them is only what they say about themselves. You would have to E-mail the webweaver about the actual authorship of the information on myths. This case for lack of authorship is common and does not especially connote poor design. Websites are often directed at the local population, and global use is not anticipated or necessarily desired.

You need to look for slightly different kinds of information about authors, depending on what they are writing. If the author is writing *summary information* on a topic, you will want to know if they have the educational and professional background that would have prepared them to write with authority in the field. If, for instance, you found an article summarizing the social work referral process written by an electrical engineer with twenty years of work experience at the local power plant, you would not consider this individual prepared to write with authority about social work practice issues. Likewise, if you decided to rewire your office based on information a social work colleague working in addictions had posted on the Web, your coworkers would probably question your sanity just about the time the fire trucks pulled into the parking lot. The connection between *appropriate* expertise is a vital one to establish when you need summative information.

When looking at *original research* posted on the Web, you would want some assurance that the author was professionally prepared to conduct research in their field and had actually done so. If you were reading a summary text about the research of others, you would want the author to have training in research methodology and the related discipline. The paraprofessional or the agency volunteer at the adolescent group home, while able to write about their experiences as a paraprofessional or as a volunteer, would not be trained to assess and summarize the research of others on adolescent development.

Lastly, when you read articles by laypersons about their *personal life experiences*, you expect them to have had the actual experiences about which they write. You would want the author describing what it is like being Chicana and growing up in Texas to be Chicana, not an Anglo who grew up in Minnesota! You will use Web information differently, if at all, depending on who wrote the information and their level of expertise.

Decide on the Kind of Information You Need

Your first task in evaluating authorship is to determine what kind of information you are seeking. This is dependent upon your purpose. If you are writing a grant, you may want empirically based statistical information or researched-based evaluation data that supports both the need for and the effectiveness of the program for which you seek funding. If you want to develop a volunteer training program for your agency, you may want to use personal client stories. If you had found that such stories really help prepare volunteers to deal sensitively and empathicly with the agency's clients, you might want to use personal accounts posted anonymously on the Web. You would not want to use actual client case material from your agency because of your commitment to client confidentiality.

Determine Who the Author Is

Once you know what kind of information you are seeking, you can begin to assess actual authorship. When you are evaluating empirically based information, it is crucial that you know the name of the author. This is the case if the information you are assessing is either an original research study or a summary of the research of others. Larger websites that post full research reports, or even abbreviated versions of an original study, usually have the author's name listed at the beginning of the article.

When no author's name is attached to an article posted on-line, *do not assume that the webweaver is the author.*[7] While this can be the case, most webweavers are technical associates who often have little knowledge about the material they post. Their expertise is in computer science. They just post what they are told to post and maintain the website technically. Webweavers usually do not decide what information to put on-line, nor do they write the actual text. Yet, they often serve as the only

---

[7] An e-mail feature can make authorship verification *much* easier. Some e-mail programs allow you to attach a small "business card" file containing contact and affiliation information. (Example: the "vCard" in Netscape Communicator.) We strongly recommend that you use this feature and encourage your webweaver to do the same. These "cards" are wonderful when you need to contact authors by non-electronic means.

contact person for the website. If it is unclear who is who on the "Send E-mail to
. . ." link, or if authorship is not posted on a website, you will need to contact the
webweaver for this information. The means for doing so electronically is usually
found in the footer. If you request information on authorship and get no response,
or if there is no place on the website to contact anyone electronically to inquire
about authorship, you will not be able to use this information. *Never use any information that purports to be empirically based where authorship cannot be determined.*

REMEMBER: Never assume that the webweaver is a website's author. View
them as a conduit to another source when E-mailing them for confirmation about
authorship. Allow time for delays.

If you are seeking narrative-based information, you should also attempt to determine authorship. You need to be aware, however, that there are individuals who
want to post their stories anonymously. Such authors may be afraid of being stigma-
tized or further victimized should their full identities be revealed in such a public
venue as the Web. For instance, "The Survivor's Page" (http://207.194.73.24/)
allows victims of sexual abuse to publicly post their stories as a means of empowering themselves as well as other survivors who live with similar painful histories.
Stories on this website are posted under a first-name-only basis, which itself is
often fictitious. Because the website posts multiple personal stories, you can learn
a lot about survivors, including common patterns and the diversity of personal
experiences. Such narrative-based information can be quite valuable for sensitizing
yourself and others to the experiences and needs of survivors, even though you
cannot determine authorship. You can, of course, contact the webweaver electronically and inquire about representativeness and the criteria, if any, that are used in
deciding whose story to post. The very nature of this information compels
anonymity, making it impossible and unrealistic to attempt to establish true
authorship.

Social service agencies or advocacy organizations may also post anonymous
stories about the clients they have served or on whose behalf they advocate. In
these situations, your assessment of the sponsor is most important. If you have a
clear sense of the reputation of such an agency or organization, you have some
assurance that the client's story is either real or representative of the population.
Again, if you need more information about authenticity and representativeness,
you can E-mail the webweaver or sponsor and ask for this information.

Web Background Checks

Once you have an author's name, your next task is to find out something about
their background. Sometimes you can click on the author's name and view their
résumé or a statement about their background, including their reasons for posting
the information on the website. Most authors do not bother with or are not comfortable posting their full résumés. Some list a means of contacting them by indi-
cating their E-mail or snail-mail addresses. This enables you to follow up with the
author and ask questions regarding their background to help you determine their
level of expertise. For example, one of the writers read an article on-line entitled
"Chatt(er)ing Through the Fingertips: Doing Psychotherapy Groups On-Line,"
which appeared in an on-line journal, *"Women and Performance: A Journal of Feminist Theory" (http://www.echonyc.com/~women/)*. Electronically requesting information from the author on her background resulted in her E-mailing her résumé,

which gave her educational background, current employer, professional affilia-tions, and the following additional background information:

> The article I wrote was based on my experiences with the first two general therapy groups I facilitated on-line. I continue to do on-line work for my agency, Cancer Care, in NYC. I facilitate an ongoing patient support group and just finished a 12-week group for the partners/relatives of brain tumor patients. I also oversee on-line support groups facilitated by other social workers—in the last year we've done three time-limited family groups and we're about to launch a time-limited bereavement group. These groups have been part of the pilot study for my dissertation. I'm having participants complete pre- and post-group measurements. . . .
> (Yvette Colón , E-mail correspondence, 8/5/98)

This is a superb example of what you would expect from a professional colleague engaged in conducting legitimate research.

If no means of contacting the author electronically is available, E-mail the web-weaver and ask them to forward your inquiry on to the author. You can also see if the author has an E-mail address listed in one of the E-mail directories such as Bigfoot, Netscape People Finder, or WhoWhere? Be aware, however, that these electronic white pages often have small databases. If you find no way of contacting an author electronically, you can search for the individual on the Web using a search engine or two. Until you can track down information on the author's background—information you must have to assess expertise level—you cannot safely use the information they have provided.

It is also important—once you have tracked down an author's educational background, work experience, and professional affiliations—to attempt to confirm this information. If the author tells you that they are associated with a particular university, professional association, or social service agency, you can search for them at that institution's website. If they are not mentioned on the institution's website, these institutions can be contacted by E-mail or by telephone to confirm both the association and the specific nature of the relationship. If the institution itself is suspect, consider abandoning the information as unverifiable.

When assessing an author who is a layperson telling their personal story on-line, you will want to know whether or not the author has actually had the per-sonal experiences they report. This is difficult to do when the personal story has not been posted by a reputable organizational sponsor who can vouch for authen-ticity. In this situation, you are dependent upon the word of the author themselves who may have no professional or institutional associations that can confirm their personal story. Even assessing the author's credibility is difficult to do electroni-cally since the nonverbal cues are missing in this form of communication. Multi-ple personal stories are your best insurance against an author who has manufac-tured a fictional life experience or even cultural identification. The Web certainly affords those with Munchausen syndrome an unusual forum!

CASE STUDY EXAMPLE

Continuing to search on-line for information that will help you with the Slankowski family and with your work at the shelter, you find the personal story of the Sjoblom family threatened with homelessness on the "National Coalition for the Homeless" web-site (http://nch.ari.net).

(continued)

This story recounts the frustration of the family as they struggle to maneuver the social service system in their time of need. Their struggle certainly makes a case for the need for a case management approach to servicing families who are only a few paychecks away from homelessness. In this situation you know of the family's identity since they have chosen to be public with their story. The National Coalition for the Homeless, a reputable sponsor, has also included documentation of their story on-line.

You also encountered at several websites the name of a James Baumohl who had edited a book entitled *Homelessness in America*. You decided to find out what Mr. Baumohl's background was before considering purchasing his book. You search several E-mail directories but cannot find an E-mail address for him. After searching on-line, you find a reference to his background that said he was associated with Bryn Mawr College. You search for him on the college's website and find him listed as a faculty member of the college's "Graduate School of Social Work and Social Research" (http//www.brynmawr.edu/gsswsr/welfac-ak.html), where a description of his background was provided. You find that Dr. Baumohl has considerable expertise in the area of homelessness. You feel quite confident that the college has posted reliable information about their employee. You feel that you have enough information at this point to invest in his book.

TIP: Don't be bashful! Ask 'em! E-mail 'em! Fax 'em! Phone 'em! Do what you need to confirm authorship! It is not realistic to expect sponsors, webweavers, and authors to always post confirming information!

DETERMINING CURRENCY

As a social worker, you are expected to keep yourself well informed regarding developments in your field. This ensures that you can provide the best possible service to your clients. Maintaining your state license or certification is also dependent upon your documenting that you have participated in ongoing continuing education efforts. To keep yourself current, you will want to have access to the latest up-to-date information. Quality information is cutting-edge information. Information in print can be out of date by the time it reaches your desk. Most journal articles and books take a couple of years to move through the publishing process before appearing in print. The beauty of the Web is that it can give you access to information that is posted immediately upon its becoming available.

This can be information on the latest eligibility requirements for food stamps or the latest research findings on literacy programs. How effective you can be with the client sitting in front of you, or how successful your grant application will be, can critically depend upon the currency of the information you are using. Unfortunately, you cannot assume that the information you are viewing on your computer screen is more current than that back article you read in a journal.

What is technically possible (posting the latest information) and what is actually done (keeping it current) can be worlds apart! You will find that you have to look closely at what is posted to determine if it really is current. You just cannot assume it is. Sometimes information can be dated and yet still useful. An article describing historic welfare cases, by definition, would not change, and there would be little reason to update it. On the other hand, a three-year-old article on treatments for AIDS victims could be lethal if not understood in context.

Look for Posted Dates

Look for dates that tell you about a website's currency. These can often be found in the footer of a webpage, but they may also be found in the header. In the ideal situation, you will find both the date that the webpage information was originally posted and the last date it was revised or updated. Many websites contain either one or the other date but not both. Sometimes a missing date can be tracked down by checking under View on the menu bar in the Navigator browser, which you may have tried in Chapter 3, Exercise 3D. By selecting Page Information in the View pull-down menu, you may be able to find the date the webpage was last modified. On the other hand, do not be surprised if the "Date Modified" is blank. For whatever reason, the webweaver may not have filled in a date. If you are using the Explorer browser, this level of detail is not available.

If no dates can be found anywhere, E-mail the webweaver and ask about currency. If you cannot get a reply from the webweaver, or you get one that is ambiguous, play it safe: Do not assume currency!

A word of caution is in order here. Even when you know that a webpage was very recently updated, it does not guarantee that all the information posted has been kept current. Recent changes may have had nothing to do with the quality of the text. Maybe the update to the webpage consisted only of a change in background color, but if the statistics posted four years ago have not been altered, they may now be useless for your purposes.

Evaluate the Webweaver's Maintenance Efforts

Maintenance of a website, especially one that is rather large, requires considerable time and effort. Even conscientious webweavers can be hard-pressed to keep their websites current. Often, you will see posted a notice that the website is being revised or that sections are still under construction. While an encounter with this type of warning can be frustrating, it at least lets you know currency cannot be assumed. If you are not sure how current a particular piece of information posted is, you can, of course, E-mail the webweaver and ask.

Another indicator that a website may not be current is the number of dead external links found. An external link can change overnight since sponsors often change ISPs. Finding one or even two dead external links on a large website may not indicate much other than that the webweaver has not checked the links this week. (There are programs that automatically do this.) However, if you find several dead links, then it is best to assume that the webweaver is not minding the store. You have no way of knowing how outdated the information posted may be. As a rough and subjective measure, a list of resources usually has about a 15-percent link change every year (writers' estimates based on experience).

Note the Currency of Bibliographic Information

If you find an article on a website that you have determined is being maintained, you still have no assurance that the article itself contains information that is most current. Information that is outdated could have been posted yesterday. In this situation, the recent posting dates and the active links are not an indication that the sponsor was committed to posting only the most recent information on their website.

Articles written in standard form come with references. You should scan these references or bibliographies to determine currency for the information in the article itself. Are the references themselves outdated? Is relatively current research cited? Scanning bibliographies is something social workers need to do whether an article appears on-line or in the print media. Alas, not everything changes with the Web!

In the article itself, you can look for information that indicates an outdated social or political environment. For instance, if an article was using statistics on families who were homeless and referred to the AFDC era, you would know this article was written prior to 1996 when AFDC was eliminated. Given the differences in TANF with its work requirements and time limits, you would wonder how different current statistics on families who were homeless would be since the safety net developed some large holes.

CASE STUDY EXAMPLE

The information you gathered from the Slankowski family indicated that the family had been using a space heater all month to heat their apartment. Marian told you that the landlord had given them the space heater to use until he had the furnace replaced. This was over a month ago. You check out the website for the "Low Income Home Energy Assistance Program" (LIHEAP) in Illinois (http://www.commerce.state.il.us/dcca/FILES/COMM_DEV?LIHEA.HTM) to see if this family could qualify for some assistance with their electric bills. Financially, they should qualify for the program, so you make a note of how they can apply. Unfortunately, you find out it will take thirty days before their application can be processed. You know the LIHEAP information is current because the website states on the main page: "Governor Edgar Encourages Low Income Families To Apply For Energy Assistance for the 1998–99 Winter."

Next, you try to find some information on tenant rights in relation to heat. You access the "Metropolitan Tenants Organization" (http://www.cnt.org/~mto/mtphome.htm) and find some information on what a tenant can do if their landlord is not furnishing heat. However, you can find no dates posted on this website, and the View page Information functions on the browser tell you that the webpage has not been updated for over two years. You want to make sure you have the most current information pertaining to tenant rights in Illinois before you discuss any options with the Slankowski family. False expectations are sometimes the worst. "The Chicago Bar Association" website (http://www.chicagobar.org/public/diallaw/28.html) also provides similar information. At this website, you find a copyright date of 1998 in the footer and the View, and the Page Information function in the browser says that the webpage was updated a couple of months ago. You find out that local city ordinances vary somewhat and that you need to contact the specific city hall for your town. Your search has provided you with some possibilities, however, such as withholding rent, getting the landlord to pay for the electric bill, and getting the landlord to pay for any housing costs the tenants may incur over and above their rent should the furnace continue to not function. You also find out that what is written in the Slankowski's lease (if they have one) will also have an impact on what this family can do.

DETERMINING SCOPE

As you begin to look at the actual information on websites, you become aware of the range in scope that exists in cyberspace. You will need to assess a website's **scope,** or the adequacy of its posted information, in terms of the level of coverage. This needs to be done in the context of your particular information.

A website's scope can have considerable breadth, covering multiple facets of a topic, or can quite narrowly address a highly specialized single area of a topic in great depth. Breadth and depth are determined in part by the audience for whom the website has been designed. For example, the "Administration on Aging" website (http://www.aoa.gov) is an example of a website with a broad scope covering a wide range of topics related to aging. In comparison, the "Home Modification Action Project" (http://www.usc.edu/go/hmap/) focuses in great depth on one facet of aging: specialized information on environmental modification needed to keep the elderly in their homes.

The kind of breadth and/or depth you need as a social worker is determined by professional purpose. If you are making a short community presentation on homelessness, you will most likely find websites that give you breadth more helpful because they will enable you to prepare an overview for community residents summarizing important aspects. If, on the other hand, you are writing a journal article, preparing a lengthy report for a task group, or researching information for a conference presentation, you will probably want much more depth. In these situations, you will be preparing information for other professionals who are already familiar with the topic. You will be looking for more specialized, in-depth information to present to your audiences.

The scope of a website's information can also be quite wide or narrow in relation to time and geography. A topic can be covered but only in relation to a particular time span. The 1990 United States Census data posted on the census website (http://www.census.gov) has a narrow time span, as does "The Orphan Train Riders History" website (http://www.hamilton.net/subscribers/hurd/index.html), which covers a child welfare approach to adoptions from the 1850s to 1930s.

Geographic parameters also narrow or widen the scope of a website's information. An international website such as the "World Association of Persons with disAbilities" (http://www.wapd.org) will have a much broader scope than a national one like "Japan Council on Disability" (http://www.vcom.or.jp/project/jd/) or a local one such as the "Georgia Developmental Disabilities Council" (http://www.ga-ddcouncil.org).

Determine Your Information Needs

You cannot evaluate the scope of a website without a clear sense of the kind of information you need. The "ideal scope" does to a considerable extent reside in the eye of the beholder. If you are disappointed in how general the information on a particular website is, obviously this website does not have the scope to satisfy your information needs. Another visitor to this same website might be delighted with what they find. On the other hand, if you find yourself lost in the contents, you are probably at a website with way more depth than what you need. You may find yourself struggling to keep your head above the water in a sea of specialized information that is difficult to fathom. The degree of professional sophistication usually determines the depth you seek. In a time when information changes as quickly as it does, staying current as a generalist practitioner will place many demands on you to access a wide range of information spanning the breadth of human experience.

In those areas of practice in which you specialize, you may find yourself quite frustrated with the lack of in-depth information you find on the Web. The Web still is a long way from permitting a social worker to remain current in a targeted field of practice (i.e., corrections, child welfare, income maintenance). This will probably change over time as social work journals and conference proceedings move to electronic formats. Greater access to specialized information has considerable potential to change the nature of the social work–client relationship *as information*. What was formerly only in the possession of the social worker is now available on-line for all clients to access. This will make it much easier for clients to empower themselves and has the potential to put an entirely new spin on the self-help movement. The potential for self-inflicted harm may increase, too.

Identify the Audience

Webweavers and sponsors have a certain type of individual in mind when they design their websites. The intended audience can be a student or an expert, a client, a social work professional, or a social science researcher. The intended audience determines the language used, the level of technical detail, and the degree to which prior knowledge is assumed. With some websites, sections in the header identifying the website's mission or purpose may give you information on the nature of the audience toward whom the website is pitched.

More frequently, you will have to determine the intended audience by perusing the body of the website. At a professional social work website, you would see social work terminology used with the expectation that you are familiar with the professional language. A good example is the "Council of Nephrology Social Workers" (http://www.kidney.org). This website assumes you are a social worker with an understanding and interest in renal social work issues. It uses terms such as *end stage renal disease* (ESRD) and dialysis outcomes quality initiative (DOQI). It is assumed the visitor knows what *dialysis* is and what is meant by *biopsychosocial risk factors*.

In contrast, at a website geared to clients, you would expect a subject to be discussed in layperson's terms with more basic information that is presented from a client's point of view. The "American Association of Kidney Patients" (http://www.aakp.org/aakpteam.html) offers information on support and treatment options written in simple lay terms. When treatment options like automated peritoneal dialysis (APD) are referenced, they are described in simple, straightforward terms. It is assumed that the visitor may not know or understand either the treatment or its abbreviation.

By looking at a website's content, especially its language, you should be able to determine the intended audience that, in turn, will tell you a great deal about the scope of the website.

Take the Tour, Review the Contents

In most cases, you will need to peruse the website to get a sense of its scope. If a table of contents, website map, or an index is provided on the home or main webpage, you may be able to get some sense of the website's breadth. The table of contents or index gives you a summary of the website's content. "The Minnesota Center Against Violence and Abuse" (http://www.mincava.umn.edu/index.asp) is a good example of a website with an extensive table of contents that shows the breadth of information posted.

The presence of a built-in search engine for the website is another indicator of breadth, depth, or perhaps both. The absence of such a search tool, however, does not suggest a lack of breadth or depth. You just have to eyeball the website yourself, checking to see how many aspects of the topic are covered and with how much detail. Websites that focus on breadth may provide external links for the details (depth). This avoids duplicating information on similar websites. Some websites have such a limited scope that you wonder why anyone bothered to put the website on-line. You will find some websites that have little substance to back up their vision.

Do Comparison Shopping

Limited scope can be intentional and misleading as a reflection of the sponsor's or author's bias. All of the topic or issue may have intentionally not been covered because certain aspects did not support a favored position. This can be problematic for you if you know little about the topic. You may be recruited to support a particular viewpoint without even knowing this is the case. Of course, a narrow scope does not always mean a website's information is biased. The sponsor or author may have wanted to purposely focus upon only one aspect of a topic. When this is the case, this is usually stated in the "About This Website" or "Read About" sections of the website, and external links are provided to address those aspects of the topic not being addressed. In this case, the information may be accurate but represent only a small piece of the whole pie with no intention to promote a particular viewpoint.

How thoroughly a topic is covered may also reflect the degree to which the webpage itself is still under construction. Webpage construction is a time-consuming process and is frequently tackled in stages so that a webweaver may have put on-line only a few pieces at a time. As annoying as those "Under Construction" messages and graphics are, they do alert you to the fact that more information is coming and that promotion of a particular view is not the website's intent.

TIP: To avoid being taken in by a website with an intentionally narrow scope that is misleading, it is best to always *search other websites for the same information.* Looking at other websites covering the same topic can uncover bias even when you are yourself not very familiar with the subject area.

CASE STUDY EXAMPLE

After the Slankowski family settled down for the night, you reflected on your discussion with the family. You were very aware of how little information or sense of Marian's Aunt Florence you got from your interview with the family. You wondered if she was just too tired and hungry or disoriented. You heard Marian raise her voice a couple of times in addressing her aunt, which you did not encourage since others at the shelter were trying to sleep. When you asked Marian if her aunt could hear, she acknowledged that this was a problem. You have had no background in working with people who are hard-of-hearing, so you search for information on how to interview such individuals. You are hoping to communicate more effectively with the aunt the next day. At the Administration on Aging website (http://www.aoa.gov) you discover a handy list of tips on talking to people who are hard-of-hearing. The specific tips really address your needs since they give you an overview of how to approach Florence without your having to wade through specialized and detailed information on communication with those who are hard-of-hearing. The scope of this information fits the overall scope of the Administration on Aging's website: general information about a wide range of topics related to the elderly. And in this case it fits your needs, too!

DETERMINING ACCURACY

Even after you have checked out a website's sponsor, author, currency, and scope, there are still no guarantees of **accuracy,** that is, that the actual content of the information posted in the body of the website is accurate. You want to know if the information is based on sound facts or just an author's personal opinion. Personal opinions, while interesting, and at times entertaining or infuriating, are not the basis for professional knowledge. The Web offers sponsors and authors the opportunity to post both opinions and facts. Your job is to tell the difference.

One of the first things you will discover is that you cannot judge content accuracy by the way a website visually looks. Professionally designed and spiffy looking websites do not mean you have found accurate information. You really cannot judge a website by its artwork. You may find some of the best data on plain, visually unattractive webpages and those old gopher servers. A fast webweaver can crank a forgery out in an hour or less.

It is easiest to spot facts and opinions if they are labeled as such on a website. Websites that have a section labeled *"Facts About . . ."* will often provide a fact sheet with basic statistics about the topic at hand. For instance, the "National Institute for Literacy" (http://novel.nifl.gov) has posted a *"FAST FACTS on Literacy"* webpage that gives you basic information about the scope, impact of illiteracy on poverty rates, and government expenditures on adult education and family literacy programs. Compare this to the letter to the editor, *"Handouts Only Promote Vagrancy,"* posted by the newspaper, the *Arizona Daily Wildcat* (http://wildcat.arizona.edu/papers/90/85/04_2_m.html). This information is clearly identifiable as personal opinion.

Even if the sponsor did not refer to this posting as a letter to the editor, one only has to read the item to discern that it is clearly the author's personal account of her experience. She writes in the first person and makes no reference to factual information like statistics or research findings. The author's personal distaste and distrust of young "panhandlers" in her community, as well as her separating the "worthy" from the "unworthy" needy, is quite clear.

Not all personal opinions are easy to spot. Some websites have personal opinions posted to look like they are scientifically based and well informed. You, of course, want to be able to spot these so you do not embarrass yourself professionally by using inaccurate information. Accuracy is the most difficult to assess when dealing with a topic about which you know very little. Probably the less you know about the topic, the more difficult this is to do and, therefore, the heavier the burden of verifying accuracy.

Errors and Omissions: What Is Wrong and What Is Missing?

Errors and omissions can suggest a less-than-scholarly approach to information accuracy and tip you off to the possible presence of other inaccurate or purposely misleading information. When you encounter obvious and frequent *spelling and grammar errors,* do not just ignore them. The lack of attention to these details can indicate a lack of attention to the veracity of the information posted as well. It seriously undermines the author's credibility unless it is a personal narrative.

Errors in content also suggest the information posted is of poor or questionable quality. If, for example, you found inaccurate estimates for the poverty level for a family of four—something the United States Census has been measuring for decades—you should be alerted to the possibility that other factual information on the website may be inaccurate as well. If, by looking a little more closely, you found additional factual errors, perhaps in the number of females currently incarcerated in your state—often available from state-level criminal justice websites—you would want to check *every* piece of information on the website before you could safely use any of the information. It would probably be better to seek the information you need elsewhere. One error: a typo? Two errors: no spell checker? Three errors: a plot!

Being able to pick up these errors is, of course, contingent upon your knowledge of the facts. While it may seem hard to believe that you will spot errors of fact on-line, this will occur. Your training and professional experience have given you a considerable range of professional knowledge upon which you are drawing. Certainly, if you were working in an agency with low-income families, you would know the financial poverty line for a family of four; and if you were working for the Department of Corrections in your state, you would be quite familiar with the incarceration statistics of women in your state. Perhaps you would not know the exact numbers, but your professional practice wisdom should give you the ability to spot glaring errors.

When you spot an error, bring it to the attention of the Web sponsor or author. If the information is not meant to be purposefully misleading and is strictly a typo, you should expect an appropriate explanation or correction. If you get no response to your electronic inquiry, do not use the information. Play it safe and assume no accuracy.

Omissions can also throw into question the accuracy of the information posted on a website. Leaving out important facts or conflicting viewpoints can be very misleading. Even among the experts there are differences of opinion on many issues related to social work practice, especially in those areas where the research has yet to produce conclusive evidence. In these situations, social workers often rely on their professional experiences, which can vary considerably from practice setting to practice setting. Someone working in the field of domestic violence with one ethnic group may view this social problem quite differently from someone working in another.

Authors committed to accuracy will be quick to point out such differences and acknowledge that universal dynamics may not exist. Check on-line bibliographies cited to see if conflicting points of view are referenced. If relevant factual information is available, but missing, you should question the soundness of the information posted and the intention of the author who may be so committed to a particular viewpoint that they have sacrificed their commitment to accuracy.

Verify References

Look at the sources of the information posted. What sources are cited and listed in bibliographic information, and are they credible? If links to original sources of information are provided in the on-line text or in the references cited, *follow them* to ascertain if the original information has been accurately presented. It is always important to track down the bibliographic sources cited. You may find a reference to an article published in the *Journal on Sidewater's Syndrome,* only to find out that such a journal does not exist! Websites have been known to list bogus bibliographic sources like the "University of Santa Anita" for a variety of reasons, ranging from the legitimate to the frightening. (See footnote number 5 in this chapter). A trip to the library (either on foot or on-line) to verify bibliographic references, including how accurately the information was used, is crucial. REMEMBER: The reference can be real, but the information can still be misrepresented.

When no references are listed, you should E-mail the webweaver or author to find out the sources of the information posted. If you cannot verify accuracy, you are then relying on the credibility of the author or the sponsor. This is very risky when you are not familiar with either, and even riskier if they are not referenced by other credible sources. Glowing eyes in the back of the cave. . . .

Check out the accuracy of the information posted on the external links. Always follow external links and assess the quality of information. (By their links ye shall know them! Remember?) Authors and sponsors committed to content accuracy are cautious about the types of websites to which they choose to provide a link. Conscientious webweavers give you brief evaluations or annotations of their external links. For example, a small nonprofit homeless organization may post information on illiteracy rates and also provide a link to the Census Bureau for greater detail and verification of the summary information they post. It only takes about three minutes to do this when crafting a webpage.

If an external link takes you to a credible, well-known website with accurate information, check to see if there is reciprocity. Does the linked website have an external link taking you back to the original website you are evaluating? Such mutual links increase the likelihood that the accuracy of the information can be trusted.

TIP: Be very suspicious of websites with no links, especially when you would expect to find them because of the topic. Be *very* careful. You are probably on shaky ground.

Websites with Drama: Avoid the Unbelievable

Inflammatory, outrageous, or misleading statements are big warning signs that the information is very slanted and represents nothing more than a virtual propaganda soapbox. A website promising to teach adults with dyslexia to read twenty-five thousand words a minute in two weeks sounds outlandish. It is. Remember that you are looking for scholarly information that you can use as a professional social worker. If you read statements that appear unbelievable (make excessive claims, present facts out of context, or spout popular stereotypes), they probably are just that—unbelievable.

Secret solutions to social problems or medical cures known only to the owners of a website or their sponsors are always bogus. Most such websites are trying to persuade you to purchase their service or product. They pitch their websites to vulnerable individuals who are in a lot of pain (emotional or physical) and desperate for help. Instead of using facts to back up their claims, such websites often rely on glowing testimonials.

CASE STUDY EXAMPLE

Since Marian Slankowski told you that she might have dyslexia and that probably accounted for her difficulties in school as a child and her difficulties with reading today, you decide to search on-line for information about dyslexia and what resources are available to address individuals with this disability. At the "National Institute for Literacy" (http://novel.nifl.gov/nalld/R_P_Fink.htm), you find considerable information on illiteracy and learning disabilities, including an article by Dr. Rosalie Fink on her research on successful adults with dyslexia who have learned to read well. You scan the references Dr. Fink has cited and then search for the books and journal articles she has cited. You are pleased to discover these references all check out so that the information in this article appears to be accurate as well as current and written by someone with the expertise to write credibly about dyslexia.

You also find the story posted on this same website of a woman who was herself homeless and who learned to read as an adult. You bookmark this website to share this information later with Marian. You know that giving Marian hope that perhaps something could be done to help her develop the reading skills she needs for finding and keeping another job—even a better one—may be crucial. You know you will need to do more than just instill hope. You will have to be able to find assessment and remedial help for Marian as well. The credible websites that you have found on the Web that provide information on remedial programs are all attached to universities. You decide to contact the two universities in your area to find out if any such remedial programs are available.

TIP: When references lead you only to testimonials that "prove" a clinical approach, service, or product are effective, hit your favorite search tool and find another website. Do not buy that Brooklyn Bridge! It has already been sold to another gullible Web viewer!

DETERMINING OBJECTIVITY

You need information that is objective with a minimum of bias. Objective information is based upon facts that are verifiable. In contrast, opinions can range anywhere from thoughtful analysis of the facts to blatant propaganda unrelated to anything factual. The verifiable facts and the blatant propaganda are the easiest to spot on a website. The opinions require you to have a scientific background and an understanding of social work values so that you can make professional judgments regarding the quality of the opinion.

Since you cannot take what you find on a website at face value, you have to be able to read between the lines. Look for the assumptions underlying what you find, separating the fact from the opinions. Some websites clearly identify editorial comments, biases, and opinions. Unfortunately, many do not. It is therefore, extremely important to assess a website's **objectivity.**

Ignore the "Awards" and "Seals of Approval"

Websites often display seals of approval and awards from various external organizations that rate websites. Indeed, there actually are professional organizations that legitimately evaluate websites. Be wary. If you need to verify a seal or award, find the evaluating organization's website and completely review it.

There is no way for these organizations to rate all of the websites that can be found in cyberspace on a particular topic. As a result, most of these are awarded because the webweaver submitted them to the evaluative organization. Many webweavers do not do this and may be totally unaware of any evaluative organizations. As a result, the *absence of any seals or awards is meaningless.*

It is also very easy to swipe an award or seal off of one website and stick it on another. The images are only graphics files, and this process can take all of five minutes. In addition, unless the legitimate awarding organization is informed about a theft, there is no way to track down fraud. (If you were stealing the award or seal, would you tell 'em?) The only assurance that you have that an award theft has not occurred is to E-mail the evaluating organization and ask them about the specific website on which you found their seal.

Moreover, some of these evaluating organizations are not even interested in objectivity but only in the website's design. Just because it got an award for being pretty does not mean it is factual!

TIP: In addition to irrelevant and stolen awards and seals, beware of the phony! A clever webweaver can cook up a bogus "Seal of Planetary Approval" or "Best Website in the Known Universe" in about ten minutes.

Peer Review: The Ultimate Scrutiny

Peer-reviewed information represents scholarly work in contrast to personal or organizational information. While few journals post free-of-charge copies of their journals, you can often determine whether or not an article has been juried or not.[8] Reputable professional journals have established peer-review processes that are explained up front. They also identify the experts on their editorial review boards. For example, *Social Work Research* (http://www.nasw-press.org/publications/journals/research/research.html), published by the NASW, informs visitors that its articles undergo an anonymous review process in which three members of its editorial board and/or consulting editors read manuscripts submitted for publication. This is traditional peer review. When you encounter these or find them listed as references in other articles, you can be assured that an effort has been made to ensure that the information is objective, it is reasonably researched, and the methodology and assumptions are sound. The article must pass these standards for legitimate scholarly journal publication.

Professional organizations also publish expert opinions that are *not* intended as scholarly research but instead as summative observations and points of view. For example, Leon Ginsberg's "Show me the money: Eight observations on giving and soliciting funds," in *The National Networker for Social Work Managers* (http://www.socialworkmanager.org/ginsberg.htm), provides practice wisdom accrued from *decades* of experience. In cases such as this one, the nature of the hosting and sponsoring organization is helpful for assessing objectivity and accuracy, along with the author's earned reputation. As in the case of authority, check for supporting references if in doubt.

Do be aware that anyone can call their website a *journal*. The key is to look for a reputable and traceable sponsor, editorial board, and peer review process. In addition, just because a journal calls itself one does not mean that it is committed to publishing objective scientific articles. Some journals such as *Policy Review: The Journal of American Citizenship* (http://policyreview.com), published by the

---

[8]   While on-line free journals are fairly uncommon, some publishers are making back issues available on-line, a true gold mine!

Heritage Foundation, provide no information about a peer-review process or an editorial board. The mission of this journal, as clearly stated on its website, is one that supports conservative public policies, a limited government role, free enterprise, individual freedom, and a strong defense. These types of journals may be more invested in representing a particular ideology than presenting objective information. There are many across the political spectrum.

TIP: If information on the sponsor, peer-review process, editorial policies, *and* the reviewing editors is missing or suspect, or if the biases of the journal are not clearly stated, forget it! The cave is dark, and something is purring close by.

Put the Information in Its Context

When Web information is not peer reviewed, begin your own review process by putting the information in its context. If the information is posted on-line in the context of selling a product or service, expect the advertising to bias the information. If the Web author is affiliated with an organization that has a strong political or ideological point of view, expect the author to share this bias. Information found in the context of a commercial or political agenda should be viewed with suspicion until verified by other sources that do not have a stake in a product, service, or ideology. Also, if you find yourself at a website that is not clearly identifying itself contextually (the commercial or ideological agenda is disguised or buried five webpages away from the homepage), the real agenda is to sway your opinion, not to give factual information.

TIP: Responsible sponsors and authors present biases on or near the homepage. If you have to click and scroll forever to find a stated bias, the website is either deceptive or very poorly designed.

Watch for the pseudoscientific approach. Websites that just want to sway your opinion often resort to multisyllabic scientific jargon to appear objective. When the intended audience is not peer experts, you should be able to understand the text. If you encounter a website where everyone but a rocket scientist would be hard-pressed to follow the reasoning and you are sure it is not a website for rocket scientists, something is very wrong. The website is trying way too hard to impress you and, therefore, might very well be trying to deceive you.

TIP: If you cannot understand a website because of its dazzling scientific gibberish and befuddling complexities, it is probably frivolous, biased, or fraudulent. Go elsewhere.

Web authors with strong political or ideological opinions can be quite manipulative in their interpretation of the facts. They often disguise their opinions as facts. Compounding this is that you, too, have biases, both personal and professional. When you encounter a website that has information posted by a Web author or sponsor that holds the same values as yourself, you are especially prone to becoming subjective. For instance, if you personally believe in the merits of homeschooling, you will be inclined to accept uncritically Web information that reports in glowing terms the successes parents who homeschool can expect with their children, whether or not such reported successes are documented by research. In this situation, you must challenge yourself to make an effort to critically analyze the website's contents.

TIP: If you love the information you find on a website, identify what values you and the Web author have in common.

Repetition Is a Good Thing

One way that you can be assured that the information you have found on the Web is both objective and accurate is the frequency with which the same information is posted by multiple websites. Checking website information against what is posted on other credible websites is important. Consensus in and of itself does not guarantee objectivity or accuracy, but consensus particularly among those considered expert in a certain area does lend considerable weight to your placing confidence in the quality of the information you have found. Information that is reported on numerous websites is much more likely to be objective and accurate than information that you can find on only one website.

Critique the Methodology

In addition to searching for and finding information on the methodology, you need to critique what you find about the research methodology itself. You need to determine whether or not the study upon which the information is based was flawed and what its limitations are. As in all juried researched articles, look for specific methodological discussions and limitations to any findings.

Web authors committed to objectivity present reasoned conflicting research results or interpretations, at least in the citations. If conflicting viewpoints are not presented or referenced, you cannot count on objectivity. Fair presentation of a conflicting viewpoint is a reasonable expectation.

CASE STUDY EXAMPLE

The next day, you arranged for a volunteer to take the Slankowski family back to their apartment to get a change of clothes and some of the information and documentation that Marian needs to apply for unemployment compensation and LIHEAP. The volunteer reported that the apartment was too cold to be habitable and that, indeed, the electricity was disconnected. She also reported that Sophie communicated very little, taking direction only from Marian. She said that Sophie particularly seemed very confused and needed Marian to change her clothes when they returned to the shelter. Marian asked Florence to read some of the papers she thought she should bring back to the center, but Florence had difficulty being able to see clearly enough. Florence asked the volunteer to read some of the documents to her. The family returned when the shelter opened again.

That evening, you found a quiet spot to talk at greater length with the Slankowski family. You found using the tips on talking to those who are hard-of-hearing very helpful in communicating with Florence. Both Marian and her aunt reported that Sophie was very confused since coming to the shelter and that in the last year she could handle very little change in her routine. They both also said that Sophie was having a much harder time taking care of herself and that she communicated much less than she used to. When asked, Florence said that she was finding it very hard to help Sophie care for herself since she was not as strong as she used to be and her eyes were failing her. She was worried about how she would manage once Marian went back to work. Marian again brought up the pills that Sophie had been taking to make her "smarter." You knew that this family would definitely be in need of in-home services once Marian found gainful employment and the family either had heat again or was relocated to alternative housing that did.

Later that night, you returned to the website you had looked at earlier regarding the pills that Sophie had been taking. The website suggested that patients with Down's syndrome were at risk for Alzheimer's disease. You were very skeptical about this information since this website was pushing the use of these "smart" drugs and your research the night before had indicated that these "smart" drugs were not supported by the medical community. You decided to see if you could find more information at other websites. Your search efforts uncovered similar information at the "ARC" (http:thearc.org), the largest nonprofit organization that addresses the service and advocacy needs of the mentally retarded; the "Alzheimer's Research Forum" (http://www.alzforum.org); and the "National Library of Medicine" (http://www.nlm.nih.gov), which is operated by the National Institutes of Health. You found reported at these sites that persons with Down's syndrome do have a high incidence of Alzheimer's disease; Alzheimer's disease in individuals with Down's syndrome has an earlier onset than in the general population; and that early indicators are losses in communication and self-care abilities. All three websites referenced peer-reviewed literature that reported Alzheimer's disease in adults with Down's syndrome. You decided to talk to the family about what you had discovered and to encourage them to seek further medical attention for Sophie once the immediate heating and housing crisis is resolved.

TIP: Whenever you are presented with two opposing viewpoints of the same topic, stick with the one that is more credible based upon your assessment of the methodology, corroborating information, and the presentation of the information.

Summary

In working with the Slankowski family, you accessed many websites that provided you with valuable information to help in both assessing and intervening with this family. Web information assisted you in tracking down the following resources for this family:

- Information on unemployment compensation
- Information on applying for assistance with heating bills (LIHEAP)
- Information on in-home services for both Marian and Sophie Slankowski
- Information on Supplemental Security Income (SSI) for Sophie
- Information on the rights of renters
- Information on adult literacy classes
- Information on employment opportunities for Marian

You also were able to track down information that helped you communicate more effectively with Florence Slankowski since she was hard-of-hearing; and you were able to provide this family with medical information regarding vitamins and Alzheimer's disease, which assisted the family in making some decisions around Sophie's care and medical needs.

In addition to the direct services you provided the Slankowski family, you were able to track down information that would assist you in developing and funding the homeless shelter that employed you. These included

- Statistical data on both homelessness and the housing market in your county
- Statistical information on adult literacy
- Fund-raising and grant-writing opportunities
- Information on homelessness for community presentations
- Consultation resources for developing the shelter's program/services

All of these resources were readily available from the Web.

Evaluating information from the Web is the most critical task of all. Bad information in social work can lead to grim consequences. You must continually evaluate information. The nature of domain relationships is important, and different domains have varying dimensions of credibility. The nature of sponsorship for a website determines how professionally useful it is. Authorship is equally important. Website currency may, at times, be profoundly critical when clients' lives are at risk. The depth and breadth of a website—its scope—provide boundaries for understanding its intent and purpose. Accuracy and objectivity are vital because they are the hallmark of the professional practitioner.

Questions for Discussion

What kinds of Web information, if any, are OK to use without verifiable sources?

Do you believe you can really trust all government information from the Web? Why?

A friend finds a website touting a "miracle cure" that is "too new for science." What should you tell them?

You have found a website that professes to have scholarly backing for their medical products. You E-mail them, and they reply back that they would appreciate any scholarly medical citations you can provide them. What should you do?

Exercise 6A
Domain, Sponsorship, and Authorship

■ This is a computer exercise. You will need a Web-connected computer.

■ The purpose of this exercise is to sharpen your ability to trace the domain, sponsorship, authorship and webweaver in websites.

■ This work will carry over into the next exercise.

DIRECTIONS

A. Visit one *official* United States state or territory or Canadian province or territory website of your choice.

To do this, enter the URL as described in the section on Analyzing the Domain:

http://www.state. (the postal abbreviation) .us

If you want to visit United States territories:

Guam: http://www.gov.gu

Puerto Rico: http://fortaleza.govpr.org

The Virgin Islands: http://www.gov.vi

For Canadian provinces and territories, go to

http://www.info-canada.com/prov.html

Write the name and URL for the United States state or territory or Canadian province or territory:

Write the website name and URL: _____

B. Almost all state, provincial, and territorial websites have information and links to several or all of the following services: business/commerce, economic development, education, employment, and tourism.

Choose one of these services and write down the actual name or label for

the link: _____

(You can choose a social services link if one is available.)

Follow the link to the next website.

Observe: Has the *domain changed* in the Netsite/Address box? (Example: a *.gov* becomes *.org,* or a *.org* becomes a .edu.)

If no change has occurred, *keep following the path* for the issue (Example: "Education in Our State") *until the domain changes.*[9]

Write down the exact URL for the new, nonofficial website:

(You will need this for the next two exercises.)

URL: _____

---

[9]   The writers have not encountered an exception: inevitably you should find a boundary between the official and contracted realms. If you should not find it, then repeat this process using a different state, province, or territory.

How many different websites did you visit starting from the official state, province, or territory website and ending at the website with a new domain?

Number of websites from the official one to the new domain: _____

What does this number suggest about how much the state, province, or territory relies on consultants? Write one sentence.

Was a *disclaimer or notice* that you were leaving the official website(s) *available?*

___Yes ___No

If Yes, describe: _____

Why would this information be important to know? Write one sentence.

C. Examine this first nongovernmental website and *determine the actual sponsor.* Look by examining "FAQ/Frequently Asked Questions," "About Us," and similar links. From the information you gain:

Was this information available?　　　___Yes　　　___No

If Yes:

What is the name of the *sponsoring (or owning) organization?*

What contact information is provided? (E-mail? Snail-mail? Phones? Faxes?)

How does the sponsor describe themselves or their mission?
Describe in one sentence:

If the sponsor is an organization, are they nonprofit or for profit?
Nonprofit _____　　　For profit _____　　　Cannot determine _____

Is the website *title* deceptive in any way?

___Yes ___No
Describe in one sentence:

Do the website's title and mission support each other?

___Yes ___No

Describe in one sentence:

D. Look over the webpages for a *specific author credit* such as "This Webpage Designed by RazzelDazzel Websites" or "Mary Smith."

Was this information available? ___ Yes ___ No

If Yes: What is the name of the authoring firm or person?

What contact information is provided? (E-mail? Snail-mail? Phones? Faxes?)

If a specific individual is credited with authoring the information posted on the site, is background information provided somewhere on the website?

Yes No
___ ___

If Yes, does the author appear to have the expertise needed to write with authority about the topic?

Yes No
___ ___

Describe in one sentence:

If no information is provided, attempt to find background information on this individual by searching on the Web. Were you able to find any?

Describe your efforts in one sentence:

What information, if any, did you find?

Describe your results in one sentence:

E. Look over the webpages for a *specific webweaver credit* or E-mail link such as "Click here to send E-mail to Mary Smith." (This may be the same as in the author example, but you must answer No unless there is clear proof that the author and webweaver are the same person or firm.)
Was this information available?

___Yes ___No

If Yes: What is the name of the webweaver, or is it generic?

What contact information is provided? (E-mail? Snail-mail? Phones? Faxes?)

F. Circle your website's letter grade:

A = (1) Disclaimer and/or "Leaving website" notice is present, (2) clear sponsorship with contact information available, (3) clear authorship with contact information available, (4) clear webweaver present with contact information available.

B = All of the above except one element of the four is missing or incomplete.

C = All of the above but two elements of the four are missing or incomplete.

D = Only one element of the four is present in any respect.

F = No traceable information is present.

Exercise 6B
Currency

- This is a computer exercise. You will need a Web-connected computer.
- The purpose of this exercise is to sharpen your ability to analyze currency.
- This work will carry over into the next exercise.

DIRECTIONS

A. Go to the URL you recorded for the last exercise, the first nongovernmental website. (You may substitute any URL from your issue research if so directed.)

Write the website name and URL: _____

B. Look over the entire website for a specific notation about when it was created and/or modified.

Was this information available?

___ Yes   ___ No

If Yes:

What were the date(s) provided?

Creation date   _____

Modification date _____

C. What dates, if any, are included or referred to in the body of the text?

D. What does your work tell you about currency for this website?

Write one paragraph of three to five sentences.

Exercise 6C
Scope

■ This is a computer exercise. You will need a Web-connected computer.
■ The purpose of this exercise is to sharpen your ability to analyze scope.

DIRECTIONS

A. Go to the URL you recorded for the last exercise, the first nongovernmental website. (You may substitute any URL from your issue research if so directed.)

Write the website name and URL: _____

B. Peruse the contents of the website:

Is a table of contents, site map, or index provided?

___Yes ___No

Is an internal search engine provided?

___Yes ___No

C. Intuitively rate the *scope* of this website by putting an "x" on the line below:

Broad _____ Narrow

D. Intuitively rate the degree of *information depth* by putting an "x" on the line below:

Superficial depth _____ Considerable depth

E. Does the website have a clear specific time span (example: welfare statistics from 1981–1990)?

___Yes ___No

If Yes, what is it? _____

F. How specific is this website in terms of geography?
(Check only one category that is the most predominant.)

International _____

National _____

Regional _____

Local _____

Does not apply _____

G. How specialized is this website?

Intuitively rate the *degree of specialization* of this website by putting an "x" on the line below:

Generalist _____ Specialist

H. How technical is the language used?

Intuitively rate the *technical language* of this website by putting an "x" on the line below:

Very technical _____ Only lay terminology

I. Do you think this website offers information that would meet the needs of a social worker practicing in this field for five years or more?

___Yes ___No

Explain. Write one sentence:

Do you think this website would meet the needs of clients searching for information regarding a problem or concern?

___Yes ___No

Explain. Write one sentence:

Do you think this website would help a researcher looking for information on this subject?

___Yes ___No

Explain. Write one sentence:

Could you use this information for a presentation to clients, colleagues, or a community meeting?

___Yes ___No

Explain. Write one sentence:

J. Great expectations?

Review the mission or implicit purpose for this website. Does it fulfill any promises made? Put an "x" on the line below that shows your overall rating:

Very fulfilling _____ Very superficial

Explain. Write one paragraph of three to five sentences:

Exercise 6D
Accuracy

- This is a computer exercise. You will need a Web-connected computer.
- The purpose of this exercise is to sharpen your ability to analyze accuracy.

DIRECTIONS

A. Review the exercises you have done to date and select the one website you found the most intriguing concerning its accuracy. If you do not have one, then either continue with the public website from Exercise 6C or, with permission, conduct a search for a suitable website that interests you.

Write the website name and URL: _____

B. Thoroughly review this website. Based on your intuitive assessment, put an "x" inside the following triangle that represents your evaluation of the website's accuracy:

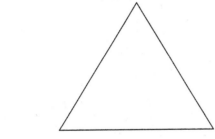

Factual Information

Clear Expert Opinion   Unsupported Opinion

What evidence have you found to support this choice?

Write one paragraph of three to five sentences:

C. Count the number of typos, misspellings, and grammatical errors in this website:

Number of typos _____

Number of misspellings: _____

Number of grammatical errors: _____

D. In your opinion, are any *factual errors* evident in the information posted?

Yes _____ No _____

If Yes, what are these errors?

E. In your opinion, is there any important *missing information* in the posted contents?

Yes _____ No _____

If Yes: Explain the nature of the missing information. Write one sentence:

Without this information, do you think a typical visitor would be mislead?

Yes _____ No _____

If Yes, in what way? Write one sentence:

If No, what assurances did you find that suggest the information is adequate? Write one sentence:

F. Are references or citations about the posted information available?

Yes _____ No _____

If Yes, are on-line links provided to references or citations?

Yes _____ No _____

If on-line links are available, *follow one of these links* and see if the information posted seems to accurately support the information from the website.

Name of linked reference: _____

Does the link support the provided information? Mark an "x" on the line to show your opinion:

Well supported _____ Not supported

If on-line links are not available but references are provided, see if you can verify the existence of one by going to any search engine, such as Hotbot or AltaVista, and searching for its title and/or the name of the author(s).

Describe your success or failure at finding the reference. Write one sentence.

G. Are conflicting viewpoints available either in the website's contents or in the list of references?

Available _____   Not available _____

H. Are external links to additional supporting resources provided?

Yes _____ No _____

If Yes:

Do the external links take you to websites that appear to have accurate information?

Yes _____ No _____

Are the links reciprocal/mutual?

Yes _____ No _____

If no links to additional supporting resources are provided, what should be added to the website in your opinion? Write one sentence.

I. Is any *dramatic language* found on the website?

Yes _____ No _____

If Yes, give an example:

Are any *excessive promises* made on the website?

Yes _____ No _____

If Yes, give an example:

Are *secret solutions or miracle cures* promoted at this website?

Yes _____ No _____
If yes, give an example:

Are *testimonials* given as evidence to back up any claims?

Yes _____ No _____
If yes, give an example:

J. Write a three-to-five-sentence paragraph that summarizes how trustworthy you think this website is:

Exercise 6E
Objectivity

■ This is a computer exercise. You will need a Web-connected computer.
■ The purpose of this exercise is to sharpen your ability to analyze objectivity.

DIRECTIONS

A. Review the exercises you have done to date and select the one website you found the most intriguing concerning its objectivity. If you have none, conduct a search for a suitable website that interests you.

Choose a website that either has or directly refers to a research article.

Write the website name and URL: _____

B. Does this website have any awards or seals of approval posted?

Yes _____ No _____

If Yes, can you find a website for this evaluating organization?

Yes _____ No _____

If Yes, what is the name and URL of the evaluating organization?

Write the website name and URL: _____

C Does the website post *statements of ideology, biases, and/or predominant values* on or near the homepage? (Check headers, FAQ, mission statements, and "About Us . . ." types of links.)

Yes _____ No _____

Describe any in one sentence:

If Yes, do these coincide with your own professional or personal values?

Check one:

Professional _____ Personal _____ Both _____

Neither _____

If No, write a paragraph of three to five sentences stating what you think *should* be posted on the website:

D. Is the context of the website easy or difficult to discern? (Is its purpose to give information? Provide explanations? Persuade?)

Describe in one sentence:

E. Is there a commercial agenda?

Yes _____ No _____

Describe any in one sentence:

F. Who is (are) the intended audience(s) for this website?

Describe in one or two sentences:

Would this website confuse the intended audience(s) with terminology beyond their understanding?

Yes _____ No _____

If Yes, give an example:

G. Is information on methodology presented either on the website itself or in the references that support the content on the webpage?

Yes _____ No _____

Describe any methodological discussion in one sentence:

Are limitations discussed?

Yes _____ No _____

Describe any provided limitations in one sentence:

Are conflicting viewpoints referenced in a fair and professional manner?

Yes _____ No _____

Describe any mentioned conflicts in one sentence:

Are any of the articles posted on the website or referenced in bibliographies *peer reviewed?*

Yes _____ No _____

(Note: If journal information cannot be found on the Web, a trip to the local public or university library (on foot or on-line) will be necessary to complete this part of the exercise.)

If Yes, is the peer-review process described?

Describe in one sentence:

Is information on the editorial board available?

Yes _____ No _____

Describe in one sentence:

Does the journal have a detectable or attributable bias?

Yes_____ No _____

If Yes, what is this bias?

Describe in one sentence:

If no references are available, *what journals should have been consulted?* Find one on-line or at the library that would be relevant to the subjects treated in the website. (Look for lists of "Journals in Print.")

Name (and URL if available): _____

J. Write a three-to-five-sentence paragraph that summarizes how objective you think this website really is.

Exercise 6F
Putting It All Together

■ This is a computer exercise. You will need a Web-connected computer.

■ The purpose of this exercise is to pull together the factors needed to evaluate most websites.

DIRECTIONS

A. Review the exercises you have done to date and select the one website you found the most intriguing or interesting. If you do not have one, conduct a search for a suitable website that interests you.

   Write the website name and URL: _____

B. Write a three-to-five-sentence paragraph describing why this website interests you:

C. Thoroughly review this website and write a one-to-three-sentence response for each of the following factors:

   Domain:

   Sponsorship:

   Authority:

Currency:

Scope:

Accuracy:

Objectivity:

References/Websites

Administration on Aging http://www.aoa.gov

Alzheimer's Research Forum http://www.alzforum.org

American Association of Kidney Patients http://www.aakp.org/aakpteam.html

ARC http:thearc.org

Bay Area Homelessness Program http://:thecity.sfsu.edy/~stewartd/welcome.html

Bryn Mawr College Graduate School of Social Work and Social Research http//www.brynmawr.edu/gsswsr/welfac-ak.html

Chicago Bar Association http://www.chicagobar.org/public/diallaw/28.html

Council of Nephrology Social Workers http://www.kidney.org

Georgia Developmental Disabilities Council http://www.ga-ddcouncil.org

Ginsberg, L. Show me the money: Eight observations on giving and soliciting funds *National Networker for Social Work Managers, The* http://www.socialworkmanager.org/ginsberg.htm

Henderson, John R. University of Santa Anita http://147.129.1.10/library/lib2/AIDSFACTS.html

Home Modification Action Project http://www.usc.edu/go/hmap/

Homes for the Homeless www.HomesfortheHomeless.com

Japan Council on Disability http://www.vcom.or.jp/project/jd/

Knowledge Exchange Network (KEN) http://www.mentalhealth.org

Libertarian.Org http://www.libertarian.org

LIHEAP http://www.commerce.state.il.us/dcca/FILES/COMM_DEV?LIHEA.HTM

Metropolitan Tenants Association http://www.cnt.org/~mto/mtphome.htm

Minnesota Center Against Violence and Abuse (MINCAVA) http://www.mincava.umn.edu/index.asp

National Alliance to End Homelessness http://www.endhomelessness.org

National Coalition for the Homeless http://nch.ari.net

National Institute for Literacy http://www.nifl.gov/newworld/

National Institute for Literacy (Dr. Fink section) http://novel.nifl.gov/nalld/R_P_Fink.htm

National Institute of Mental Health http://www.nimh.gov

National Law Center on Homelessness and Poverty http://www.nlchp.org

National Library of Medicine http://www.nlm.nih.gov

National Resource Center on Homelessness and Mental Illness http://www.prainc.com/nre/index.html

Open Group Books http://www.opengroup.com

Orphan Train Riders History http://www.hamilton.net/subscribers/hurd/index.html

Policy Review http://policyreview.com

Regional Task Force for the Homeless http://www.electriciti.com/homeless/home.htm

Social Work Research http://www.naswpress.org/publications/journals/research/research.html

Substance Abuse and Mental Health Services Administration
http://www.samsha.gov/cmhs/cmhs.htm

Survivor's Page, The http://207.194.73.24

Tederico's Page: Homelessness, Hitchhiking, Panhandling, and Homeless Programs
http://4homeless.hypermart.net

United States Census http://www.census.gov

Urban Institute http://www.urban.org

Wildcat Arizona Newspaper http://wildcat.arizona.edu/papers/90/85/04_2_m.html

Women and Performance: A Journal of Feminist Theory
http://www.echonyc.com/~women/

World Association of Persons with disAbilities http://www.wapd.org

World Socialist Website, The http://www.wsws.org/index.shtml

Additional Websites

Engle, M.
Olin Kroch Uris Libraries
Cornell University
Evaluating websites: Criteria and tools
http://www.library.cornell.edu/okuref/research/webeval.html

Grassian, E.
University of California Los Angeles Libraries
Thinking critically about World Wide Web resources
http://www.library.ucla.edu/libraries/college/instruct/web/critical.htm

Kirk, E.
Milton S. Eisenhower Library
Understanding and decoding URLs
http://milton.mse.jhu.edu:8001/research/education/url.html

Tillman, H.
Babson College
Evaluating quality on the net http://www.tiac.net/users/hope/findqual.html

University of Washington Libraries (No name credit)
Other sites about evaluating information on the Internet
http://weber.u.washington.edu/~libr560/NETEVAL/resources.html

PART III

BEYOND THE SURF

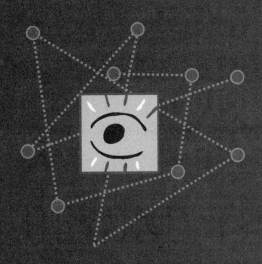

Designing Websites
for Agencies and Practice

Right now . . .

   . . . Agencies are developing webpages.

   . . . Practitioners are offering therapy on-line.

   . . . Information and referral are going radical.

   . . . The revolution is being digitized.

CHAPTER OVERVIEW

First, let's talk about a major myth: Creating webpages is easy, just a little more challenging than using your word processor. The fact is that while anyone can whip up a personal webpage showing their family, their vacation, and their cat Fluffy, creating professionally acceptable websites can be a very daunting endeavor. It is a hard-learned skill. It can be very rewarding. This chapter covers:

- It Is Not a Brochure!
- Resources You Need to Develop a Website
- The Design Process
- Determining the Website Mission, Objectives, and Audience
- Initial Webpage and Navigation Planning
- Defining the Nature of the Website
- Design Specifics for the Nonprofit Agency Website
- Getting the Website On-Line

This chapter is intended to give you a *taste* of the issues that are involved in developing a viable Web presence for your agency, practicum placement, or yourself. Creating real websites requires commitments and significant resources far beyond this book.

IT IS NOT A BROCHURE!

IMAGINE	You are working for a domestic violence shelter called "My Cousin's House." In addition to offering temporary crisis-related shelter, the agency provides counseling, job and education/GED classes, and legal assistance. The agency is staffed by six employees with varying skills and degrees. It also depends on volunteers and students for many services and tasks.

Your director tells you that the board of directors has decided that the agency needs a website. They really do not have any specific ideas other than "something like the brochure" you produced two years ago. They think that the time has come when the agency could really use one. The only mandate they have given is to develop a website that reflects all of the services and needs for the agency.

If you have been following this book chapter by chapter, you have already acquired a lot of sophistication at critically using the Web for your studies and practice. You may have even formed some ideas about what the preceding website could look like. What should you do?

Webpages are different from print media in countless ways. It is vital to remember that *you are not just producing a simple brochure* for your agency, even if that is what the board of directors thinks! A website is a much more formal resource that your colleagues, clients, funders, and other people in the community are going to access for many reasons and with many agendas. As a result, the design of your webpage is a very serious undertaking and will require a significant commitment of resources. It requires courage, too, because agency webpages are really cutting edge and there are few precedents out there to guide you.

In addition, the politics of inclusion are vital! Some executive directors and their boards know full well that creating a Web presence is a major step in out-reaching people, promoting services, engaging in information and referral, and in support funding. They may recognize that developing a website is a serious undertaking. It requires major initial support and significant ongoing maintenance. Others may be far more naïve and think they can solve the problem for a few hundred dollars and a little time commandeered from a few employees "in their spare time." Maybe they believe in the Tooth Fairy, too. The reality is that developing a professionally acceptable website is a significant task; and once it has been brought on-line, the website must be continually maintained and updated either by someone in the agency or an outside contractor.

At the very outset, the agency needs to be aware of the actual politics, expenses, and time commitments needed to provide a professional Web presence. This needs to be stressed at *all* levels in the organization. And the agency needs to be encouraged to continue! It is possible to "solve" the problem by getting some consultant to slap together some barely interactive webpages that somewhat represent the agency. These, unfortunately, are usually on a par with telephone book advertisements. The authors believe this approach is counterproductive. This "solution" neglects the incredible potential that websites can extend to the community, consumers, and professionals. Thus, the agency needs to be aware of the commitments, have a vision of the benefits a professional website can provide, and be encouraged to proceed.

While we have written this chapter from the single-agency perspective in which a social worker does most of the work, the idea of collaboration between agencies may well be worth investigating. Efficiencies are possible when several agencies pool their resources to create a common website or to host all of their websites together.[1] Pooling efforts will not be lost on potential funders because collaboration is often rewarded when agencies work together. Consider sharing efforts and resources if you are beginning to seriously develop an actual Web presence for your agency. This approach may be very helpful if developing the website means committing more resources than the individual agency has available.

Cause-related marketing should also be investigated. For example, a large pharmaceutical company that makes products used by your consumers may be interested in subsidizing your website or hosting it on its server. Corporate funders recognize websites as marketing tools and may be willing to provide support if it promotes their firm or products. Look for possible underwriters that have a direct affinity with your type of agency. Grants, too, are worth investigating.

Consider developing a Web presence over time through the agency's regular budgetary process. After all, your agency annually budgets for telephones and office equipment. Why should developing and maintaining a Web presence be any different? The more integrated the website is, with regular ongoing budgets and other standard operating procedures, the more the website will become integral with the agency.

We also think there is merit in seeking voluntary help, especially for technical assistance. Website development entails considerable technical expertise, and there may be very skilled people in your area who are willing to volunteer their services. If a friend of a board member says "I'll design a website for you," then pursue this lead. While you will certainly want to actively control the design process and contents that go into the website, voluntary expertise can not be undervalued.

Finally, generate support for the website from three constituencies: the board of directors, the staff, and your consumers. The board may be able to make arrangements for a national organization to host your website, or find other resources. Staff, especially those who do not use the Web and may not even have desk access, should be included because they, too, will benefit from a well-developed agency website. Consumer input is vital, especially if you intend to help people find and use services to a wider extent than present. None of this will happen unless there is complete support for a professional Web presence from all three constituencies. The design, use, and upkeep of the website must be completely integrated into the organization's culture for it to succeed.

RESOURCES YOU NEED TO DEVELOP A WEBSITE

You need empowerment and technical resources to actually create a real website for an agency.

---

[1] For an example of collaboration, visit the "Indiana Youth Services Association" (http://www.indysb.org).

Empowerment

You need to be empowered to proceed and not on any "spare-time" basis unless the agency is willing to wait a few years. This means getting the authority to conduct design workshops and to consult with relevant people during the design process. *This will take quite a bit of your time.* You are going to need political supervision, too, unless you *are* the director or are into taking high risks. When you link to another website, be it another agency, somebody's meta-list, or perhaps an information website, it is a political act. This can occasionally lead to negative consequences and nasty embarrassments. You need to have a peer-review process to build ownership of the website and prevent this. You also need the freedom to spend time at the computer and become proficient with using the hypertext markup language (html) software and then time to actually create the working webpages. This, too, is often a long process.[2]

If you do not get this permission, we recommend that you refuse to proceed. Do not walk away from the assignment. *Run!* If you volunteer without support, you can count on burning out from lost weekends, political flack, and the naysayers who do not have the foggiest idea about the Web but have plenty of uninformed opinions. You will regret it. Ditto your supervisors. Ultimately, you risk providing a disservice to the clients and the agency.

Let's presume that you are willing to learn how to do most of the actual work. We will also presume that you have persuaded your supervisor and others higher up that this will not be any "spare-time" project. As a result, you have the permissions and commitments to devote time to conduct workshops on design and to actually acquire the html skills needed to create the website. Great! You are about to begin a most challenging, fascinating, and rewarding task.

Technical Resources

To generate the actual webpages, you need a reasonably sophisticated personal computer. We do not have any preferences or recommendations, and chances are good that you will be stuck with what is available anyway. What you need to know follows:

Generally, html files are not much larger than regular word-processed ones. This means that if you have a personal computer that handles word processing, you should do just fine. However, if you are going to also be creating graphics files—and most websites have plenty of them—then you may need quite a bit of working memory (RAM), maybe sixty-four kilobytes if possible. This is because graphics files are quite large. In addition, while not mandatory, having a "zip-drive" type of large capacity storage device is extremely helpful. This is because these disks hold about one hundred megabytes, approximately the equivalent of seventy floppy disks. This is wonderful for manipulating graphics files when creating the website. This often makes it possible to store the complete website on one disk, making backup very easy. These types of storage drives generally cost about 150 dollars, and 10 to 15 dollars per disk. They are well worth the investment.

---

[2]　An alternative to this is to use a consultant, especially after the planning process. Once you have a coherent plan for the website, you can certainly collaborate with a technical helper as long as the agency is willing to foot the bill.

You also need html-writing software. There are two different types:

■ Programs that write the actual html script. These are like the very first word-processing programs, where you had to type in commands to capitalize letters and words, make indents and breaks, and so on.

■ Programs that are WYSIWYG (pronounced *wizzywig,* meaning *what you see is what you get*). These are graphic and do not require much knowledge about the actual html language, if any.

Each object on a webpage, be it a picture or block of text, is controlled by a specific computer code written in html. Pioneers who have spent tedious hours mastering html insist that you need to learn it, code command by arcane code command. The writers believe that the WYSIWYG software approach is quite effective and, with rare exception, all that you really need as a beginner. No one uses the first versions of word processors from the 1980s anymore, and no one should feel that they have to learn the obsolescent approach of writing tedious commands when WYSIWYG editors are far easier, give you much faster results, and, yes, produce a better website. Resources for finding various webpage-creating programs are provided at the end of this chapter. Both the Netscape Communicator and the Microsoft Internet Explorer browsers have optional—free—WYSIWYG editors that work quite well. Other commercial ones can be well worth the investment, because these may offer more sophisticated design and management features.

Unless you plan to produce a webpage that is totally void of logos, pictures, and icons, you need to be able to design and manipulate graphics files, too. Graphics editors are necessary because you have to edit and modify the graphic information you put onto the page so it proportionally fits and downloads at less than a glacial rate. As an alternative, you can contract this work out if there is money in the budget. This book is too limited to go into these programs in depth, but you *will* need to choose a graphics editor and learn how to use it. Resources for finding a graphics editor are provided at the end of this chapter, and the reference readings can be most informative. Do remember that manipulating graphics files is a real skill that will take you time to learn. Very simple graphics, however, such as fancy titles or the occasional photo of the agency, are certainly possible for most beginning webweavers.

If you plan on slick and fancy webpages for a very sophisticated audience (e.g., teenagers with an MTV outlook on life), you are going to need additional software abilities such as being able to write JAVA SCRIPT and JAVA files. JAVA SCRIPT drives the scrolling lines of text that appear on webpages, and JAVA drives the animations. These are different languages from each other and from html. The same goes for virtual reality markup language (vrml) and other features that can really get complex. We cannot go into detail in this book, but do be aware that other programs may be needed. Consider hiring a consultant to do this for you. After all, you are a social worker, not a programmer! Writing in html with a WYSIWYG editor is fairly easy. Writing JAVA or vrml is a much more demanding skill.

Extra resources include mentors, classes, websites, and books. Find a mentor or consultant who has been through the experience of crafting a website. If available, your local college or university may have helpful classes or workshops you can take. Get your agency to pay for them. In addition, there are some very good websites available for designing webpages; we have provided a beginning list at the end of this chapter. Most libraries and bookstores have books on the subject, too, and some of these can be most helpful.

Why Bother?

As you will learn in the next few pages, developing a professional website can be a fairly complex activity. Yet, the marketplace is full of consultants and commercial firms who are quite eager to develop websites. It is very tempting to turn over design and production to them. We strongly urge you not to do so! The authors think it is important for you to actually design the website with input from throughout the agency. This should be done almost totally without technical consultants, at least in the beginning. Commercial firms often do not have the vaguest notion about what social service agencies do, much less social workers. Worse yet, some actually think they do understand us when they do not. As a result, using an outside firm to design and deliver a nonprofit website risks getting a poor takeoff of a commercial design. Some design firms are excellent, but many produce websites with barely adequate information and abysmal interactivity. No one is going to come up with a better website than you, your colleagues, and the consumers.

There are several areas where consultants can be invaluable. First, a technical consultant can help write an efficient html program that is compatible with many browsers and platforms, but *only after you and your group have agreed on a design.* This person or firm should help you get the website up on the server with minimal problems, but *only after you and your group have agreed on a design.* A graphics artist can be invaluable for professionally developing design, colors, and pictorial layouts, but *only after you and your group have agreed on a design.* Finally, if you really do need the virtual reality, game quality interaction, and other bells and whistles, you also need the help of a technical consultant to design and create them, but *only after you and your group have agreed on a design.* Did we mention that you should do this only when you and your group have agreed on a design within the agency?

Finally, once the website is up and available, strive to keep its control and management within the agency. An *outside* webweaver will not be connected to the agency or understand specific details that may be quite important. Updates will take forever. Vital feedback will be lost. The best solution is to develop the ongoing maintenance expertise within the agency and use consultants only when technical support is needed. This may not be possible if you are working with a consortium of agencies but, if alone, consider developing at least the rudimentary skills associated with designing the website. This includes using a basic html editor and perhaps a graphics editor—if not you, then someone in the agency. When someone has the basic skills "in house," then editing and updating the website are quick and painless. Training clerical staff to support the website or at least to regularly monitor it and report problems is within the reach of most agencies and well worth the investment.

THE DESIGN PROCESS

Do Not Reinvent Monopoly!

You have seen several hundred webpages by now and have developed specific preferences for what you do and do not like. When faced with a new challenge, we often fall back on what is familiar and comfortable. In short, *we often mimic what we like.* Yet, developing an agency webpage is a very different process because you usually need to please several different "publics" or constituencies as much as you can, and these are sometimes antagonistic. Teens have very different Web expectations than older adults, for example. As a result, while using pages you have liked in the past as models can be helpful, *do not begin by mimicking them* in terms of design, layout, or content. This is like the person who wants to invent a new game and begins by using Monopoly as their model. What do they get? Inferior Monopoly! Really great webpages from other sources can certainly give you great ideas, but think about them only after you have generated a sound website design of your own. We strongly urge the process described in the next pages because different groups of visitors require different designs and levels of webpage sophistication.

Your Goals Are Simple

Delight your visitors! You want people to really enjoy visiting your site. You want them to bookmark it. You want them to pass your URL on to others because the website looks so great and has such important information!

Provide absolute clarity and transparency! Every webpage needs to be so clear that anyone with a minimum of Web experience and literacy can understand its purpose, scope, and identity.

Allow complete user control! People do not like getting lost in the Bermuda Triangle of a poorly designed website: They leave. You want every user to be able to get anywhere they like within your website with extreme ease. Whenever possible, scrolling should be an option, not a necessity.

Complete accuracy, good scholarship, and currency are imperative. A professional webpage for an agency is different from a personal or glamour page. It will be used by clients, colleagues, and many others. This is where using an advisory group during the design process really pays off!

The process described in the following sections will be very helpful as you proceed from a general notion of what is needed to the actual creation of a specific plan for your website.

DETERMINING THE WEBSITE MISSION, OBJECTIVES, AND AUDIENCE

We suggest that you form a committee, advisory group, task force, or blue-ribbon panel (whatever you want to call it) and *take them through a formal process workshop*—issue by issue, item by item, decision by decision, argument by argument. Include representatives from every possible constituency, such as clients, management, colleagues, and the board of directors if the executive director so decides.

The point is simple: The more input you can get into the initial design phase, the more likely you will get a satisfactory plan that is workable for everyone! When done, present it to your executive director and/or the board of directors plus everyone who has had a part in the design process. Throw a party, put the initial designs up on the walls, and invite everyone in the agency to review them and give feedback. Enthusiasm and ownership grow through inclusion and consultation! OK, this is basic macropractice 101. It *really* works!

Mission and Objectives

Decide on the actual mission for developing a Web presence. Just what do you want the website to accomplish? Are you going to directly help the clients who come to your agency? What about clients who may never set foot through the door but use the website? Are you going to use the website to outreach? Are you going to offer resources to colleagues? What about colleagues from ancillary areas or professions? Are you creating public relations visibility for your services? Do you want potential funders to really like what you are doing? Are you going to use access records of the number of hits for measuring outcomes and evaluating interests? Just what is the overall mission for the website, and what are the goals?

In the chapter's opening scenario, you read:

> You are working for a domestic violence shelter called "My Cousin's House." In addition to offering temporary crisis-related shelter, the agency provides counseling, job and education/GED classes, and legal assistance. The agency is staffed by about six employees with varying skills and degrees. It also depends on volunteers for many services and tasks.

This gives you a basic idea about what the website could contain. From this, you convene the advisory group. Compel them to debate and create a *short* list of objectives. You want a list of maybe five or less different objectives, because anything longer could get extraordinarily complex. Press them to make each objective as mutually exclusive from the others as possible. When objectives are mutually exclusive, you can address them individually during the design process. Taking "My Cousin's House" as an example, the advisory group may have decided that the objectives of the "My Cousin's House" website are to

- Clearly state the mission and organizational information.
- Provide emergency shelter information.
- List services information.
- Clarify volunteer and student recruitment policies.
- Provide resource links on domestic violence.

Does this imply that you should have five separate sections or clusters of webpages for your website and that your homepage should control this? *You bet it does!*

Audience

Who is the audience for each specific objective? This is where Web designers can really screw up! One size definitely does not fit all! Separate objectives often have separate constituencies with very different needs. The key to designing an effective website is to define the exact dimensions of needs for each constituency or group of users around each objective and to incorporate them into the exact design of each specific webpage. Think through what audiences the website will target. Who is the agency hoping will visit their website? Possible constituencies include agency clients, volunteers, agency employees, board members, funding bodies, politicians and their aides, donors, other professionals, and individuals seeking information regarding the population or issues addressed by the agency. *Define the specific constituency for each individual objective and then design the corresponding webpages on a tailored basis! Once again, one size does not fit all!*

CASE STUDY EXAMPLE

Taking the five objectives for the "My Cousin's House" website, you can now have your advisory group ponder the various audiences, their needs, and their characteristics for every different dimension that you will have on the website. Create new advisory groups at this time for each specific objective if this process works better. Consider the following design factors:

■ What, exactly, are the *contents* that must be included for each objective? Get ready to make lists!

■ How *literate* is this audience? Are they professionals with college educations? Are high-school "pushouts" who can barely read going to need this information?

■ How *technically sophisticated* are they? Will most users have some familiarity with the Web? Will there be "newbies" who are likely to get confused? What are the advantages and limitations to getting "fancy"? What navigation and linkage issues may be present or unusual?

■ What differing *abilities* should be addressed? What visual issues for users who are partially sighted should be taken into consideration? What audio helps might be warranted? Should you have companion pages in other languages?[3] Are people under unusual stress?

Have your advisory group(s) look at each of the objectives in these terms. Then convert each objective and its specific contents into *menu pages,* the first level of website organization beyond the homepage. Let's examine what each of the five menu pages could contain from the design groups for "My Cousin's House":

1. Mission, history, organizational information about "My Cousin's House" menu page

   ■ *Contents:* Users should have access to sponsorship and authorship information about the agency. This section will provide the basic information about the agency that is usually included in newsletters, reports, grants, and brochures. Our mission statement will be included, along with our history, staffing information, and a basic description of funding. Graphics of the agency and maybe a "virtual tour," would be good.

   ■ *Literacy:* This needs to be written for any typical consumer. The prose should be plain and simple.

   ■ *Technical:* No major problems. Include a "for more information . . ." link to the office staff.

   ■ *Abilities:* Text should be large and have a good level of contrast. Optional audio file availability.

2. Emergency shelter information menu page

   ■ *Contents:* This section must clearly tell clients how to contact us in an emergency. This part should be on the homepage at the very top just below the agency logo. At minimum, it should have our phone numbers, including the 800 number. Transportation

---

3 For a spiffy example of a website that supports multiple languages, check out Alateen: http://www.Al-Anon-Alateen.org

directions are needed. Bus routes are to be included.[4] Add disability access information: Text-Telephone/TTY for hearing, speech, vision, and mobility considerations.

- *Literacy:* Needs to be cast in basic writing and supported by graphics that a five-year-old child can understand. Kids call us for help!

- *Technical:* Links must be very obvious and simple. Have a very simple digital audiorecording that is redundant with the visual information. Make E-mail reply available and clearly marked.

- *Abilities:* This part must be designed for people under a great deal of stress. Include vital information in audio form that is easy to play. Also, TTY information is mandatory.

3. Services information menu page

- *Contents:* Information about the counseling, advocacy, and other services should be described. List descriptions for every different service we provide. Leave room to add new ones!

- *Literacy:* This needs to be written for any typical consumer. The prose should be plain and simple.

- *Technical:* Typical internal navigation. Either have each service on a separate page or put them all into one large document with navigation built in so people can easily skip around.

- *Abilities:* Text should be large and have a good level of contrast. Optional audio file availability.

4. Volunteer and student recruitment menu page

- *Contents:* The website should assist in recruiting volunteers and students. Information about volunteering. Include sections for social work, nursing, physical and occupational therapy, law student, psychology, medicine, education and management interns/field practica requirements. Provide specific contact information. Also provide conditions, expectations, and perks.

- *Literacy:* This needs to be written for any typical volunteer at the high-school-student level or above. The prose should be plain and simple.

- *Technical:* Have a "forms" section for initial inquiry for more information. This part directly E-mails to the volunteer coordinator.

- *Abilities:* Text should be large and have a good level of contrast. Optional audio file availability.

5. Links to resources on domestic violence menu page

- *Contents:* Resources for clients and professionals should be made available through a list of links to other agencies and services within the community, plus national-level resources.

- *Literacy:* This needs to be written for any typical consumer. The prose should be plain and simple.

---

4 From a practice standpoint, if this is a shelter for domestic violence victims, then you may not want to include specific location information because perpetrators can find the shelter.

- *Technical:* Links to websites. Have an E-mail reply so people can report bad links.
- *Abilities:* Text should be large and have a good level of contrast. Optional audio file availability.

By addressing the content, literacy, technical, and ability dimensions for each objective, a much more fine-grained vision of what the website should provide emerges.

WHO IS NOT ESPECIALLY WELCOME?   Finally, it is very helpful to decide on just for whom the website is *not* intended! One of the key mistakes in webpage design is trying to please every potential person who hits the website instead of tailoring the webpages to the target audience. This is a boundary issue, is it not? Consider whether there are any significant audiences who can be overlooked or avoided. For example, are you working with alleged perpetrators? If not, do not design the website with their needs in mind. At minimum, define the boundary issue of who is *not* the audience.

GET READY TO PLAN! When you have finished specifying the content, literacy, technical, and ability dimensions, copy the requirements for each menu page onto a separate piece of paper.

INITIAL WEBPAGE AND NAVIGATION PLANNING

If your group has carefully specified the details of what is needed for very specific constituencies by each objective, you now have menu pages that describe your website. Assume that one master page on the website will hold descriptions and links to all of the menu pages such as the five just described for "My Cousin's House." This is the homepage! In addition, while you may not know the exact number of other webpages needed just yet, we have discretely defined the different sections that are going to be covered within the website. From the "My Cousin's House" example, we know that the (1) homepage will link to different menu pages including (2) mission, (3) emergency, (4) services, (5) volunteers, and (6) resources. This means having at least six sections to the website. We can now make a preliminary **sitemap** for the website by simply laying out the separate webpages we have designated on a large sheet of newsprint (Figure 7-1). The *homepage* in the diagram's center permits linkages with all of the satellite *menu pages*.

Next, we need to decide on the internal navigation links between the menu pages. We can draw in the *beginning patterns for links* between the homepage and five menu pages by using arrows to show the direction that the links take (Figure 7-2).

In general, it is safe to presume that all of the different sections within the website should link to each other in some fashion. It is important to consider exceptions. In "My Cousin's House," let's presume that your advisory group decided not to let visitors who are in the Emergency menu page go anywhere else within the website except back to the homepage. The reason to limit internal links from the Emergency menu page is that when visitors really need emergency information they are highly stressed and possibly new to the Web. The very people who need services the most might easily get lost and frustrated. Thus, this website's internal linkages can be described as rather comprehensive with limits on the Emergency section.

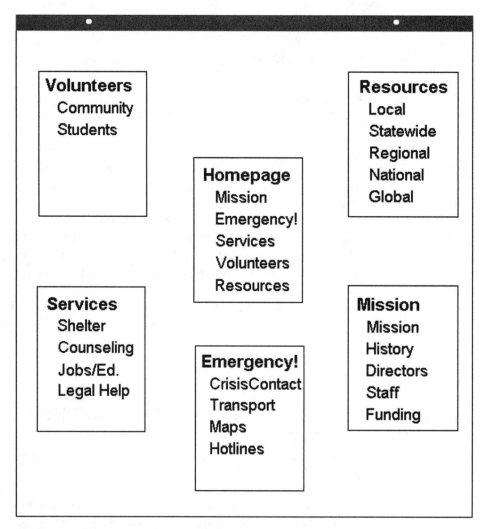

FIGURE 7-1 A preliminary sitemap with menu pages for "My Cousin's House."

The arrows in Figure 7-2 show where the main internal navigation links will be programmed into the website between the homepage and the menu pages. Note how the arrows are more limited for the Emergency menu page.

Next, think about the implications for basic navigation. The figure implies that people in need of services can go directly to the Services section from the homepage. These visitors may be the clients the agency wants to serve and perhaps the occasional colleague browsing for information. When visitors change their minds and want information on volunteering, mission, or resources, they can easily go to these sections. Yet, a visitor who has selected the Emergency choice will only be able to get to these other places by returning through the homepage of the website.

REFLECT: Is this what you want? What other combinations are possible or desirable? If your group has gotten this far, now is a good time to touch base with the executive director and/or the board of directors, revise as needed, and proceed. Inclusion at this juncture makes the next part of the process easier.

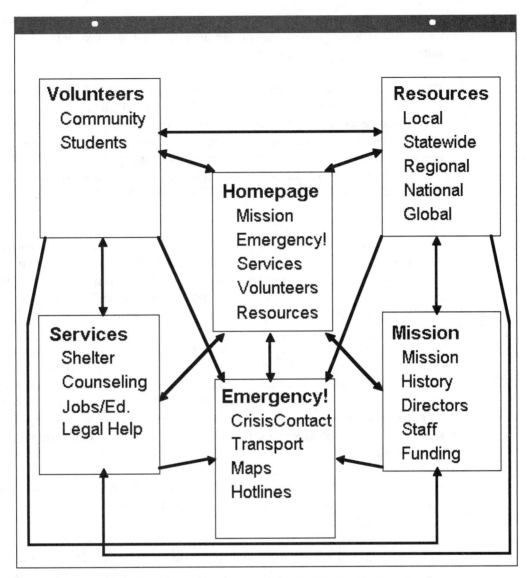

FIGURE 7-2 Internal linkages/navigation between menu pages for "My Cousin's House."

Add the Actual Webpage Specifications!

To continue with the diagram, we now know the nature of information that will be in each section of the website. We can now plan for specific webpages beyond the homepage and menu pages. One technique we have found useful at this stage is to take the homepage/menu page plan just described, put it on a large sheet of newsprint, and use sticky notes to represent each planned webpage. This way, you can easily move the notes around if you decide to move webpages or explore different patterns of links and navigation for the website as a whole. To do this, you are going to need to specify the title, file name, audience, text contents, graphics, internal and external links, and special technical requirements for each webpage; so use the largest sticky notes possible. Each webpage should contain a different concept or idea. Decide what is needed for each webpage and gather the information, making sure each supports the overall website's theme. If possible, try to limit each webpage to one concept or issue. On each sticky note, write the following specific information.

TITLE   Create an *obvious* title for each menu page and webpage. This will go into the Title box at the top of the browser, and these will really help visitors know where they are within the website. First, give each menu page a specific title that clearly describes its contents, such as "About 'My Cousin's House'" and "Emergency Services." As new pages are added to the plan, give them transparent titles too. For example, you could title the mission statement webpage "The Mission of 'My Cousin's House.'" Most browsers can display up to forty characters in the title at the top of the browser window.

FILE NAME   Next, you need to add file names. Create a system for *naming individual webpage files by menu pages* if possible. You can then tell at a glance where you are within the website and, if it can be transparent enough, so can your visitors.[5] By convention, the file name for the homepage is usually "index," and homepages are usually called "index.htm" or "index.html." The rest are up for grabs! Start by clearly labeling the menu pages.

For example, if every file in the menu page describing "My Cousin's House" relates to the mission of the agency, then this "missions" section could have all files begin with the letters "ms-," an abbreviation. The file name for the webpage containing the mission statement could thus be called "ms-state.htm." The important point is to create a system for naming individual webfiles in a way that makes sense to you and your colleagues. This will make subsequent design and maintenance much easier.

AUDIENCE   Describe the specific audience segment for whom the specific webpage is intended. For example, you might write "All visitors: clients, students, professionals, others."

TEXT   Briefly describe the text that will appear on the webpage. If you are importing text from other sources, such as a brochure file with the agency's mission statement, then jot down the name of the file and its location. The less text you have to enter by hand, the better! Decide on what information will be posted on this agency's website. Information about the agency will need to be collected from written documents and based on discussions with the advisors. The text must address the needs of the audience selected and fit with the overall theme. For example, you might write: "Use the new mission statement adopted by the board of directors last winter. Available at c:\publish\brochure.doc on the central office computer."

---

[5]   While most contemporary operating systems (e.g., Microsoft Windows or MAC-OS) will let you use longer file names. We suggest that you stick with the old DOS-*based eight-character file name plus three-character suffix* system, because you can count on its being displayed without being abbreviated (e.g., filename.htm). You cannot use different suffixes (e.g., *.doc*) because you *must* use *.htm* or *.html* as the suffix for the file's name. (The nature of the server determines which suffix you use. In general, *.htm* is used for IBM-type servers and *.html* is more common for Mac ones.) The browser will not work if you use any other type of suffix.

GRAPHICS   Decide on the images, icons, and logos that *support* the theme of the website and the function for which they are being employed. For instance, an image of a senior citizen would not support the theme of a shelter that serves younger people, and vice versa. A teddy bear icon that links the visitor to a list of the agency's board of directors would be confusing. What does a teddy bear have to do with the agency's board of directors or with the agency's mission/purpose? Icons should include images that visually echo and explain the link. Plan for any graphics that should appear on the webpage. If you are incorporating the agency's logo somewhere, then make note of it. EXAMPLE: "Include a front-shot picture of the agency and a collage of all the employees." Call the graphics files "agency.gif" and "staff.gif." Include the "cousin.gif" logo. *This is a great way to develop your list of graphics for later creation.*

INTERNAL NAVIGATION   Note the anticipated internal navigation links to other pages. For example, almost every webpage should have a "Go To . . ." ability. Optional communications links should also be specified, such as automated E-mail to the webweaver or a specific person or office in the agency for more information. EXAMPLE: "Menu page should link with all other menu pages plus the homepage." Include "E-mail to webweaver" option.

EXTERNAL NAVIGATION   Specify navigation links out of the website to other places. EXAMPLE: In the resources menu page, "Use the list of local resources being prepared by the I & R (information and referral) people. Name the file 'rs-local.htm.' Use the list of national resources being prepared by (name of employee). Name the file 'rs-natnl.htm.' Be certain to include MINCAVA http://www.mincava. umn.edu."[6]

TECHNICAL FEATURES   Flag any technically unusual elements that should be on the webpage. Note any fancy features you need such as animations or JAVA SCRIPT banners scooting along the bottom. EXAMPLE: In the Emergency section, "Make a digital recording of basic emergency contact information that will be triggered by a large, plain, clearly marked button. Tentative title for this file is 'emergent.wav.' (The .wav suffix is a common one for digitized audio files.)"

Put all of this specific webpage information on a large sticky note and place it on the newsprint near its menu page. An example of a sticky note for an individual webpage might look like the one in Figure 7-3.[7]

Add the specific webpages, one per sticky note, to the newsprint. Place each individual note/webpage close to the most relevant menu page (Figure 7-4). The advantage to doing this with newsprint and sticky notes is that you can still have flexibility in the design process if revisions are required.

You now have a very crowded piece of newsprint with a lot of sticky notes stuck all over it. It may look a little ratty, but *you also have a wonderfully helpful overall plan for building your website!* Spend some time reviewing this plan with the advisors to be certain that the design is what everyone wants. Try putting your

---

[6]   MINCAVA, by the way, is an actual resource. It is a superb clearinghouse for information on domestic violence.

[7]   If you can find one, use a typewriter for the sticky-notes! Old technology still has its place!

Webpage Title: Mission of My Cousin's House

File Name: ms-state.htm

Audience: All visitors: clients, student, professionals, others.

Text: Use the mission statement adopted by the board last winter. Available at c:\publish\brochure.doc on the central office computer.

Graphics: Include a front-shot picture of the agency and a collage of all the employees. Call the files "agency.gif" and "staff.gif." Add logo.

Internal Links: Go to all other menu pages and index: Index.htm, em-menu.htm, vl-menu.htm, sv-menu.htm, rs-menu.htm.

External Links: None

Technical: Include "welcome.wav" digital audio file. Also include an E-mail reply ability to the clerical office.

FIGURE 7-3 A typical sticky note describing an individual webpage.

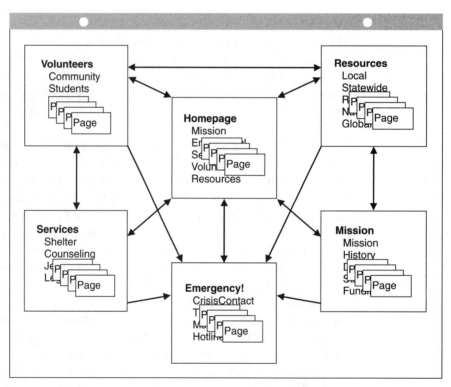

FIGURE 7-4 The overall plan for the website "My Cousin's House."

finger on each "webpage" and, following the described links, imagine what it will be like when visitors click to other pages. Show your work to the constituencies who have helped to design it. Revise as needed so that the plan becomes as clear as possible, and reflects all of the contents that have been specified. Then try the plan out on new people who have not been in the design process. Revise again! Once done, copy it!

DEFINING THE NATURE OF THE WEBSITE

Congratulations! you now have a very clear idea of just "What?" will be going on the website. Now the question becomes "How should it look?" Designing print and Web publications is as much a profession as social work. People go to college, study it for years, and then spend an awesome time practicing it! We are not going to attempt to give you a crash course in all of the thousands of choices you need to consider when "publishing" the webpage—such as layout, text positioning, proximity relationships, typeface choices, white space use, graphics layout, text-size ratios, justification choices, or color balance—though some of the resource books and websites at the end of this chapter do address these issues. We are, however, going to call your attention to some basic design issues and questions you and your team are going to have to consider as you begin to translate your concepts from ideas to real webpages.

Technical Help

Getting technical help during this phase of webpage design is very important. We recommend three sources. First, *graphic designers* can be of immense help as consultants. Consider using them and paying them what they are worth, especially if you want your website to reflect a professional presence and coherent visual theme. At minimum, ask them to help you design a basic format or template for your webpages. If you are in a larger agency, a consortium of agencies, or on a college campus, you may have free access to professional graphic designers with Web experience. Use them as resources! If you have specified the exact number and nature of graphics during the planning process, you should be able to get fairly specific estimates for consulting costs.

A second source for help is *the Web itself*, and there are several dimensions to this. While we advise against mimicking pages you like, do spend some time looking at them (and the ones you find abysmal too!) for the features within them that work well or make you want to exit. *Put yourself in the visitor's seat and choose features that are workable for each menu page's primary visitors.* You may want something rather pretty and generic for the homepage, but you do not want to scare, lose, or confuse that five-year-old who is in the Emergency section! Good resources for Web design are *on the Web!* We provide a few URLs at the back of this chapter, but consider searching for more because new examples and resources emerge every day.

Third, *read.* Most public libraries and bookstores have books on designing webpages. Acquire a few select books and master them. A good strategy is to review what your library has, and then buy your own copies for reference. We suggest that you only choose books with very recent publication dates because Web design books quickly get out of date. A basic list is provided at the end of this chapter.

As you begin to actually design the specific webpages, keep the following concepts in mind. First, you are going to need a coherent visual theme that will orient visitors and provide visual continuity. People need to know when they are in your website and when they are somewhere else because browsers make jumping around so easy. This suggests a rather uniform and predictable layout for most of the webpages, typefaces, color schemes, art work, and other major visual cues. Next, you need to think about how Web savvy your audience is. This too directly shapes the theme and "look" of the website. Finally, you should plan for the different types of computers and browsers that are currently available. People use vastly different systems that produce very different visual results. Each of these three factors plays a critical role in how the webpages should look and interact with visitors.

Choose a Theme

Decide on an overall visual and textual theme for the website and stick to this theme throughout the design and construction process. The theme should complement the goals for the website and the agency as a whole. If you are offering shelter, you may want to choose subdued pastels and muted colors that are tranquil, not jarring and garish. You may want to use an informal and inviting typeface such as Comic Sans Serif or an Arial instead of a more formal Times Roman or other serif typefaces. When considering theme, it is important to focus on what is unique about the agency. If several agencies provide services to children in the area, what is unique about your particular agency and its services? These should be reflected in the overall theme. The nature of your audience is going to determine the actual look for each page.

At the risk of fostering a generation of hopelessly uniform websites, the authors recommend the following. Remember the How to "See" a Webpage discussion in Chapter 2? Follow this basic layout with three distinct parts to each webpage:

- *Header*

  Put logos and at least the name of the agency at the top! *Do this on every single page.* Make the logo visually largest for the homepage/index page, scaled down in the menu pages, and even smaller in the subsequent ones. *The goal is to maintain visual continuity.* The reason for this is that if you have a visual graphic such as a logo, and if you repeat it consistently, then users will automatically know they are in the website and will not get easily confused. At minimum, put the name of the agency at the top of every webpage. If the webpage is going to be considerably long, perhaps more than two complete screens, then also consider adding an internal navigation bar or table in the header so people will not have to scroll to jump around within the website.

- *Middle/Body*

  Put the principle title/nature of the webpage at the top of this section just below the header or navigation. You want people to know what they will find on the webpage without hunting and scrolling. Strive to keep the body as short as possible, especially if it is the homepage or a menu page. Avoid making people scroll for more than two or three screens, and do not make them scroll at all for the homepage. When this is unavoidable, such as in a long list of resources or a large body of text, then periodically add internal navigation in the page such as "Return to the top of the page" links. This is technically very easy to do and well worth the effort because it adds to the visitor's comfort.[8]

---

[8] One exception is the document text. If you are making large documents or forms available on the website and expect people to make prints of their own, then do not add the periodic navigation within the document's text. This will just get in the way. An alternative is to provide large documents in both the html and text versions with an accompanying link for downloading the textfile. A button with a "Click here to download a textfile" caption is quite helpful. This type of programming is not difficult.

Clearly label all resource and navigation links in the body. "More goodies here!" types of buttons really do not belong on professional webpages for adults. Spell out what the links will do. Do not make your visitors guess. And do not just list the URL to another site. Instead, provide at least the name of the website the link will follow and a short sentence or key words describing it. The more your visitors know where they can go without guessing, the happier they are going to be.

■ *Footer*
The footer is where you tell about your authorship, sponsorship, and legitimacy as an organization. Post revision dates. At a minimum, include the agency name and address plus telephone numbers and an E-mail return link for the webweaver. Include city, county, state, *and country!* Think internationally: Someone in Israel or Italy may not know that *Indiana* is in the United States. (There are people in Indiana who have serious doubts, too.) Be thorough: Put contact information on *every single webpage* throughout the website!

Be certain to put internal website navigation links in the footer. These can repeat the same ones you put into the header, or you can add more to this part of the document if you like.

Level of Visitor Sophistication

Just how comfortably can your users access and get around the Web? What kind of supports will they have? Are they likely to have friends or relatives in a network, or are they more likely to be alone? Just how much experience does a typical user bring to your website? There is no high ground in this issue. You will always have some visitors who are far more capable than you or your colleagues. Others are just beginning, and yours will be among the very first webpages they see. They may not even know enough to scroll or click the mouse.

As a rough gauge for how technically complex you may get, consider the following. If users are generally accessing your website from home, they have gone to the trouble of buying a computer, connecting it, and subscribing to an ISP service. This *generally* means that they—or someone in their personal network—have at least a modest competence. As a result, the webpages can be fairly sophisticated. Instead, if a substantial amount of users are accessing from public workstations such as libraries, schools, or other nonhome places, they may be inexperienced and have less available help. The website needs to be technically simpler in these circumstances.

Technical Limitations

Not all computers are created equal. Some people may labor on older computers with limited monitors, while others have stunning multimedia systems at their disposal. Worse yet, some people will be using commercial connections that download text and graphics in a flash while others still connect with that s-l-o-w 14,400-baud modem or worse! Furthermore, not all browsers are created equal. Graphics often appear different on various browsers, even on the same machine with the same monitor. Backgrounds can vary from the innocuous to the irritating with different browsers. Finally, the options the user has chosen impose space, size, and feature limitations on the amount of visible space one can see without resorting to scrolling. All of these factors impose serious design considerations. *We recommend the following:*

- Use features common to all major browsers. The time may come when commercial browser developers have features available only on their own idiosyncratic browsers. To counter this potential, do not use browser-specific features. Instead, keep to the universal html features available on all common browsers.

- Test! Revise! Test again! Revise again! Be certain to test with multiple platforms such as IBM and Mac. Try multiple browsers and different versions of them. Disable the graphics features and test the text-only appearance, too. REMEMBER: What may appear really snazzy on one platform and browser may appear wretched on another.

DESIGN SPECIFICS FOR THE NONPROFIT AGENCY WEBSITE

Standards and conventions for agency websites have not yet emerged. Some agency websites are marvelously transparent, full of information, easy to navigate, and clearly credible. Others leave great room for doubt. Some very wealthy agencies have really crummy websites, while some very poor ones are really splendid, and *vice versa*. There is no high ground. We offer the following ideas toward building professional websites that clients and social workers can use and trust. Each of these issues should be considered, even if they are not included in the final website.

Agency Information

AGENCY'S MISSION/PURPOSE/GOALS   Provide clear details about the agency's mission, purpose, and goals. Include auspices. Echo previous mission statements, and update these on the website when necessary.

AGENCY'S HISTORY   Give a succinct history of the agency. Pictures are very helpful for conveying a sense of welcome, evolution, and development. Just be certain you have written permissions for any graphics.

BOARD OF DIRECTORS/COMMITTEES   List the current members of the agency's governing board and its committees. List who the officers are and their terms of service, including expiration dates. Provide institutional affiliations and even links if available. Also give contact information such as E-mail addresses or other means for contacting board and committee members *if* they approve of this.

LEGAL INFORMATION RELATED TO THE AGENCY'S EXPERTISE   Include specific and accurate information on agency accreditations, memberships, certifications, and licensures relevant to service provisions, regulatory entities, and the law. When possible, link to these organizations.

INFORMATION ABOUT THE ORGANIZATION'S NETWORK AND AFFILIATIONS   Provide descriptions of formal linkages, affiliations, and common referral patterns between the organization and other agencies. Is your agency a United Way member? Show it!

If your agency is part of a consortium or national association, then let consumers know it. It is also advisable to provide linkages to affiliated organizations if warranted.

STAFF INFORMATION   Depending on the comfort level and agency personnel policies, consider listing staff by name and job title or service. Be certain to include relevant degrees, licenses, certifications, and other important credentials. Be certain that staff members are aware of this and have given their approval. Provide limited contact information if appropriate, such as pilot phone numbers or E-mail addresses. *Avoid providing any personal information about any employee or volunteer—ever!*

Services

SERVICES AVAILABLE   List all specific services the agency provides, and perhaps give a brief—one-or-two-sentence—description. Avoid jargon and acronyms! Does "CD" mean "chemical dependency" or "community development"?

ELIGIBILITY AND GEOGRAPHICAL ISSUES Clearly state any eligibility requirements. If the agency is in a specific catchment area, provide a map so people can decide if they want to visit or contact another agency closer to home. Be as inclusive and clear as possible, because people often do not understand the nuances of eligibility issues and catchment policies.

APPLICATION PROCEDURES   Just what do people need to do to apply for services? What do they need to bring with them? Is an appointment necessary? Birth or vaccination certificates? Referrals from other agencies? Clearly explain application procedures, requirements, and routines.

DIRECT APPLICATION FOR SERVICES   If appropriate, you can create electronic forms that can be filled out. These can be E-mailed or printed out and brought to the agency. E-mail scheduling of appointments is sometimes possible, too.

AGENCY FEES   Post any current fee schedules or provide a description of any sliding-scale fee policies, third party reimbursement participation, and other dimensions of payment for services.

Additional Important Issues

The following issues constitute the major "whats" that should be included somewhere on the website. The results will be most worthwhile, especially if careful attention to details is followed.

VOLUNTEER AND STUDENT OPPORTUNITIES   If you do not advertise volunteer opportunities, other agencies will. Guess who will get them? Student recruitment via the Web is also a possibility. Some professional programs actively encourage their students to find their own placements, and the Web is one place to start!

FUND-RAISING AND FUNDING INFORMATION   Describe annual fund-raising events and activities. Remember to list those recent grants, donations, endowments, and bequests! Potential funders are lurking out there! While you are at it, discuss in-kind contributions too if your agency accepts them, or at least state any policies on receiving donations such as clothing, food, or other salient goods and services. Put all of this in a specific place within the website so people do not feel nagged from every page.

JOB LISTINGS   Vacancies? Post them!

UPCOMING EVENTS   Depending on need, provide an organizational calendar for the weekly, monthly, or even the yearly listing of major events for the agency. Consider including local events in the neighborhood or community. When possible, link to them.

ANNOUNCEMENTS (PRESS RELEASES)   Interesting news? Take that press release, edit it, and post it!

EXTERNAL LINKS RELATED TO THE AGENCY'S MISSION   Again: "By their links ye shall know them." Consider providing at least a minimum of external links that support the agency's mission. Foster cooperation and collaboration!

CONTACT INFORMATION   One more time! Be absolutely certain to include relevant contact information including maps and directions, phone and fax numbers, E-mail addresses, and snail-mail, too! Nothing is more discouraging than visiting a really engaging website and then discovering you have not the foggiest idea where the agency is located or how to contact them. Every webpage should contain the name of a contact person, including their E-mail address. This allows visitors to know who and how to contact someone for further information or to give the agency feedback on the website.

Audience Issues

The following suggestions will help aid the design and development process.

ADD ADVOCACY   Consider using your agency website for political advocacy. An agency's website can be used to empower clients, colleagues, and supporters for your agency's mission. Post agency positions on relevant issues, publicize lobbying efforts, and encourage visitors to your website to take action on proposed legislation and the development of administrative regulations related to legislation already approved. In addition, website visitors can be provided an opportunity to join mailing lists and listservs that will permit your agency to target interested constituencies with important legislative alerts via E-mail. Such mailing lists can also be used, of course, to provide other information of interest to supporters as well.

PAY ATTENTION TO DISABILITY ISSUES   Always presume that people with verbal, visual, and/or cognitive challenges will need to view and use your website. Protocols for this are just beginning to emerge. Resources for making disability-friendly webpages are provided at the back of this chapter.

PAY ATTENTION TO DIVERSITY ISSUES   Should you create a mirror website in another language? Are your graphics culturally acceptable to people from different backgrounds? What may the colors mean? Is the language gender neutral? While it is impossible to completely forecast how the website will be received by all diverse peoples, at least consider specific issues that are salient for the specific populations served.

INCLUDE WARNINGS AND DISCLAIMERS   Think through whether or not the information posted could be offensive to some visitors. Post a warning for visitors to this effect. This allows visitors to decide whether or not they want to view specific pages within a website. For instance, a shelter dealing with child abuse may post photos of abused children that would be offensive to some readers. A large, red, flashing WARNING notice prevents unwittingly offending visitors and demonstrates respect.

CONSIDER USING FAQ PAGES   Lists of "Frequently Asked Questions" or FAQs can help visitors quickly zero in on specific information. Consider the most commonly asked questions related to a particular content area. For instance, a FAQ for potential agency volunteers may include questions and their answers such as:

- *How can I get information on volunteer opportunities?* "Persons interested in volunteering at 'My Cousin's House' can contact the volunteer coordinator, Mary Smith, at 123 555-0000 or by E-mailing her at . . ."

- *Why is a background check required of all agency volunteers?* " 'My Cousin's House' is legally required to conduct a background check on all volunteers having contact with our agency clients. Background checks serve as a protection for . . ."

- *How many hours a week are volunteers expected to work?* "Volunteers at 'My Cousin's House' are asked to contribute from three to fifteen hours per . . ."

IDENTIFY CREATION/MODIFICATION DATES   Let visitors know when the website was created and when it was last updated. Creation and last-modified dates should be listed on all webpage footers.

INCLUDE E-MAIL FEEDBACK   E-mail links are very important because they permit the visitor to easily E-mail the agency with a question, idea, or a request. This E-mail function also permits the individual who maintains the agency webpage to quickly get feedback on the website itself. Often, a viewer will spot an error, make a suggestion on the website's design, or suggest additional information for inclusion. This feedback can lead to improvement in the design of the website. Programming these in the actual html script is very easy. All you have to do is code the link for the E-mail address in the format: "mailto:e-mail@address." Substitute the actual E-mail address for the "e-mail@address" part. There really is no excuse not to build this into every webpage!

Look and Layout

Now that you have an idea of what you should include, think about how you want your website to look.

EXAMINE SIMILAR WEBSITES   Look at other, similar websites serving similar populations or issues. Remember that companion websites can be found anywhere in the country or perhaps the world. What elements of other sites are appealing and what elements are annoying? Consider incorporating *your own custom version* of elements that appeal or work well, and avoid those that do not. Learning from what already is on the Web will be of great assistance in the design effort once you have a clear idea about your own website's requirements. You also want to know this so you do not inadvertently make a copycat version of another website.

Avoid duplicating information that is already available on other websites. If a well known website on domestic violence has a good posted list of diagnostic criteria for abuse, it may make much more sense to link to the website rather than reposting the same information. Do investigate how often updates take place and what maintenance goes into the resource website before linking to it. As a matter of professional courtesy, notify collegial websites that you are linking to them.

PAY SPECIAL ATTENTION TO THAT HOMEPAGE!   The homepage is the most important part of an agency's website. Since this is the first webpage a visitor views, it is vital that it be attractively designed with a brief description of its purpose and a good table of contents. An unattractive or visually boring homepage will discourage many visitors from exploring the agency's website further. The brief description of the agency's purpose in mounting the website tells the visitor what they can expect. Is the site designed to educate the public about the agency or a particular problem, to recruit financial supporters, to assist professionals making referrals, or to provide support to a specific population? A good table of contents outlines what is available and answers these questions. Again, no scrolling if possible!

HONOR COPYRIGHT RESTRICTIONS   Always check to see if an image or information being posted on a website is copyrighted material. While information and images free of copyright restrictions can be found on the Web, verify this before using any "public domain" materials by contacting the website host or webweaver. Materials restricted by copyright may still be used, provided permission has been obtained. Exchange snail-mail addresses and get all permissions in writing!

CAREFULLY HIGHLIGHT SIGNIFICANT INFORMATION   The most important information should be displayed at the top of each webpage. Not all visitors will scroll down an entire webpage. Some people will not know that they *should* scroll down a larger webpage. Important information should also be highlighted on a page using headings and formats that help it stand out. Avoid burying important ideas in lengthy text. If something is really vital, then surround it with white space.

Divide text into short paragraphs. Lengthy paragraphs are harder to read. Emphasize only the most important contents. Emphasizing too much material with headings, flashing graphics, or bolded or italicized lettering results in nothing standing out. Do not overkill!

BE CAREFUL ABOUT PAGE LENGTH   Visitors may give up scrolling through pages that are longer than three screens. Also, webpages that offer only a half-screen of information should probably be combined with information from another webpage. Adjust your webpage lengths for balance.

USE HEADINGS   Use headings to assist visitors in spotting the information they are most interested in reading. Compare the layout between the two homepages in Figure 7-5. Why is the left better?

USE "UNDER CONSTRUCTION" LABELS SPARINGLY   Many visitors find "Under Construction" labels and icons annoying. Avoid putting pages on the Web that have nothing but "Under Construction" labels on them. It frustrates visitors to go to a page that contains no information. If "Under Construction" labels are used at all, they should be used sparingly and combined with an announcement that additional information will soon be available. They should not be found on every webpage and should not be posted eternally on a website. Little is more embarrassing than to see an "Under Construction" notice and then discover the "last modified" date in the footer reads "1995."

USE COLORS PURPOSEFULLY   Choose colors carefully. A nice green that looks beautiful when displayed on one browser can take a sickening turn when viewed on another

My Cousin's House
Homeville, Illinois
"Taking Families Off the Streets"
 	
Our Mission
  Goals for 2001
  History of My Cousin's House
  Families We Serve
  The Homeless in Homeville
 	
Our Services
  Emergency Housing Program
  Counseling
  Jobs/GED
  Legal Help
  Skills Classes
 	
Resources
  Emergency help
  Local agencies
  National advocacy
	My Cousin's House
	Homeville, Illinois
	"Taking Families Off the Streets"
	Our Mission, Services, Resources
	  Goals for 2001
	  History of My Cousin's House
	  Families We Serve
	  The Homeless in Homeville
	  Emergency Housing Program
	  Counseling
	  Jobs/GED
	  Legal Help
	  Skills Classes
	  Emergency help
	  Local agencies
	  National advocacy

FIGURE 7-5 Why is the left homepage better?

browser. If the agency has a color scheme associated with its logo, brochure, or even its building exterior, you may want to highlight that color on the website. The "Little Red Door Cancer Agency" in Indianapolis provides a great example of color use (http://www.littlereddoor.org). A Web designer who loves purple may have to forego their favorite color if designing a website for a Girl Scouts of America chapter. Color coordination is also really helpful!

Keep in mind that individual webpages within a website should be tied together by common logos and colors. Do not switch color schemes drastically from webpage to webpage. For example, if the Mission webpage is done in greens, do not switch to oranges on the Volunteer page and pinks on the Services page without good reason. Visitors may get confused and wonder if they are still at the same website. As an alternative, you can also create a scheme for color coding various webpages. If you do this, be certain to be consistent and always incorporate one visual element such as the logo into each page so people know they are still in your website.

BE CONSERVATIVE WITH BACKGROUNDS   Many types of backgrounds can be used for webpages. Plain colors can be easily programmed, and fancy ones with subtle pictures or patterns are possible, too. The color you choose may look pitiful when viewed from another browser, so test backgrounds on multiple machines. Be consistent in the use of background colors throughout a website. Background colors and graphics visually remind the visitor that they have remained in the agency's website. Also, many backgrounds can be found or created using a small graphic and repeating it across the entire screen. If you create a unique custom background for the website by repeating a small image, make sure that the background image does not have visible edges or seams or it may be very distractive. Avoid images where the end result is a background that is so visually busy that it appears to have a life of its own. Smaller is usually better when it comes to backgrounds since large background images increase the amount of time it takes for a page to appear on a screen. Backgrounds should also not overwhelm a webpage making it difficult for the reader to focus on the printed information. Backgrounds should remain just what they are: backgrounds.

INCREASE INTEREST WITH IMAGES   Images can make an agency website so much more interesting and inviting. Children's art work could be displayed on the "My Cousin's House" website. Photographs of the agency, its staff, and programming activities can give the potential client a sense of the agency prior to their first visit, making the visit easier and less intimidating. In addition, complex concepts often can be easily explained using graphics such as maps, diagrams, or an organizational chart. Be selective in choosing any image or graphic to be incorporated into a webpage's design. Good images serve a specific function and do not just clutter up the webpage. Transfer speed also needs to be considered in image selection. Large graphics take longer to bring up on a screen, and, since most visitors will wait only ten to fifteen seconds to view a website, it is important to use only fast-downloading images. REMEMBER: Some people disable the graphics ability for the browser when they surf just to speed up the downloading time, so do not depend on just graphics for conveying information!

After putting in the time and work necessary to design a website, it makes no sense to lose a visitor's interest and risk the likelihood of their premature departure. Downloading speed for graphics can often be increased by two tricks. First, graphics can be compressed into smaller files that download faster, and visual quality may not be especially compromised when this is done correctly. Second, graphics do not have to be huge to be effective. As a rough rule of thumb, never use a graphic larger than a quarter of a screen.

There are many sources for images. These include the following.

Clip Art   Copyright-free clip art is included with many word-processing programs or as separate commercial packages. The image for the webpage must be in either a .gif or .jpg format. If converting commercial clip art from word-processing to Web use, check copyright restrictions and usage limitations first.

Scanned Images   Images can be scanned into .gif or .jpg files and then placed on the agency's webpage. This is one way to include an agency's logo and photographs on the website. When scanning images, it is important to make sure that copyright restrictions are followed.

Web Images   You can use several of the major search engines to find graphics clearinghouses. Make sure you comply with copyright restrictions or licensing fees.

Creating Images   Two approaches are possible. First, graphics programs can be used to create your own icons, fancy types, and edited images. Creating a specific image gives the freedom to design a website that is unique to the agency. This approach also avoids copyright problems. Professional graphics programs can be purchased, and the names for several are provided at the end of the chapter. Do remember that these programs require time, practice, and skill to master.

An alternative, especially for photographs, is to use a digital camera. While expensive, these are often within the financial reach of the agency. Consider budgeting and acquiring one for agency use. In addition, some digital cameras can be used to copy existing photographs and artwork, making scanning unnecessary. *Always pay attention to liability and copyright issues with graphics. At minimum, photographs that include identifiable clients should never be used. Use posed pictures with models instead, and still get signed releases!*

GO EASY ON THE ANIMATIONS AND MOVING FIGURES   Many public-domain moving figures or graphics (usually known as "animated .gifs") can be found on the Web and incorporated into the design of an agency's website. These include cute thumbtacks that change color, colorful bars, dancing cartoons, and many other visually engaging works. Yet, the more moving parts that exist on a webpage, the more potential there is for distracting the visitor from the most important part of the webpage's message. Restrict yourself to one moving graphic per screen, if any, to avoid overwhelming the visitor. Choose moving graphics purposefully by taking into consideration the overall theme and purpose of the website.

Links and Navigation

INCORPORATE CLEAR NAVIGATIONAL TOOLS ON EACH WEBPAGE   Creating good navigational tools on each webpage is very important if the visitor is going to be able to move around the website easily. Navigational tools should permit the visitor to move both farther into the website and also back to earlier webpages that have been explored. At minimum, include navigational tools in the footer of each webpage that will allow the visitor to return to the homepage of the site, and to link to the most relevant other webpages. For large websites, this means that the visitor's needs must be considered when designing navigational tools since internal links to every webpage cannot be included in the footer of each webpage.

EXAMPLE: A visitor viewing a large child welfare agency website may be interested in becoming a foster parent. The visitor should always be able to explore further information about the agency's foster parent program when viewing any one foster care related webpage *without going back to the homepage.* If the agency has the following foster care webpages—(1) a description of the foster care program; (2) a FAQ page for prospective foster parents; (3) general descriptions of children needing foster homes (minus identifying information and pictures, of course!); (4) a foster care application and screening procedures page; and (5) a foster care training page—it would be important for the visitor to be able to access any of these pages no matter which foster care webpage they had up on their screen. They probably would not need a link to a "day-care licensing" webpage or other departments. They would, of course, be able to get to the "day-care licensing" department by going back to the homepage.

If a single webpage is very long, navigational tools within that page can be very important. Visitors often do not want to have to scroll through a long webpage to find what they are looking for. It is best with long pages to include navigational links in both the header and the footer, with internal links within the individual page as well.

PAY ATTENTION TO HOW LINKS ARE PRESENTED   Be descriptive. Always use words or phrases that describe each link. Avoid general phrases like "Click Here." Also watch the colors of the links. Most webweavers highlight links using the color

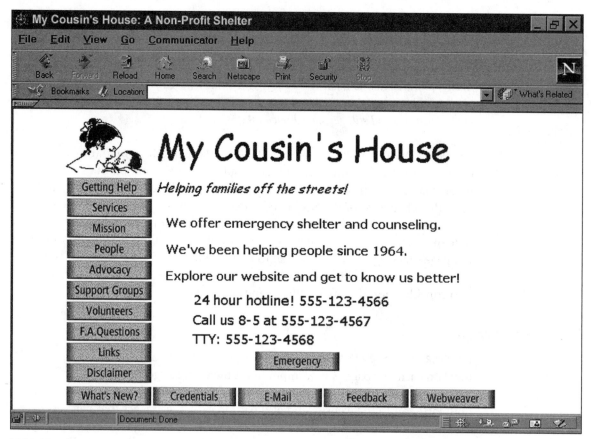

FIGURE 7-6 Eventually you will get there!

blue, the common default value. Visitors have come to expect that *if the text is blue it contains a link*. Web-editing software, however, often gives the ability to change this default link color. Alter the default link colors only if needed to make a web-page more navigable.

EXAMINE THE QUALITY OF ALL EXTERNAL LINKS Always be *fully* familiar with any externally linked sites. Make sure that these external links lead to relevant and quality sites with information that supports your website's goals and mission. Periodically check back to be certain that the website continues to work and present the same information. If an external link is not clearly identifiable from the website's name, an annotated comment can be most helpful in assisting the visitor in determining whether or not to pursue it. A single sentence such as "This website shows all of the domestic violence centers for the state" or even a couple of words such as "More statewide shelters" can be extremely helpful.

USE LINK MENUS Display internal links in a menu format such as a small table or bar, particularly if many links are being provided or if you are only providing links between menu pages. Consider having the same link menu in both the header and footer, especially if the webpage has two or more screens of content.

INCLUDE TEXT DESCRIPTIONS WITH GRAPHIC LINKS Always include a text description with graphics used as links. It may be hard for the visitor to determine where a graphic will take them. Never assume that a graphic alone will be self-apparent to the visitor. Remember: People may have their graphics viewing abilities turned off or may not understand the meaning of the picture or icon. Does a graphic of a pencil and paper link you to sending E-mail notes, a word-processing feature, or maybe a list? Without a label, many graphics are ambiguous.

Proofread

Finally, proofread all webpages before they are put up for public viewing. Avoid embarrassing the agency by carefully checking spelling and grammar. Mistakes devalue the agency's credibility. Use more than one proofreader!

GETTING THE WEBSITE ON-LINE

While this chapter is intended to give you a taste of website design, some readers may want to seriously begin the Web-planning process. If you are among these fortunate individuals, you have several additional technical requirements that need to be solved in order to actually put up a website.

You will need a server computer. This is a dedicated and very robust computer that generally runs twenty-four hours a day, day in and day out, with multiple user access abilities. You will also need the gizmos and widgets associated with the care and feeding of this expensive machine. Server choices are well beyond the scope of this book, but it is important to know that this is an expensive investment that the agency may need to consider.

You will need an Internet connection. Direct Internet access connections cost in the thousands of dollars and are usually well beyond the resources of most agencies. This problem can be solved by contracting with a commercial ISP. There are many firms that do this. While it usually costs more, your agency can often get a "virtual domain" URL that is quite transparent for users. For example, a typical, cheap ISP-supported URL might look like

> **http://www.gibberish.com/somewhere.out.there/finally/your-agency.org**

while a "virtual domain" URL would look like

> **http://your-agency.org**

The extra expense is well worth the additional fees, especially if your visitors are new to the Web.

Depending on what you contract for, the ISP firm may furnish you with space on *their* server, making the preceding requirements go away. ISPs will often take care of other vexing issues such as registering your URL with appropriate domain regulators, search engines, and databases. This makes access possible for many human service organizations. As an alternative, some commercial firms may be willing to let your agency "guest" on their system. This is a nifty problem for your board of directors to solve. Just be certain to *get as stable a URL as possible*, one likely to last a few years. This way, you can print the URL in brochures, newsletters, and stationery with confidence.

Afraid someone already is using the URL you want? The "Network Solutions InternNIC" organization provides domain name registration for the domains .com, .net, .org, and .edu. Their website has a custom database that allows you to look up URLs for these domains and find out if they are in use or not, along with additional information. Their URL is

http://www.networksolutions.com

You are also going to need security. Generally, this can be arranged with the ISP. In the "My Cousin's House" example, you can safely assume that there are people and organizations out there who have some very nasty attitudes toward the clients. Ditto *any* at-risk population. You can also assume that at least a few of these people know an awesome amount about computing and are perfectly capable of ruining everything you and your colleagues have labored so hard to create. Act accordingly! At minimum, back up the entire website and safely store multiple copies of the disks in several places! Back up the website every time you update it!

While the authors think that generating your own pages without benefit of consultants is feasible, the use of a professional consultant for getting your website finally out on the Web is well worth the money spent unless your organization or field placement has someone in-house who can do it. Ask around for contacts, get references, and look at their websites before you agree on a contract! Get a mutually acceptable written contract. The advantage of using a consultant at the end of the development process is that they can help ensure that your website runs most efficiently in terms of the server-computer's needs and requirements and the ISP characteristics. Often, the ISP that has been chosen can provide this help at a modest cost.

Summary

Designing and creating a website can be one of the most rewarding activities in a new and growing area for practice. When you think about it, you are addressing all of the practice issues in the profession. You are working at the microlevel with clients who will directly access your agency. You are also practicing at the macrolevel by making your agency available to the largest community that ever existed. The process we have described works! If you strive for getting input into the design process from every constituency, then you will probably produce a website that everyone is proud of. In order to do this, you do need to advocate to have adequate authority and technical resources. Once you have gained this, then the process for designing the website can proceed from creating a large-scale sitemap to the fine-grained definition of every single webpage. With this plan in hand, you can then build the website yourself if you want to master the technical skills or work with a consultant in a most efficient way.

WEBWEAVER WISDOM: *You never really complete a website, you simply stop working on it! ;-)*

Questions for Discussion

What, in your opinion, constitutes the worst in website design? Describe an example. Why is it awful?

What, in your opinion, constitutes the best in website design? Describe an example. Why is it appealing?

What are the major political issues involved when deciding whether or not to include an external link?

Just how skilled at creating websites should social workers become?

Exercise 7A
Website Proposal

- This is a paper exercise. You do not need to use a computer.
- The purpose of this exercise is to develop a proposal for developing a website around the issue you have worked on in the previous exercises.
- This proposal would be a useful prototype for one that you could present to various constituencies for support and funding.
- This work will carry over into the next exercise.

DIRECTIONS

Write a description of a website that you would submit to a possible funder.

Give a tentative name that includes at least one key word that reflects the mission of the website.

Tentative name for the website: _____

What type of organization or agency is the website designed to serve?

(Specify the owners, authors, and possible sponsors for the website.)

What is the mission of the entire website?

(What specifically is the website supposed to accomplish?)

What are the primary objectives for the entire website?

(List and describe the specific objectives that will lead to menu pages.)

Provide a name and brief general description for each of the menu pages that would be required, including the nature of the links. (Give the specifications for the type of links desired, not the actual links to specific websites.)

Name: _____

Description: _____

Name: _____

Description: _____

Name: _____

Description: _____

Name: _____

Description: _____

Name: _____

Description: _____

Specify the principle audience segments for whom each menu page is intended and how they will be using it. (Who will be using the website, menu page by menu page. How?)

Menu page name: _____

Audience segment: _____

Menu page name: _____

Audience segment: _____

Menu page name: _____

Audience segment: _____

Menu page name: _____

Audience segment: _____

Menu page name: _____

Audience segment: _____

What special design considerations need to be taken into account?

(What are the social, diversity, and ability dimensions, menu page by menu page?)

Menu page name: _____

Design considerations: _____

Menu page name: _____

Design considerations: _____

Menu page name: _____

Design considerations: _____

Menu page name: _____

Design considerations: _____

Menu page name: _____

Design considerations: _____

Why should a funder subsidize this website?

(What makes your website important?)

Exercise 7B
Website Design

■ This is a paper exercise. You do not need to use a computer.

■ The purpose of this exercise is to develop an initial design or "sitemap" that could be used to develop the actual website proposed in the previous exercise.

■ This work will carry over into the next exercise.

DIRECTIONS

Generate a graphic plan for the website that includes its homepage plus all menu pages. Be certain to draw arrows showing the internal patterns for linkages. Provide the name and purpose for each menu page. Specify internal navigation linkages within the website by drawing connective arrows. A one-way arrow shows a link that does not return. A two-way arrow shows internal linkages that are reciprocal. Depending on instructions, add general descriptions or specific URLs for external links where appropriate. Refer to Figure 7-2 as an example.

Now *footnote the plan* with an annotated discussion showing how your website addresses the objectives from the previous exercise. For example, if you have designed a website to promote social justice for a specific population at risk, then footnote each part of the planned website that specifically addresses this, such as "These links go to national advocacy organizations" or "This webpage contains sample letters that can be E-mailed to politicians." Use additional sheets of paper.

Tentative website name: _____

(Choose a name that includes at least one good key word reflecting the issue.)

One-way linkages: ——————————————————————→

Two-way linkages: ←——————————————————————→

Exercise 7C
File Designations

- This is a paper exercise. You do not need to use a computer.
- The purpose of this exercise is to develop a system for titling files and designating file names based on audience segment needs as proposed in the previous exercise.
- This work will carry over into the next exercise.

DIRECTIONS

A. Specify a title for the website's homepage and menu pages. Add the titles and file names for the additional webpages for each menu page if so directed. Briefly describe the audience segment for whom the webpage is intended. Strive for visitor-friendly titles that are clear and unambiguous for the intended audience segments. Use file names that will allow you and others to easily guess the menu page for any subsequent pages.

Homepage:

Title: _____

File name: _____ .htm

Audience segment: _____

Menu page:

Title: _____

File name: _____ .htm

Audience segment: _____

Menu page:

Title: _____

File name: _____ .htm

Audience segment: _____

Menu page:

Title: _____

File name: _____ .htm

Audience segment: _____

Menu page:

Title: _____

File name: _____ .htm

Menu page:

Title: _____

File name: _____ .htm

Audience segment: _____

B. Refer to Figure 7-3, and create sample sticky notes that you would use to detail the homepage, menu pages, and any subsequent webpages. You can use real sticky notes and attach them to this sheet. If you do, then be certain to tape each one individually so they do not fall off! Instead, you can append reproduced copies of the following page.

Title:

File name:

Audience:

Text:

Graphics:

Internal links:

External links:

Technical:

Exercise 7D
The Look of the Website

- This is a paper exercise. You do not need to use a computer.
- The purpose of this exercise is to develop a sketch for what the actual home-page will look like.

DIRECTIONS

Draw a picture in the box that shows what the homepage for your website should look like. Be certain to include the header, the body, and the footer. Show all links. Provide any necessary annotations and comments in the right-hand margin.

The square represents the screen area the visitor first sees. The dashed area is for unavoidable scrolling for the homepage, if any.

Additional Readings

Castro, E. (1998). *HTML for the World Wide Web.* Berkeley, CA: Peachpit Press, Inc.

Heid, J. (1997). *HTML & Web publishing secrets.* Foster City, CA: IDG Books Worldwide, Inc.

Lemay, L. (1998). *Sam's teach yourself Web publishing with html 4 in 21 days.* Indianapolis, IN: Sam's Publishing.

Rose, C. (1998). *Adobe Photoshop 5.* Indianapolis, IN: Sam's Publishing.

Shneiderman, B. (1997). *Designing the user interface: Strategies for effective human-computer interaction* (3rd ed.). Reading, MA: Addison-Wesley Publishing Co.

William, R. (1994). *The non-designer's design book: Design and typographic principles for the visual novice.* Berkeley, CA: Peachpit Press, Inc.

Williams, R., & Tollett, J. (1998). *The non-designer's Web book.* Berkeley, CA: Peachpit Press, Inc.

Additional Websites

Disclaimers/Privacy Examples

The Chicago Bar Association Website *Terms, Conditions, and Disclaimers*
http://www.chicagobar.org/copyright.html

American Association of Retired People *Statement on Privacy*
http://www.aarp.org/privacy.html

html Authoring Software

Get the latest! The resources below are popular html editors, but there are many more. To find out about what is available, go to the HotBot search engine, http://www.hotbot.com, and conduct a search using the key words "html editor reviews," using the "exact phrase" option. Look at the Top Ten list first. To find out more about other html editors, go to HotBot and search using the key words "html editors" as a phrase.

Additional Websites

Adobe PageMill www.adobe.com

Macromedia Dreamweaver www.macromedia.com

Microsoft Internet Explorer: Front Page Express (Available free with full Internet Explorer download) www.microsoft.com

Netscape: Netscape Communicator with Composer (Available free with full Communicator download.) www.netscape.com

Learning html

National Center for Supercomputing Applications
University of Illinois at Urbana-Champaign
http://www.ncsa.uiuc.edu/General/Internet/WWW/HTMLPrimer.html
Yale Web Style Guide http://info.med.yale.edu/caim/manual/contents.html

Graphics Editors

Adobe Photo Shop www.adobe.com
Paint Shop Pro www.jasc.com

Website Design

For many resources, go to AltaVista, http://www.altavista.com. Choose the "Computer and Internet" category and follow the "Internet and the Web" and then the "Website Design" prompts.

Backgrounds

Netscape's Background Sampler
http://www.netscape.com/assist/net_sites/bg/backgrounds.html

Graphics

Lycos Pictures and Sounds http://www.lycos.com/picturethis/
AltaVista Photo Finder http://image.altavista.com/cgi-bin/avncgi
WebRing (visit the computer section) http://webring.com

Disability Access and Design

Specific populations at risk have unique needs. For help and guidelines, visit the World Wide Web Consortium at www.w3.org and the Web Accessibility Initiative website. The specific URL is www.w3.org/WAI/

The "Accessibility Internet Rally" website contains helpful resources along with examples. www.main.org/AIR-Austin/

"Bobby" offers an automated review service for disability access www.cast.org/bobby/

Organizations

html Writers Guild (Many resources!) http://www.hwg.org/
InterNIC http://www.network solutions.com/index.html

CHAPTER 8

Future Social Work Practice and the Web

 One of the most vexing questions we can ask is "Just where is all this technology taking us?" Maybe not much will really change, and our future roles will remain very similar to what we do now. But paradigms do shift from time to time, and the immense changes in communications technologies could fundamentally alter our vision of social work.

CHAPTER OVERVIEW

This chapter explores some of the future issues we need to think about. Just as we adapted to telephones a century ago, we must adapt to the Web and to many other technical changes and challenges on the horizon. Some of the issues we will explore include:

- A Guess at Our Future
- A Child Protective Services Case
- Some Trends to Think about

A GUESS AT OUR FUTURE

If you have ever looked at "futures" literatures—forecasts on what the future holds—you may note a peculiarity about the dates the various authors choose to write about. Futures literatures are shaped like dumbbells: There are many articles written about the near future, maybe within the next ten years or so. These are "safe" because the writers simply extend current developments and make incremental predictions. And there often are articles that look way beyond the present day, maybe fifty years or more down the road. These articles are safe, too, because the writers will be long dead before their predictions can be judged. They will not have to face up to their mistakes. But very little is said or written about the middle period of the next ten to thirty years or so.

We forecast that the next two decades are the most important period to think about because the paradigm used for social work education and practice is most likely to radically change during this time period. The nine core areas for studying social work may remain, but just who teaches them, who learns them, and how they are taught and learned may be fundamentally altered through distance learning and the widening embrace of communications technologies in social work practice. We think the change may be as fundamental as the transition of Western civilization from the Middle Ages to mercantile capitalism. After all, the "post-industrial society" is just that: fundamentally different from the world that preceded it.

At the risk of being very, very wrong, we present the following fiction for you and will ask you to reflect on some of the ideas it raises. Who knows? Maybe we will be very right and smug, or maybe you can visit us in our retirement homes and we will laugh together over just how far we missed the mark!

A CHILD PROTECTIVE SERVICES CASE

CASE STUDY   CHARLES STEWARD, JANUARY 11, 2025

Carla descended the basement stairs carrying the full laundry basket. She went over to the washer and dumped the basket into the open top.

"Do it!" she said directly to the washing machine.

The machine chirped twice and cheerily responded, "As you wish, Barb. Whites on top as usual?" She winced and made a mental note to teach it her own name instead of her ex's. She spoke to the console on the machine, "Sure. Hot and warm. Use more enzymes than you did last time, and no extra rinse."

"I'm working on it now, Barb," replied the machine. She heard the hiss of water running through the pipes overhead and then moved over to her cubicle.

It had been a difficult morning, and the afternoon did not look any more appetizing. She had arranged two foster placements, done nine spot checks in foster homes, and programmed a final on-line hearing/disposition/judgment session on the Wilkes case for tomorrow. She wolfed down the earthly remains of lunch on top of the flat gray surface in front of her.

"Back to work." she commanded. Her words echoed in the dim cubicle. "Hello! Is anyone there?" More echoes. Louder now, "Back to work, damn it!"

The wall in front of her sputtered and glowed. Blurry images floated just above the gray desktop as a cacophony of unintelligible sounds filled the cubicle. The glowing lights finally gelled and froze just above the gray surface into what appeared to be a shining glob of melting ice cream.

"Stupid county always uses the cheapest equipment and the worst voice-recognition software. . .," she thought as she pounded the desk in front of her. "Hello! Child Protective Services, Marion County. Caseworker Carla Adams. Code word is `Pearlmuter!', Hey, Earl, I'm back from lunch!" She pounded the desk and wiggled her right hand in the ice-cream glob.

The glob organized itself into a miniature 3-D copy of Earl, her supervisor. "Welcome back from lunch, Carla. While you were gone, you had one urgent message and three memos. Would you like to know them now?"

"What's the 'urgent' this time?" She stifled her urge to squash Earl.

"The message concerns Charles Steward, case 127 from last month. It is from his foster care mother, Ms. Colleen Blanchard. One memo is a reminder that you have to take a three-hour continuing education course within ten days to keep your license up. The other is from the Delegate Assembly asking you to comment on the last proposed policy statement. The third is a reminder about our face-to-face staff meeting next month."

"Play the message, and confirm me for the continuing education course tonight at 10:00, Earl," she responded. "Nag me in a couple of days about the delegate assembly, and in two weeks about the face-to-face." She wondered whether or not Earl was being real or virtual. It was hard to tell most of the time. His responses tended to be more direct and to the point when he was virtual, but he could be this way, too, when he really was on-line in realtime with her.

Earl disappeared, and a matronly woman, hair in curlers, appeared in Earl's place. The figure was about ten inches tall. "Face." Carla spoke, and the image morphed into Colleen Blanchard's face.

"Carla, you get this little son of a bitch out of here by tonight or he's on your doorstep." Ms. Blanchard's face contorted as she spit out the last words of the message. Two curlers fell out of her hair as her face got redder and redder. "Just watch the video from this morning!"

The state's *Foster Care Supervision Act of 2010* had been a response to custodial child-care scandals some years before. All foster parent homes now had two-way Web television that continually monitored home life back to the county Child Protective Services unit. No one watched for abuse all the time anymore—it was too expensive—but foster parents had learned to use the system to their own advantage when they needed to document problems with their charges.

Ms. Blanchard's face disappeared, and two small boys appeared in front of Carla. One was Charles Steward, and the other was a toddler, Ben, whom Carla had placed with Ms. Blanchard some six months earlier. Both boys were in a bedroom, and Charles was reaching under the mattress. He took a lighter out and furtively looked around the room to see if anyone was watching. Charlie whispered, "Give me the doll or I'll hit you again." Too quick to be recorded beyond a fuzzy blur, the doll was aflame as Ben ran screaming out of the camera's field, whimpers coming from a corner.

Ms. Blanchard's face, still red, appeared again and she said, "You didn't tell me about his fire setting now, did you? Call me now or find someplace else!" Ms. Blanchard vanished. The cubicle was silent and dark.

"Earl, get me the case, 'Charles Steward'. You know, you *could* have brought it up when you gave me the message. I think your intelligence is *really* getting artificial these days. Are you being virtual with me or are we in realtime?" Carla spoke into the empty cubicle.

Earl's voice came from nowhere, and then he reappeared where Ms. Blanchard's face had been above the desk. "Sorry. You know the last union contract won't let me answer that question. I had two consultations and some supervision to do. Do you want to read the case as visual-only or multimedia?" Earl continued.

"Multimedia/historical. And I'm sorry I snapped," Carla lied. She absently mused about how she remained a Class III CPS worker, and Earl had risen quickly to become District Supervisor. She had met him in a virtual seminar during grad school and had not been impressed then. Time had not improved the relationship. She preferred him in virtual mode instead of realtime because he was more predictable and actually a little smarter.

"Earl, please bring in two consultants on childhood arson while you are at it," she continued, absently glancing on the floor for Ms. Blanchard's two missing hair curlers. Even though she had grown up on virtual communications, she still could not completely separate reality from virtuality, especially when she was pressured.

"You must review the case first. Standard procedures," Earl replied.

Earl disappeared, and an image of a small Caucasian baby appeared in his place. The image morphed into an infant. Carla watched it grow into a toddler, then a preschooler, and then into the shy, withdrawn second grader she had placed a month ago with Ms. Blanchard. As the child grew in front of her, the image momentarily stopped at regular intervals, an artifact from the legally required developmental scans that the federal *Missing Children's Act of 2014* required for all children born in the United States after January 1, 2015. She heard statements ghosting in from the wall with each pause. "Normal development consisted of. . . . Inoculations records indicate that. . . . Genetic predictors showed. . . . Identity chip implanted. . . ." And then the litany of the horrors that had happened to this frail little boy during the past year echoed through the cubicle. "Parents' accident. . . . Aunt dies. . . ."

"Earl, can I have the two consultations now?" she asked when the final image of Charles disappeared.

Earl appeared in front of her. "The first consult will be virtual, an archived conversation with Dr. Ayano Yamamoto at the University of Kobe School of Human Technologies, made in 2023. You can proceed to the second realtime consultant, Dr. Latesha Drury at Michigan State, but only if the first isn't adequate. If you do, please keep it to under twenty minutes so we can break even on your consultation budget. You are still $387 in the hole."

"Did you add a cross-cultural dimension? The kid's European American, you know. Minority issues *are* important," Carla said.

Earl responded, "Can't right now. Haven't the resources. Would adding an artificial intelligence consult substitute? This one is free."

"That's the best you can do?" she replied, nervously drumming on the desk. The image of Earl jumped with each finger tap. Carla wondered if Earl knew this and kept on tapping.

"That's all, unless you can show me something serious. You aren't the only caseworker in the county, you know." Earl spoke as he jiggled on the gray desk.

"Thanks, I'll remind you of that at my next performance review unless the lawsuit comes first. The kid appears to have snatched a doll from another little boy and set it on fire. He looked like he knew what he was doing. It's your call and your problem, Earl. Blanchard is more of a resource than you can imagine. You lose her on me and I won't forgive it or forget it. Got me? Give me the free artificial and Dr. Yamamoto," she said.

"Here is the information," Earl responded, his voice trailing off. The morph of Charles Steward appeared again as Earl dissolved over the gray desktop. A mechanical voice spoke from nowhere, "Nothing unusual detected. The social and economic indicators for both of the deceased parents and the aunt were typical for Caucasian/European families of the period. First two years showed cultural coherence. Early child rearing, as indicated by direct adrenaline monitoring, shows no unusual spikes or traumas beyond expected norms for the child. Instances of trauma and excitement appear initially after the death of the parents and intensify after the death of aunt. Guardianship history is first with Hispanic foster parent during initial custody month: no frequency change and positive record. Followed by like-culture matched Caucasian foster placement until last month when ward moved to current placement because of suspected/unconfirmed abuse attributed to routine visual medical scan and adrenaline spike correlation comparisons."

"Archive?" She spoke into the morph of Charles.

Another voice came from nowhere, and the black-and-white image of an Asian woman appeared next to Charles. The woman was speaking Arabic.

"Oops. Sorry. Wrong translation parameter. I'll get it," Earl echoed. The image blacked out for an instant and then reappeared. "This is Dr. Ayano Yamamoto at the University of Kobe School of Human Technologies, archive consultation 1420B: year 2023. Sixteen dollars and fifty cents for the first three minutes," said the voice. "We can have a conversation on adolescence and fire setting. My current research will be updated in June, 2026. Would you like to begin now?" The voice seemed to surround the morph of Charles. The convention of always showing dead people in black and white was a cue for Carla.

"No, thank-you, Dr. Yamamoto. The child isn't old enough. Thanks anyway." Carla thumped the desk and Earl's image jumped. "Earl, that was useless. Dr. Yamamoto was certainly eminent in her field, and yes, she probably still is for that matter, but you chose the wrong age group. Charlie won't hit puberty for four years. Besides, I still have problems interacting with simulated people when they are dead. Gives me the creeps. And no, don't you bring that up again at my next supervision session. Get over it. Dr. Drury, are you there?"

"Hi Carla. Latesha Drury here." An older African-American face appeared next to the little boy's. "Yes, simulations from dead colleagues are unnerving, even for me. And I'm in my eighties now. I remember you from that child welfare seminar at Case Western when you were getting your MSW. How have you been?"

"Fine. I don't remember you. Were you in the seminar too?"

"No, I lurked a few months after it ended when I was doing some research, but I do remember you. You have real talent! How can I help?" the animated face replied.

"Did you see the morph?" Carla asked.

"Yes, but it was garbled at the end. You folks must be using the old version of Bell/Netsoft. Earl, can you play the last part again, please?"

"I'll be back in a sec," Carla said as the morph began replaying itself. She got up and went to check the washing machine. As she neared the machine, it said, "Its ready, Barb. I set the fuchsia dress and didn't press it. Its battery is down and you need to recharge it. And I won't be able to read the instructions on your black Honduran sari in three more washings so renew its chip, please."

She touched the sorted pile of clothes that the machine had slipped into the laundry basket. "I weigh 3.2 kilograms, Carla. I'm safe for you to lift," chirped the basket.

"It never ends," she thought. She turned and went back to the cubicle.

"Carla, I don't see any abnormal problems, although given this little guy's history and the poor foster placement several months ago, I wouldn't rule them out. I tend to think, though, that this is simple preadolescence behavior and not all that unusual for boys his age. It's probably normal, but needs attention. What does the artificial say?" Dr. Drury asked.

The mechanical voice spoke from nowhere. "No conflicts are present at this point. Dr. Drury's hypothesis is supportable."

"Is your artificial intelligence just cross-cultural, or does it do class and gender, too?" Dr. Drury asked.

Earl's voice chimed in, "Series Nine Preadolescence Consultant Software, U.S. Department of Human Technologies: beta version from last year. No complaints so far. We get the best we can afford, Dr. Drury."

"Not bad, considering other places I've consulted," Dr. Drury replied. "Is Blanchard a capable foster parent?"

"One of my best. Took all kinds of begging to get her to take this kid," Carla said.

"I think you could give her a quick session on normal child development and fire-setting and then a follow-up in a day or two. But do ask her if this is the first time she's seen the behavior. If there is more to it, then get back to me immediately," Dr. Drury suggested. "Also check out what he's being taught lately. Maybe he's seen something on fire safety and is reacting to the lesson. Is he in real school?"

"No. Virtual. We keep all of our kids in virtual during their first year. It makes for better transitions if we have to change the foster placement because they keep their playmates. So you think this may be just normal behavior? Can I get back to you this afternoon if I need to?" Carla asked.

"I have a faculty meeting from three to four, so I'd be delighted if you can inter-rupt," Dr. Drury winked. "By the way, did you stick with the consortium?"

"Yes, my MSW was built on Michigan/Auckland and a little UIC. Even had time for policy from San Diego State/Case Western. What I really enjoyed was the diversity work from Dunghai and the New University at Lagos. Really opened my eyes," Carla replied. "I'll cell you if I need to after I talk with the foster mom, Dr. Drury. Thanks!"

Dr. Drury's face was replaced by an image that read: "Consultation: $128.62/ nine minutes."

"Thanks for keeping it short. I appreciate that," came Earl's voice.

"She isn't really that expensive, Earl. Damage control time," Carla said. "Connect me with Ms. Blanchard, and, uh, reprogram that continuing education tonight to juvenile arson if you can find a session."

SOME TRENDS TO THINK ABOUT

We crafted the preceding fiction to illustrate some points and raise questions. We think that the scenario is entirely plausible, although not especially desirable. Other futures are just as possible for both the professional self and daily life (Johnson, 1995).

Structural Stability and Change

Note that Carla still works for a county Child Protective Services unit. In addition, state and federal acts and legislation affect her resources and activities. These policy and regulatory structures have not changed. Yet she now works in her home, and we assume that the many civil buildings that once housed child welfare along with the many other social services are long gone. Earl, for that matter, is probably working at home, too, along with all of the other characters in the story.

This scenario is entirely plausible for two reasons. First, future technologies will make home-based professional work commonplace. This is a growth industry. Family counselors and psychologists can be found on the Web right now, charging for their services with E-money.

Second, there are economic incentives. The county does not have to shelter, heat, and support thousands of workers anymore. Instead, workers now do this out of their own pockets. They are doing this now when they take work home. The net savings results in a lower—and politically more acceptable—tax base. As a result, any move to make workers provide their own infrastructure is likely to meet with success. Thus, the purpose for the work (e.g., child protection) may not change but the place where it is practiced may be drastically altered. "Hotelling," where people work out their own homes and occasionally go to rented office spaces, may indeed become more common as some have predicted (Butterfield, in press).

Shifting Communication Patterns

Practitioners often engage in synchronous communication (communication between two or more parties at the same time). Asynchronous communication is common, just as we leave messages for each other and play phone tag today. What may be very different in the future is that the distinction between these may blur. Carla is able to have a synchronous conversation with someone who is dead! This may not be as far-fetched as it seems. The ability to record facets of a human personality is possible right now— just think of what you have entered onto your own computer's hard disk. Artificial intelligence programs may evolve and produce virtual human beings from recorded data who have a life of their own within the computers. Dr. Yamamoto evidently continues to conduct research. Science fiction now, but a possibility. As a result, the boundaries and structures of human communications may take on altogether different dimensions we can only now imagine (Gilder, 1998).

Gender and Empowerment

Carla remains a woman supervised by a man, something that is quite common in social work practice today. Note that she not only has a male supervisor who is her equal but works out of the home with other traditional role obligations such as doing the laundry. This is not empowerment, is it? One of the critical issues surrounding communications technology is how it changes or supports the status of different groups. Access to technologies and familiarity with them may be empowering, and Carla certainly is capable of using the available technologies in the scenario. Yet, instead of empowering, mastery may simply become a requirement to participate. Earl remains in power. The technology has had no effect on this. If anything, this may get worse. The percentage of women college graduates in computer science has fallen from 37 percent in the early 1980s to 28 percent in 1995, and this trend seems to be continuing (Hamm, 1997).

We submit that if socialization to the technologies is genderless, then it will not affect the distribution of power between the sexes. Thus, technology may generally have a marginal effect on social change and the empowerment of oppressed groups. It is simply another vehicle for communication, but no group has any edge. Negative effects are certain for groups deprived of electronic communications access. Sexism in the computing industry is reported as commonplace (Hamm, 1997). Ms. Blanchard also remains in a traditional role. We do have two female consultants with power, at least in charging fees for consultation, but we have this now, too.

In addition, look at Carla's caseload and other responsibilities such as monitoring placements and taking care of legal routines such as custody determination. If anything, the technology may have made her caseload larger than that of contemporary workers!

Technology Intent and Drift

How technologies are really used is often vastly different from how their creators originally intended. In the scenario, we have ongoing supervision of foster placements because of a past scandal that resulted in legislation and the directed use of available technology. Two-way cable TV is on our near horizon, maybe within the next five years. Presumably, all of the foster homes available to Carla and her coworkers are now continually monitored. Yet the intent of the technology is different than the actual use: Foster parents have evidently turned the tables and find it more of a resource than the workers. We take the position that computing technology *per se* is value-neutral. The actual uses to which it is applied are not determined by what it can do but by *what the users want it to do*. A hammer can build houses or become a murder weapon; it all depends on the intent of the user. Expect surprises. Technology bites! (Tenner, 1996)

Social Work Education

This part of the scenario is a radical departure from contemporary social work education. Note that Carla and Earl have received degrees from *virtual* institutions. Coalitions are suggested such as Michigan/Auckland. The core curriculum she evidently studied is based on three different institutions. International experiences seem common through distance learning: Carla has studied at schools in New Zealand, Taiwan, and Nigeria. This is evolving now. International institutional relationships are beginning to develop such as the one between Western Governors University and the Open University of Great Britain (*Chronicle of Higher Education*, 27 November 1998).

Another dimension of change seems plausible: CSWE accreditation. At present, CSWE accredits social work programs in their entirety. What may happen when various "chunks" of social work education can be provided by different colleges and universities on-line through distance-learning technologies? You could conceivably study policy from one program, diversity from another, practice from a third, and so on. Accreditation could move from examining complete programs to accrediting parts of curricula as well. Someone studying social work might approach CSWE *as an individual* and submit a personalized educational plan for combining work from multiple on-line institutions. CSWE might thus move from only accrediting programs to screening and accrediting individual students as well. While this seems remote, distance-learning technologies certainly will have many effects on professional education, and we can only guess at the directions they may take us. At present, there are over fifty BSW and MSW programs with a distance-education feature (Raymond, Ginsburg, & Gohagen, 1999). This trend will grow.

Also note that Carla no longer has to go "somewhere" to get those "CEU Credits" (Continuing Education Unit) to maintain licensure. This has now become available on-line. Presumably, her license may be automatically renewed as well when she takes a course.

We submit that distance-learning technologies and opportunities, especially as they become technically cheaper, seamless, and politically acceptable, may produce major paradigm shifts in social work education and various regulatory activities.

Political Institutions

Note that the "U.S. Department of Health and Human Services" is not mentioned. Instead, we learn of a "U.S. Department of Human Technologies." We do not know what this means, but this book should have given you a few hunches. At minimum, the change of an entire department within the U.S. Government implies a serious restructuring of political and economic functions, relationships, and roles. It happened when the "U.S. Department of Health, Education, and Welfare" was cleaved into the "U.S. Department of Health and Human Services" and the "U.S. Department of Education." It can certainly happen again within your practice lifetime. At minimum, the current technology is changing how we access information about candidates, legislatures, and the political process (*Investor's Business Daily*, 30 October 1998/Edupage). Far more widespread forms of political and democratic change are also possible (Anderson, Bikson, Law, & Bridger, 1995).

NASW has changed too. Carla is a member of its "Delegate Assembly." There has been a subtle change in how it operates. The NASW Delegate Assembly currently meets every three years to make policy pronouncements and interpretations. This meeting is very similar to a political convention. Yet the Delegate Assembly has now shifted from "batch processing" issues every few years to "continuous processing" on-line. This makes the association far more resilient to emerging issues but also makes keeping up an ongoing task for members. (You *are* a member, are you not?)

Computers Everywhere!

Talking clothes baskets, washing machines, and even computerized clothes are alluded to in our story. We currently live in a world where cars cannot run without their computers. Some may soon run without their drivers. The same can be said for almost all other complex appliances and utilities. This trend may continue well beyond Carla's future (Gehl & Douglas, 1999). Yours, too.

The System Remains Imperfect

Carla has access to much better information than we do, or at least much more information, but this has not affected many of the issues future workers face. Charlie remains a victim of circumstance and has already had one failed foster care placement. While technologies may have helped detect these problems and resulted in swifter action than is common today, the problems of viable placements are still with us. Abusive foster homes still exist in 2025. Kids still need protection.

Summary

This book has taught you how to access, find, evaluate, circulate, and ethically use information from the Web. The Web empowers our abilities to practice social work on a much more solid footing. Yet the footing can erode. Technologies seldom "fix" social problems and often make them worse. The systems perspective our profession uses so well should remain at the forefront of our thoughts. As the systems in which we practice adapt to the Web and change because of it, we must remain vigilant.

Questions for Discussion

Would you want to practice in the same manner as Carla? If so or if not, why?

Is a "live" consultation from a dead authority any different than reading a book whose author is deceased?

What futures do you foresee for other areas of practice besides child protective services?

Exercise 8
Future Scenario

■ This is a paper exercise. You do not need to use a computer.

■ The purpose of this exercise is to sharpen your awareness and understanding of how some of the ideas in this chapter may affect and influence the issue you have worked with throughout most of the exercises in this book.

DIRECTIONS

If you have completed most or all of the exercises in this book, and especially if you have used a single issue as your focus, you now must know quite a bit about it. Review and reflect on all of the work you have completed and write a brief essay regarding the issue you have worked with on the Web. Address the following questions:

■ Will the Web change the patterns and processes of communication?

■ Will there be any impacts on gender, race, culture, economic, religious, diversity, or similar factors?

■ What unanticipated changes and consequences could the Web have on your issue?

■ How could social work education change for your issue because of the Web?

■ What changes in political institutions and how they impact your issue can you imagine?

■ Based on what you have written, what do you forecast for your issue and the Web within the next twenty years or so?

References

Anderson, R., Bikson, T., Law, S., & Bridger, M. (1995). *Universal access to E-mail: Feasibility and societal implications.* RAND Corporation. [On-line]. Available: http://www.rand.org/publications/MR/MR650/

Butterfield, W. (in press). Human services and the information economy. *Journal of Computers in Human Services, 15* (2/3).

Gehl, J., & Douglas, S. (January, 1999). From movable type to data deluge. *The world and I.* [On-line]. Available: http://www.worldandi.com/article/ssjan99.htm

Gilder, G. (April, 1998). The second half of the chessboard: The limits of Moore's law and the rise of the telecosm. *Gilder Technology Report, 3* (4). [On-line]. Available (needs Adobe Acrobat Reader plug-in assistance, available free from http://www.adobe.com/prodindex/acrobat/readstep.html): http://www.gildertech.com/html/archives.html

Hamm, S. (1997). Why women are so invisible. *Business Week,* 18–25, 97. Electronic archive: http://www.businessweek.com/1997/34/b354184.htm

Johnson, J. (1995). Scenarios of people using the NII. *Computer Professionals for Social Responsibility.* [On-line]. Available: http://www.cpsr.org/cpsr/nii/niiscen.html

Raymond, F., Ginsburg, L., & Gohagen, D. (Eds.). (in press). Information technologies: Teaching to use—Using to teach. *Journal of Computers in Human Services, 15* (2/3).

Tenner, E. (1996). *Why things bite back.* New York: Alfred A. Knopf.

Edupage Citation

Investor's Business Daily. (30 October 1998). Election info on the Web. [Reported in Edupage November 1, 1998].

Additional Readings

Chronicle of Higher Education (27 November 1998). *Western Governor's U. teams with Open University.*

Johnson, S. (1998). *Interface culture: How new technology transforms the way we create and communicate.* San Francisco, CA: Harper San Francisco.

Spender, D. (1995). *Nattering on the Net: Women, power, and cyberspace.* North Melborne, Australia: Spinifex Press Pty Ltd.

Stoll, C. (1995). *Silicon snakeoil.* New York: Doubleday.

Tapscott, D. (1997). *Growing up digital: The rise of the Net generation.* New York: McGraw-Hill.

Additional Websites

Mankita, S. *Cyber Social Work: The Internet Meets Social Work's Professional Purpose*
Society for Social Work Leadership in Health Care
http://www.sswlhc.org/mankita.htm

The Politics of Cyberfeminism Conference
http://www.peg.apc.org/~spinifex/cyberfem.html

Articles and Stories at Computers in Human Services http://www.uta.edu/cussn/

Write a Future Scenario of Your Own!

Visit: *Computers in Human Services* http://www2.uta.edu/cussn/fictfut.htm

GLOSSARY

accuracy   Website evaluative criterion. Degree of agreement between sponsor's mission and actual contents. Credibility of resources, materials, and hyperlinks provided.

authorship   Website evaluative criterion. Person or organization responsible for the website's contents. See also **webweaver.**

Boolean search   A multiple key word search that uses Boolean Operators to define the relationship(s) between the key words.

browser   A computer program that allows the user to visit, view, and manipulate websites on the Web.

cache   A folder within the computer that saves and holds website files after viewing them.

clearinghouse   A website with listings of resources around specific topics or subjects. Similar to but larger and more complex than **meta-lists.**

concept search   Searching for an idea that is reflected in but not limited to the literal key words used in a search engine or directory.

cookie   A program used by websites to gain specific information on how the user(s) at a specific computer have examined webpages, including the viewing record for each page, length of time reviewed, links followed, and specific information about the computer and connection. Also known as **magic cookie.**

coordinated search   Search within a database that has been compiled by both a search engine and hierarchic directory in which the results are integrated together.

currency   Evaluative criterion for websites. Degree to which website contents are updated and maintained.

database   Stored information about a subject or topic that is stored and organized for retrieval by a search engine or hierarchic directory.

directory search   A hierarchical search that proceeds through descending levels of ever-more-specific categories of information.

domains Six sectors within the Web that reflect the characteristics of the website's sponsor or owner: .gov—government; .edu—education/research; .org—organizations; .com—commercial for-profit firms; .net—network related; and .mil—military.

false drops Irrelevant documents retrieved during a search.

full-text indexing Search tool characteristic where the search tool reviews and indexes the contents of the complete website instead of only part.

history file A semipermanent record of all websites viewed within a period of time at a specific computer.

hits Listings of websites and their URLs retrieved by a search tool.

hierarchic directory A search tool database of information about websites. Often built and added to through intentional contributions by website sponsors.

homepage Primary webpage for the website. It is usually the first webpage shown. The file name is often "index.htm" or "index.html."

html (hypertext markup language) The computer programming language used to create most websites.

hyperlink General term for words or images on a webpage that, when clicked with the mouse, bring about some change such as going to a new page, playing a recording, or accessing some other additional feature. Also known as **hypertext links, hypertext,** and **links.**

hypertext links See **hyperlink.**

Internet The extensive network that enables computers to link and communicate with each other and to share information as individual machines or groups. See **Web.**

Internet service providers (ISPs) Commercial providers who provide access to the Web and the Internet. In addition, they provide storage space for websites.

intranet An internal Internet, often within commercial firms, that provides E-mail and other communications features within an organization.

key word search Specific words chosen for use with a search tool to discover Web resources and URLs.

link See **hyperlinks.**

magic cookie See **cookie.**

meta-list A large list of resources intentionally provided, updated, and maintained for website visitors. Smaller and simpler in organization in comparison with **clearinghouse** and **search tool** lists.

meta-engine See **multiengine.**

meta-search engine See **multiengine.**

multitasking The ability of a computer to perform and display more than one task at the same time, such as viewing the Web and using a word processor.

multiengine A search tool that consults several databases from various search engines and directories and provides a list of resources in an organized manner. Also known as **meta-engine.**

objectivity Evaluative criterion for websites. Degree that the materials, resources, and hyperlinks are presented within an acknowledged value base.

operator   A rule or specific instruction for inquiring into a database with key word(s).

platform   Common name for the "type" of computer operating system in use, such as Macintosh, Windows, and Unix.

profiling   Data taken from users through registration or surveys on websites and used to compile a database describing the user's characteristics.

robot   A search program that actively looks for new websites and URLs and adds them to a database for a search engine.

scope   Evaluative criterion for websites. Depth, breadth, comprehensiveness, and narrowness of topic's or issue's treatment within the website.

search engine   A search tool that actively looks for new websites, indexes their contents, and adds them to a database for subsequent access and use.

search tool   Generic term for search engines, hierarchic directories, and specialized databases on the Web.

server   A computer designed for storing webpages and dedicated to providing access to multiple users.

session history   Temporary history of a browsing session at a specific computer that is erased once the browser has been turned off.

sitemap   A general listing of the website's contents and organization. Often presented as a table of contents.

specialized search tool   A search tool/database that is dedicated to one specific topic, issue, or process.
A searchtool/data base that is dedicated to one specific topic, issue, or process.

sponsor   Website evaluative criterion. Firm or organization that owns a specific website.

stemming   The use of the root form of a word to search for words that are derived from it.

URL (uniform resource locator)   The unique address for a website usually consisting of the server name, the subdomain, and the domain.

Web   A part of the Internet that permits visitors to view text and graphic files known as **websites**. Also known as the "World Wide Web," "Information Superhighway," and "Infobahn."

webpage   An html file that, with other files such as animation, audio, and graphic files, comprises the webpage viewed in the browser's window.

WebRings   Closed circles of websites that are linked together by WebRing software.

websites   A collection of webpages organized into a coherent whole.

website manager   See **webweaver**.

webweaver   Nonsexist term for the person that designs and maintains websites. Also known as the **website manager**. May or may not be the author that decides and approves contents. See **authorship**.

INDEX

TO THE OWNER OF THIS BOOK:

I hope that you have found *Social Work and the Web* useful. So that this book can be improved in a future edition, would you take the time to complete this sheet and return it? Thank you.

School and address: _____

_____

Department: _____

Instructor's name: _____

1. What I like most about this book is: _____

_____

_____

2. What I like least about this book is: _____

_____

_____

3. My general reaction to this book is: _____

_____

_____

4. The name of the course in which I used this book is: _____

_____

5. Were all of the chapters of the book assigned for you to read? _____

   If not, which ones weren't? _____

6. In the space below, or on a separate sheet of paper, please write specific suggestions for improving this book and anything else you'd care to share about your experience in using this book.

_____

_____

_____

_____

_____

_____

OPTIONAL:

Your name: _____ Date: _____

May we quote you, either in promotion for *Social Work and the Web,* or in future publishing ventures?

    Yes: _____ No: _____

    Sincerely yours,

    Bob Vernon and Darlene Lynch

FOLD HERE

BUSINESS REPLY MAIL

FIRST CLASS   PERMIT NO. 358   PACIFIC GROVE, CA

POSTAGE WILL BE PAID BY ADDRESSEE

ATTN: Lisa Gebo/Social Work Editor

BROOKS/COLE/THOMSON LEARNING
511 FOREST LODGE ROAD
PACIFIC GROVE, CA   93950-9968

FOLD HERE